Tending
the
Perennials

# Tending the Perennials

## THE ART AND SPIRIT OF A PERSONAL RELIGION

## ERIC BOOTH

BETTERYET PRESS

Library of Congress Control Number: 2019940826
ISBN: 9780578482781

HALF OF ALL PROCEEDS FROM SALES OF THIS BOOK
WILL BE CONTRIBUTED TO ORGANIZATIONS AND PROJECTS
THAT EFFECTIVELY EMBODY ITS VALUES.

This book is dedicated to the spiritual hunger,
the yearning, that I find in so many people
that resonates with my own.

# CONTENTS

Introduction . . . . . . . . . . . . . . . . . . . . . . . . . . . . . . . . . . . . . 9

## Part I: The Foundations

1: Uniting the Long-Separated Siblings . . . . . . . . . . . . . . . . . 17

2: Aesthetic Education . . . . . . . . . . . . . . . . . . . . . . . . . . . . 26

3: The Paradoxical Facts of Who We Are . . . . . . . . . . . . . . . 30

4: Yearning for The More . . . . . . . . . . . . . . . . . . . . . . . . . . 43

5: Wonderful Problems . . . . . . . . . . . . . . . . . . . . . . . . . . . . 50

6: Tending the Perennials . . . . . . . . . . . . . . . . . . . . . . . . . . 62

7: Oh Lordy . . . . . . . . . . . . . . . . . . . . . . . . . . . . . . . . . . . 84

## Part II: Skills and Tools

8: Coming to Attention . . . . . . . . . . . . . . . . . . . . . . . . . . . . 95

9: Putting Us on Notice . . . . . . . . . . . . . . . . . . . . . . . . . . . 102

10: Response-ability and Making Connections . . . . . . . . . . . . 116

11: Symbols, Metaphors and Myths . . . . . . . . . . . . . . . . . . . 123

12: Believe-ability and Satisfaction . . . . . . . . . . . . . . . . . . . 130

13: Skills of Inquiry . . . . . . . . . . . . . . . . . . . . . . . . . . . . . . 146

14: A Grain of Sand . . . . . . . . . . . . . . . . . . . . . . . . . . . . . . 156

## Part III: Skills of Action

15: The Ten Commencements . . . . . . . . . . . . . . . . . . . . . . . 161

## Part IV: Past, Present, and Future

16: The Past as Prologue. . . . . . . . . . . . . . . . . . . . . . . . . . . . . . 211

17: Personal Religion, American Style . . . . . . . . . . . . . . . . . . 221

18: Challenging Isms . . . . . . . . . . . . . . . . . . . . . . . . . . . . . . . 230

19: Now What? Implications for... . . . . . . . . . . . . . . . . . . . . 246

20: Seven Deadly Sins . . . . . . . . . . . . . . . . . . . . . . . . . . . . . . 268

## Part V: An Evolving Inner Nature

21: Knowing Evolution . . . . . . . . . . . . . . . . . . . . . . . . . . . . . 273

22: Thriving Creatively . . . . . . . . . . . . . . . . . . . . . . . . . . . . . 282

23: Method Acting . . . . . . . . . . . . . . . . . . . . . . . . . . . . . . . . 293

24: Auxin and Improvisation . . . . . . . . . . . . . . . . . . . . . . . . 297

25: Coming Home . . . . . . . . . . . . . . . . . . . . . . . . . . . . . . . . 302

Epilogue . . . . . . . . . . . . . . . . . . . . . . . . . . . . . . . . . . . . . . . 304

Endnotes . . . . . . . . . . . . . . . . . . . . . . . . . . . . . . . . . . . . . . . 307

Index . . . . . . . . . . . . . . . . . . . . . . . . . . . . . . . . . . . . . . . . . . 311

Personal Note From the Author . . . . . . . . . . . . . . . . . . . . . . 318

Acknowledgments . . . . . . . . . . . . . . . . . . . . . . . . . . . . . . . . 319

About the Author . . . . . . . . . . . . . . . . . . . . . . . . . . . . . . . . 320

# INTRODUCTION

SLOWLY AND ATTENTIVELY as a bridegroom, I walk the hot side of the desert mountain, acknowledging everything I see. I pick my path carefully because the backpack is top-heavy for my urban balance. Stream on my right, sharp orange peaks with ridges on my left, with trees and rock outcroppings sloping down to one small excited man, all alone. One of those ridges holds my site, the level place I had selected for my week-long solo in the wild.

This is my first wilderness solo retreat, 1996, and I worry less about becoming a snack for hungry mountain lions than about the experience of extreme boredom. I am rarely bored, but I live (as we all do) in an endless parade of distractions. What happens to the mind when there is absolutely nothing to do for seven days? Does one go bonkers from boredom?

My friend Jane had inspired me to this act of lunacy, and to this spectacular Colorado location, where she has taken several wilderness retreats, once for a whole month. (If Jane can endure a month and come out ecstatic, surely I can survive a week.) The sponsoring organization called Sacred Passage owns the land of this mountain area, so there will be no hermit-hating thugs combing the mountain for sport. Sacred Passage gave me three days of preparatory training, and Jane gave me friendly reassurance. I gave myself pep talks about how quickly a week can seem to pass, but I remember that the zippiest weeks in my regular life were those filled with activities and fun. How long is a week of nothingness?

The first day of preparation at base camp, I was guided on a hike of the mountainous region to select a site where I would spend my week alone. The options were not numbered campsites with stone-circle fire pits around which to sing "Kumbaya" alone; they bore no evidence of any person ever being there before. They were just flattish areas with highlight features like a stone that looked good for sitting, and with legends of centuries of Native American use in holy rites. I immediately recognized a site that was right for me. It was the furthest from base camp, had no remarkable features, but it "felt good" in a way I couldn't name but knew. I found out later this was the very site where Jane had spent her month. I made careful note of landmarks that would guide me to this site when the solo began.

NOW, SEVERAL DAYS LATER, I head for my site. I follow the memorized landmarks. I find just the right place to cross the brook. I stay by the brook before heading up the rocky scree to transverse the slope from part-way up. I am hot, concentrating on the landmarks, and trying to ignore how much the backpack hurts. On and on I go, for a long time, seeing none of the landmarks I am repeating, mantra-like, to myself. Eventually I have to admit I have gone too far; I overshot my goal. I turn around and head back by a higher route, now looking mostly down to my left for the split pine tree, the eagle's nest, or the unremarkable knoll of my site. I try to be hawk-eyed like an Indian brave, feeling neither. The endless, hopeful transverse until I know I have gone back too far produces no sign of recognition.

So I turn again with a new and desperate plan, not designed for a tired body. I walk big diagonals, climbing across the mountain face at angles from the brook below to high above, up and then down, to give me various vantage points to search from. It makes logical sense to me, but not to my legs. After the seventh diagonal tack I am exhausted. My jelly-legs tremble; my hiking boots squish with sweat; it is getting close to dusk. I am angry at myself, worried, and out of good ideas. "What an omen. I can't find my place—I can't even get started." I don't know what to do. So I stop. I take off my pack, and feel better immediately. I sit on a rock, close my eyes and breathe to calm down. I note the smell of some herb-like tree, hear a bird laugh. I stand up, open my eyes, and look around. I am at my site.

TENDING THE PERENNIALS

All my planning, thoughtful execution and dogged physical effort had failed, while a quiet, overlooked, unnamable part of me knew where I belonged and led me there. All I really needed to do was relax, pay attention, and enjoy the gift of that inexplicable truth. I bask in the wonder of that mystery and laugh back to the bird. That bird will stay close by all week, a totemic figure perhaps, singing improvised arpeggios—a friend reminding me to lighten up and use a different kind of attention.

In subsequent years, I have told this story to various people, and its inexplicability prompts various reactions. Practical friends call it dumb luck; some New-Age friends give credit to an angel; religious friends mention God; and others talk about psychic phenomena. I still have no name for what happened, but the truth of the incident continues to guide me. I rely on that subtle navigational system— not just to find good solo sites out in the wild, but also to choose which consulting jobs I should take, to select which books I should read (and write), to find a site in a friendship where I want to stay, to help me identify what I should be noticing.

I am hardly the first to discover this subtle inner guidance system. Mystics and artists, holy people and ordinary people throughout history have navigated their way to places of meaning by the same invisible compass. As Ramakrishna said, "The fabled musk deer searches the world over for the source of the scent which comes from itself."

I take at least one retreat in the wilderness every year to restore my spiritual vitality. I go out alone, bushwhack my way to find a place far from trails that might bring human intrusion, and establish a 104-foot diameter circle (a Native American tradition) marked off by stones and sticks. I stay in this circle for a week, with a tent and minimal food (I mostly fast), with no books, no paper, no campfire— nothing that could distract me from doing nothing. Years ago I saw a Buddhist bumper sticker—"DON'T JUST DO SOMETHING, SIT THERE!" That is what I do somewhere deep in nature to restore a balance I bring back into the world of action, people and king sized beds.

I learn different things every year in my solo week. But the lesson I re-discover annually is about the richness, the pleasure, the mysteriousness of the life under the surface of daily life. The subsurface action guides me to experiences where I feel most alive, to holy sites along this short secular journey of a lifetime.

The psychologist William James wrote a century ago: "The life of religion consists of the belief that there is an unseen order, and that our supreme good lies in harmoniously adjusting ourselves thereto. This belief and this adjustment are the religious attitude in the soul."[1]

This book is filled with some of the things I know in the wild. I know them at home as well, but there I lose focus, forget them sometimes, and diffuse what I know through so much activity. I may have discovered these truths through personal experience, but others have discovered them too. I may paint my particular plum blossoms in these pages, hoping to suggest some of the invisible forces that led to them, but many others have painted them too. Modern and not-so-modern writers have expressed them. Millions of non-writers, from cave days to Hard Rock times have known the same things. You know these things as well, at least some of them. This book aspires to surface more of what you know, and to inspire fresh intention behind it. This books seeks to illuminate our spiritual common sense.

Please don't assume or project any "should" onto the offerings in these pages—nothing good happens when you *should* on people! I share my practices in hopes they clarify or spark your own ideas; I do not think you should adopt any parts of my personal practice. Of course you can try out anything that interests you, and I offer some activities for you to try that may bring concepts down to personal earth, but always know that a personal religion is exactly that, and requires our individual experimentation and discovery to serve us well.

In the four years of writing *The Everyday Work of Art* (1997), I came to see the natural, overlooked artistic abilities, the verbs of art, that all of us have and use to create the greatest satisfactions in our lives. I noticed that bookstores tended to stock it in the "spirituality" section, even though the publisher indicated to shelve it with either "art" or "self-help." That pattern intrigued me and sparked further thinking about the spiritual themes in that book.

In the subsequent twenty years it took to write this book, I came to recognize the overlooked spiritual abilities that all of us have and use to find the truth and meaning we yearn to know. I now see that these abilities in art and spirit are mostly the same; these verbs of art and spirit play together upon this common ground. You might call that common ground a personal religion.

# PART I
# THE FOUNDATIONS

# · CHAPTER 1 ·

# UNITING THE
# LONG-SEPARATED SIBLINGS

RELIGION IS THE WORK OF ART in the medium of spirit.

Spiritual and artistic experiences do not just happen to us; we create them. Whether consciously or not, we create our spiritual experiences using the same internal abilities and processes that we use to create artistic experiences. Many teachers and traditions are dedicated to the development of these spiritual skills and practices; many teachers and traditions are dedicated to the development of these skills in the arts. This book explores the ways that art and spirit are the same. We will inquire into the skills and practices in both realms that overlap to make a difference in our everyday lives.

The domains of art and religion are usually seen as separate. Both are identified by their nouns: paintings and symphonies, beliefs and rituals, media (like clay and oil paint) and stylistic schools (like impressionism and abstract expressionism), denominations and sects. Nouns specify; they distinguish this from that, this maple from that oak. Noun-focused definitions disconnect oil paintings from clay sculpture, Catholics from Baptists, atheists from agnostics. The institutions that support art and religion are invested in their differentness; the distinctive features of their specialty create their livelihood, their identity. How often do classical violinists seek to identify themselves with country fiddlers? Do mullahs get a turn in a Methodist pulpit?

If different areas within art and religion seem separate, then the larger arenas of "art" and "religion" seem even further apart. They are separate fields altogether, separate industries, with their own buildings and histories, their different purposes, professionals, politics and income streams.

But underneath that surface separateness live the verbs. The verbs tend to unite. In the heart, mind and spirit, Methodists do mostly the same things that Muslims do; actors do many things that dancers do. And further, playwrights do many things that prophets do, stage managers do many things sacristans do, and choirs sing inspirationally in both worlds. We must remember this in our noun-centric world: nouns tend to separate us, verbs tend to unite us.

This natural union of religion and the arts flows like a water table underneath the surveyor-delineated and legally owned parcels of land, the houses and businesses on the surface of all of our lives. Yet, we all rely on this subsurface water to keep us alive, to provide the sense of meaning and personal fulfillment that we struggle to find in our aggressively materialistic and just-getting-by culture. The long mysterious life of the water table doesn't care about the topographical legalities, about what it's called or where the well is dug; it just flows, providing what we need to stay alive. We all do many things that artists and religiously creative people do. We all engage in the same actions that underlie the surface separateness of a world addicted to nouns.

Right under our noses, beneath the surfaces and necessities of daily life, we use the skills of art and spirit in bits and pieces, even when we don't think of ourselves as artistic or spiritual. In our everyday lives, we have artistic moments; and we relish occasional spiritual flashes. (And we languish if we do not get enough of such moments, even if we cannot identify what ails us.) However, we tend to apply these skills intuitively, haphazardly, without the attention and intention it takes to transform any object into a symbol (a basic artistic act), any moment into a connection with the divine (a basic spiritual act). This book seeks to illuminate and coordinate these natural practices, to help us all build the satisfactions that artists and spiritual adepts use to shape, enjoy and deepen their lives.

*What seems wrong to you is right for him*
*What is poison to one is honey to someone else*
*Purity and impurity, sloth and diligence in worship,*
*These mean nothing to Me.*
*I am apart from all that.*
*Ways of worshipping are not to be ranked as better*
*or worse than one another.*

*Hindus do Hindu things.*
*The Dravidian Muslims in India do what they do.*
*It's all praise, and it's all right.*

*It's not I that's glorified in acts of worship.*
*It's the worshippers! I don't hear the words*
*they say. I look inside at the humility.*
*That broken-open lowliness is the Reality,*
*not the language! Forget phraseology.*
*I want burning, burning.*
*Be friends*
*with your burning. Burn up your thinking*
*and your forms of expression.*[2]

RUMI, 12TH CENTURY POET

## In the Beginning Were the Words

DEFINITIONS STRUCTURE THE WAY we think. Let's loosen our traditional thinking about some key terms, starting with art, religion and spirit. The common definitions of art and religion allow them to live among us comfortably and tamely; they have their defined locations and they keep to them. Personal spiritual and artistic experiences, however, are hardly comfortable or tame. They are unpredictable, idiosyncratic, not tied to designated buildings and challenging to the status quo. The inner events of religion and art are as rugged and old as humankind; their evidence appears in our earliest relics and can still rock us if we allow them.

People resist changing definitions, of course, especially understandings of significant words. This daunting task of shifting definitions is eased by the invisible fact that we already know things are out of whack. There is a gap between our peculiarly limited contemporary definitions of art and religion and the vibrant perennial human necessities they have addressed for millennia. This gap creates the feeling of an empty place, of incompleteness, the sense of "spiritual homelessness"[3] that permeates American culture.

Art means more than paintings and ballet. Religion means more than sermons and formal prayer. Spirituality means more than vague nice feelings, more than a large tent to house mendicant New Age ideas.

Let's glance at the etymologies of these keywords to rediscover the innate impulses from which they arose. (Attending to word etymologies is a habit of mine. I find they often hold clues for something crucial we have forgotten.) Using those word origins, and a microscopic view of the actions involved, we can propose three re-definitions that hold the alternate perspectives of this book:

The word *religion* originally had no divine or denominational overtones; it came from the Latin *religare*, meaning *to bind tightly*, and later *to make a binding obligation. Religion is what we do to bind ourselves to personally relevant absolutes, the ways we put together committed bonds to things beyond ourselves.* Religion begins the moment self-centeredness becomes inadequate.

The word *art* originally had nothing to do with artistic media, or beauty, or special talent; it came from the Indo-European root *ar-*, meaning *to put things together. Art is how we invest ourselves in creating things, how we put things together, be they objects, ideas or experiences, that matter to us*—let's call those things "worlds." Artistry in any field begins when an individual chooses to make something that holds personal relevance. Any medium into which we invest deep parts of ourselves becomes a medium for the work of art. While artistic media like musical notes and water colors can reward the work of art profoundly, engaging in the actions of art—making worlds in any medium—satisfies the universal craving to create meaning.

The original source of the word *spirit* is the wordless sound of exhalation, release. It became the Latin *spirare*, meaning *breathe*.

In the Golden Age of Rome, *spirit* became the word for *soul*. Spirit began as the animal instinct that keeps us alive; it provides oxygen for the soul. If religion begins the moment self-centeredness becomes inadequate, then spirit sustains its fulfilling expression, its inquiries. *Spirit is the human oxygen that enables us to burn.*

Let's draw a distinction between spirituality and religion. The words not only derive from different human functions (breathing and binding), they carry different connotations. If we were to ask a random group of people to compile a list of associations with the two words (as I have), we would find more negative terms (among the positive) on the religious list, including hypocrisy, bigotry, intolerance, even violence. We find more vague terms on the spirituality list, and a lot more gesturing with hands to try to find terms. People intuitively recognize that spirit is universal and ineffable, and that religions are particular and local. Spirituality is the impulse, the human urge to reach and connect beyond the bounded self. Religion is what we do to make those connections. Spirit is the intangible, untainted, raw material; religion is how we work with that material to make something with it. The spiritual impulse remains pure, even within fallible individuals; the religious impulse can become tainted by human needs, fears and desires; it is vulnerable to literalization. Organized religions provide various ways to shape and express spiritual urges—ways that work for many of their faithful—but there are also many other ways. The writer Pico Iyer posits that spirituality is like water, and religion is like tea. In her book *Becoming Wise*, Krista Tippett proposes to Iyer (to his delight) that spirituality is like water, and that religion is like the cup that carries it over time.

ALTHOUGH WE PREFER TIDY DEFINITIONS, art, religion and spirit have always suffered pesky blurring at the edges. Look at this mess. Religious settings are usually filled with art, which is intended to fulfill spiritual purposes. Stand in a beautiful artistic place, and we get a spiritual feeling. We feel spiritual when we "get into" some works of art. The mind and spirit start racing any time we get excited by an important new idea in religion or art. Yet despite all that natural convergence, common thinking has it that art is art and religion is religion; sometimes they overlap, but not much more than fashion and golf. Intellectually, we divide the terms, but experientially they merge. Nouns and verbs. Of course they blend. Religion and art are composed of the same creative actions. They merge as we begin to make sense of life.

In traditional thinking, we give Art and Religion capital letters. Religion is, and always has been, the United States' middle name, despite our purported separation of church and state. Religion brought the first immigrants, and America is still widely described as the most religious nation on Earth. When we think of Religion, we think of the big names, the founders and leaders, the denominations; we were taught to spell these nouns with capital letters.

Art carries a capital letter in our minds too, even though in America its profile is lower than Religion. A sliver of the American public have been educated in Art, and hold its achievements in high regard. Many more have little background in the arts, but give Art a capital identity because they know it is important to important people. It is housed in significant buildings; it provides leading tourist destinations; it gets significant philanthropic support; it requires training and talent; it has produced many of humanity's greatest hits, whose value is affirmed with money. When we think of Art, we think of the superstars and the institutions that present them—nouns spelled with capital letters.

To revitalize our traditional definitions, we will give art and religion lowercase status—the humble view, which etymologically means *close to the ground*. We will examine them through the modest lens that sees the natural artistry, spiritual impulses and creative flair in everyday life. All people engage in them, and such experience is essential to a good life. We have attitudes and opinions (nouns) about Religion and Art; meanwhile we go about the quiet work of making sense of our lives with daily creative engagement in art and spirit (verbs). Lives are made or wasted in the play of the lower case.

When I use the word religion, I refer to a variety of actions all people engage in. Of course, religion includes practices inside sanctuaries, meditation groups and prayer huddles of athletes, but it goes much further to include things we do in our heads and hearts throughout the day. We engage in the action of religion as we pray in many ways (only a few of which resemble Norman Rockwell prayer images); as we discover sacred texts (in holy books as well as works of art, in stories by our children, in phrases that stick in our minds); as we perform small rituals (finding wonder in bathing a child, beauty in washing dishes) and practice our beliefs (conversing with friends, choosing how we spend our discretionary time and money, etc.). What finally counts for people is neither the edifice nor the label, nor even the actual rituals, but the personal experience within a religion, the internal spiritual action. As the author Linda Sexson writes, "Religion is a quality of experience, not a category of experience. Religion is a way of doing things."[4]

Similarly, with the word art, I mean the actions of art, such as making connections and relating to symbols, which are not limited to the classical art forms. Throughout our lives, when we tell a story well, or when we decode the hidden subtext in a friend's hello, we put things together the way artists do. Of course, art includes the marvelous "things," the nouns, presented inside performance halls and museums. But the "*work* of art" includes the actions artists engage in to make those performances and paintings, as well as the actions we use to make personal connections to the objects they create. Art goes much further to include work we all do when we put things together in particular ways.

MANY YEARS AGO, when I was playing the lead role in a production of *Hamlet*, a lifestyle magazine reporter interviewed me near the end of the run. The reporter didn't realize that an actor playing Hamlet has no lifestyle; he spends his days in rest and preparation so dull that the story of a typical day would make any reader rush to Buzzfeed for movie star gossip. The reporter asked reasonable questions about what I ate, and my "tricks" of the trade. I answered her honestly, telling her I fasted all day before every performance because it gave me just the right mental energy to think the way Hamlet did. I talked about my daily regime of stretching and running, of breathing exercises and vocal warmups using long repetitive vowel sounds. I spoke of the secret, sweat-stained piece of paper I carried on me at all times as I performed, of my half-hour backstage sitting in silent contemplation noticing my heartbeat before the play began, of the songs I would quietly sing. The reporter looked increasingly desperate about the lousy article I was going to make. Quite thoughtlessly, I said, "I guess I play Hamlet religiously." In a flash, I understood that art and religion had naturally merged in these idiosyncratic daily practices. A decade earlier I had been heading for divinity school when I was cast in a play and made a quick turn into the theatrical lane; now the two separate tracks had reunited.

I was after the heart of Hamlet. I pushed myself to find and share mystical truths through performance, and my invented practices helped me get under the surfaces. Using my artistic skills, I had intuitively developed meditative practices that relied on sacred texts, music, and breathing and physical exercises similar to those in religious traditions of both the East and West. Fasting is an ancient, universal tool for religious exploration. (The play tells us Hamlet himself fasted in *his* struggles to cope with inexplicable mysteries.) Right before his death scene, Hamlet concludes "the readiness is all"—that phrase became a spiritual guideline for me, and that echoes the guidance of many wisdom traditions Shakespeare never heard about.

Over the years, I have heard many people state that they do something "religiously." "I run religiously." "I ride my motorcycle in the back country religiously." "I go to choir practice religiously." "I garden religiously." You have probably used the phrase yourself. (Ironically, I have never heard anyone say they go to church religiously.)

What do we mean when we say we do something religiously? We mean we do it often—not just when we feel like it, but regularly, even when we don't feel like doing it. We also mean something less overt. We mean we are personally invested in the act; we commit to it as part of our identity; we put our hearts on the line; we bring our spiritual side into play. We are deeply committed in some way; we believe, with the certainty of faith, that this activity is somehow essential. And we develop little practices. The motorcycle rider talked about polishing his Yamaha after each outing. The choir singer told me of the importance of having tea with her fellow singers before singing. These practices and the impulses that create them are of the highest importance in our lives. Faith in these practices enables us to sustain our aliveness amid the uncertainties, ambiguities and indignities of daily living. These practices we invest ourselves in provide *confidence*, which etymologically means *with faith*.

To sum up: in these pages, we will think of "personal religion" as the set of intimate individual practices, intuitive and intentional, we use inside and outside formal religions to fulfill our spiritual yearnings. We will consider "lowercase-r religion" as *the ways we put together committed bonds to things beyond ourselves*, "lowercase-a art" as *how we invest ourselves in creating worlds that matter to us*, "lowercase-s spirit" as *the human oxygen that enables us to burn*.

We will look under the surface of our everyday practices to explore the artistic and spiritual experiences they provide. We will discover the small ways we live religiously, often without even knowing it. Hopefully, we will also discover a wealth of new practices that will expand, illuminate and enrich our experience of personal religion.

# CHAPTER 2

# AESTHETIC EDUCATION

THE ACT OF CREATION LINKS ART AND RELIGION. As with "art" and "religion," there are capitalized and lowercase expressions to the word "creator." We experiment as creators to enhance our experience of the Creator's work. C's of both sizes play with the raw material of daily life. Etymologically, "creativity" has no genius or special-person-ness in its lineage; it came from the Latin *creare* meaning *to make or produce* (in any medium, not just artistic media) originally from *crescere*, which meant *to grow*. Small "c" creativity is the natural way we make ideas and connections with meaning— all the ways we invest ourselves in the mysterious urge to grow, improve, understand more, feel more connected to that which is just beyond our grasp.

Perhaps the smallest act of small "c" creativity is making a connection. Look at the idiom—we *make* that connection. Because it is a connection between our personal experience and something else, it is a unique creation, one that no one else has ever made before. Our days are filled with small "c" creative action. Our personal religion is built by small "c" creative action.

I found my preferred style of creative action when I discovered aesthetic education. Four decades of exploring this practice, the most powerful approach I know for teaching and learning in the arts, has shaped my habits of mind, heart and spirit. Since its key ideas inform many perspectives in this book, I will outline some of those ideas briefly here.

Aesthetic is a stuffy-sounding word and an elusive concept. The philosopher John Dewey admitted that he couldn't quite define aesthetic, but he remarked that he knew its opposite was anesthetic. Aesthetic equals awake. This book is aesthetic education in the artistic medium of spirituality; it proposes practices to escape the numbing of modern life, a support for coming awake with the skills we already have and use.

Although aspects of aesthetic education have been explored since ancient Greece, the modern version emerged as a philosophy in the 1960s. It appeared as a teaching practice in several parts of the U.S., and was shaped and honed by a smart group of creators at Lincoln Center in the early '70s[5]—including philosopher-in-residence Maxine Greene—into the practices by which it is best known today. The practice still thrives at Lincoln Center Education, and in many other settings that use the same proven-reliable education approaches without using its fancy name. I have taught at Lincoln Center Education since 1979, and still do. Though we rarely speak explicitly about spiritual issues with our workshop participants, aesthetic education practices constantly resonate with spiritual overtones to me.

One of the basic principles of aesthetic education is that people learn best by doing. As aesthetic educators, we design very specific hands-on activities for learners, the doing of which opens up experiential capacity. For example, let's say we are focusing on Shakespeare's *Macbeth*. Our goal is an enriched experience when participants attend a performance; aesthetic education does not rely on talking about the plot and structure of the play, or telling its history, or watching video clips of scenes, or even singing Shakespeare's praises. The teaching artist (a specially trained, practicing theater artist in this case) designs theatrical challenges for us to explore what Shakespeare was working on when he created *Macbeth*. We might improvise scenes in which our own secret ambitions are named and set aflame by supernatural creatures. We might design a game called Choice and Consequences in which players are invited to take progressively more drastic actions to fulfill their own fondest ambitions, and see how terrible a consequence to others they are willing to tolerate.[6] We might write a soliloquy reflecting on life from a failed, broken perspective, akin to the Macbeth's at the end. Of course, none of us have the playwriting skills to solve those challenges as amazingly as Shakespeare did. But we all have dramatic competences that enable us to enthusiastically engage in simplified but authentic challenges related to his artistry. Then, when the curtain rises in the theater, we recognize the choices that our colleague Will made in working on this problem whose relevance we share—and wow, he was good.

Aesthetic education works because *personal investment in a creative challenge dramatically opens the capacity to empathetically enter related creations*. This is a common sense notion: if you have woven a tapestry, you have a much fuller appreciation of a tapestry woven by someone else. Those in the bleachers who have played baseball have a deeper sense of the game on the field.

This same approach works in other artistic disciplines. When I say it works, I mean this: When it comes to the critical opportunity, with that individual facing the work of art, all on her own in the theater, she has the courage, motivation and confidence to invest herself in the complex, ambiguous world of that artwork. She is able to make personal connections, make meaning for herself. Instead of feeling overwhelmed by the enormous complexity of the world of a work of art, or trying to identify the aspects that "the expert" told her to focus on, she can engage by herself and co-create the beauty and meaning beyond words.

We can also apply aesthetic education practices to the artistic discipline of personal religion. So, we make small worlds to empathetically expand our capacity to engage with large-world complexities. The etymology of the word world comes from two prehistoric German words—*weraz*, meaning man (the root of werewolf and virile) and *ald*, meaning age—together meaning something like the age of humankind. When early humans spoke this word *world*, they referred to the mysterious aspects of human existence on Earth. Over centuries, we have literalized the word; time has brought our sense of the world down to earth. Personal religion restores its mystery, and aesthetic education activity is way to explore it.

In making worlds, we make creative choices as we construct something we care about; we notice the impact of those choices; we revise and share these creations that hold the meaning we intend, imperfect as they are. This enables us to more fully experience the magnificence of the master artist's work. In creating worlds, we become colleagues with the divine in the ongoing process of creation. A world is any creation in which we invest ourselves—a work of art in any medium—be it a story well told, a painting well painted or a project we put our hearts into. Just as aesthetic education practices enrich the experience of the theatrical world of *Macbeth*, the same practices, used as described, can open up the experience of the world.

A good teaching-artist includes time in each workshop for participants to share their work. The enthusiasm is infectious as the group discovers various solutions to the same challenge—how different six small group dances can be, despite originating from the same dance phrase. Similarly, in the discipline of personal religion we wholeheartedly explore the divine worlds others have made in the same endeavor. These include the masterworks we call the great religions, the great religious artworks and any artworks that evoke a spiritual response in us. These also include the small compositions made by friends, family and co-workers—the ways they *bind their worlds together* creatively, the ways the person behind the persona connects everyday life and the divine. Those who are working on the same essential questions are our community of inquirers. Together we are investing ourselves in spiritual work, making small worlds in a holy effort to more fully see the sacred in the everyday. The etymological root of *holy* is *whole*.

In these pages, I will sometimes serve as a kind of teaching-artist in the medium of personal religion. I will offer activities and experiments for you to try that seek to enhance spiritual capacity. The overall perspective of personal religion is that it is an ongoing experience experiment, an aesthetic education inquiry into the things that matter most.

# · CHAPTER 3 ·

# THE PARADOXICAL FACTS
# OF WHO WE ARE

A PERSONAL RELIGION is the everyday art of consecrating our experience. It encompasses all the ways we apply the human urge for stronger connections to that which is beyond what we understand. Personal religion is an ongoing inquiry into "the more"—this yearning drives artistic endeavors and spiritual practices, and it also supports all organized religious practices.

What shapes this yearning that underlies art, spiritual practices, personal religion, and even organized religion when it is working well? In this chapter, we explore some of the raw materials that enable us to create a personal religion, and the logical-mind-boggling paradoxes within which a personal journey unfolds.

For starters, what's the difference between an organized religion and a personal religion? Humor provides a good analogy. Humor is institutionalized in clubs, ticketed performances and broadcast programs, but it appears throughout our lives; we all participate in humor, for many reasons. Life without it is much diminished, and the life that engages with humor only during broadcasts or trips to the comedy club is impoverished. Humor appears everywhere in a healthy life—in jokes, in finding moments and events funny, in appreciation of irony, in wordplay and in the comic perspective that keeps us sane and keeps our relationships alive.

Similarly, religious experience certainly appears in institutional settings and broadcasts, but it does not automatically arise because of the setting—just as a night in the comedy club can be unfunny. Natural religious impulses appear in practices like saying grace and evening meditations at home. Just as humor appears in a hundred little ways we think and turn a phrase—just as we tell jokes away from the comedy club—so creative religion appears in the way we think and look at things, in an insight, or a connection with a friend. Personal religion adheres to no calendar or clock, and we each have our own private denomination and practice. Even individuals who faithfully attend the same religious institution, sitting or kneeling next to one another every week, practice different personal religions throughout the week and during the service they share. Each parishioner or member of the faith listens and responds, has different experiences, makes different meanings in entirely personal ways. The critic Edmund Wilson once said that "no two persons ever read the same book"; similarly, no two religious practitioners ever practice the same religion. William James, America's pioneering thinker about religious experience, wrote, "Religion ... shall mean for us the feelings, acts, and experiences of individual men in their solitude, so far as they apprehend themselves to stand in relationship to whatever they may consider the divine."[7]

The inner playground of a religious service is not entirely a pandemonium of idiosyncratic response. The participants share many experiences; they soar with the singing and reflect upon the message of the designated leader, but each in his or her own way. Outside of formal service-going, an individual's personal religion develops patterns and strategies at work under the surface; it may appear disorganized, but it is actually organized by subtler schemes.

When we enter the studio of most artists, a first glance usually says "disorganized"; if we spend some time there, we discover an inherent organization. It's arranged organically, not logically, entirely to suit the idiosyncratic creative process of the individual. Whether we are aware of them or not, the crucial concerns of our lives inform the choices we make and the structuring themes and shapes of our days; these life priorities even inform the way we construct our experience.

Sit by a rushing brook, and watch the water flow. Fairly quickly, we notice that the seeming chaos of turbulent action clarifies into consistent patterns on the surface, as water pounds over hidden rocks and flattens over smoother sections. We function similarly. We have inner landscapes that somewhat predictably determine the flow of thought, feeling and response over our riverbed of understandings and beliefs. I have a friend who noticed he got emotionally vulnerable and needy every late summer; his wife had come to dread August. He withdrew to read deep searching books and provoked troubling conversations. One year he realized this pattern appeared around the same dates every late summer, and then he recalled that it was when he was a child, that was when his father had died. This pattern was a covert shaping priority in his personal religion, and his discovery of its source released the grip of this annual cycle, allowing him to inquire into the need for a father in more satisfying ways. His step back from the grip of the cycle enabled him to see the formative cause, its resulting life patterns, and then redirect the way he invested his spiritual yearning. Creative spiritual inquiry looks into the inherent topography that shapes the experiential flow of our daily lives; as we make discoveries in this inquiry, we can redirect the flow toward deeper awareness.

HERE ARE "THE FACTS" that shape personal religion. I do not mean statistics. I mean *facts*. Etymologically, a *fact* is *something that is done*; if you are sitting at a symphony concert, thinking about repairing the broken oven at home, the *inner fact* is that you are working on your oven even as the orchestra is working on its Strauss. The high school boy staring out the window in history class is actively generating images and ideas, a lively set of inner facts, even as his external action seems detached from the "facts" of the Industrial Revolution.

Attention must be paid to those inner facts. Those facts announce what is actually going on inside us, underneath the stories we think and tell of ourselves, underneath the behaviors we adopt to be appropriate and to succeed and to make an impression on others, underneath the busyness of our many doings. For the quality of our lives, those inner facts of experience are far more important facts than the number of dollars in a checking account or a measure of weight on the bathroom scale. Inner facts include thoughts and feelings, intuitions and ideas, images and sensations.

Those experiences tell truths, truths that shape our personal religion. They are not lasting truths—indeed, their very nature is transitory—but they matter. We must attend to those experiences, and we must inquire into the truths they contain. That is the ongoing work of a personal religion—to psychically step back enough to see what is going on inside us, what we rely on as truth, and to inquire courageously into the deepest veracity of those truths.

The facts of inner experience are facts—experiences that are happening—even though they don't have the scientific assurance of mathematical and sensory processes that let us rely confidently on two plus two equalling four, or a finger on a hot stove getting burned. Inner facts are ephemeral and subjective, often scientifically unreliable or illogical, but etymologically they are facts because they are happening.

I know I am pushing this semantic point, but I do so for a reason. We tend to dismiss the validity of personal experience, and we can't do that if we are going to successfully practice a personal religion. Recognition of the inner play of these experiences is essential to moving past them to more profound truths. So, please accept the alternative, etymologically supported redefinition of a *fact—something that is done*—so that we can succeed in the spiritual inquiry of a personal religion, a process that includes the scientific pursuit of greater truth within us.

As if that weren't complex enough…

Our inner facts of experience that announce the truths we rely on may not align with truths for others and accepted truths in the lived world. None of us, even the psychologically healthiest of us, lives in complete congruence between what happens in the world and what happens inside us. Life presents us with so many ambiguous events that we are constantly interpreting, judging, imposing assumptions that put a spin on our inner facts, separating them from the inner facts of others. Even intimate, many-decade partners check in with one another to compare inner facts in response to ambiguous moments.

Everyday garden-variety neurotics like me have to stay aware that our inner facts may not be the ostensible truths others see. Those who are more neurotic, or not given to self-awareness as a priority, live with some or many disconnections; their inner facts, and the resulting personal "truths" their life choices are based in, do not match the consensus truths of others. This can produce psychological pains and problems that fill their lives. People with psychological disorders, deep neuroses or psychoses, live with inner truths and resulting experiential facts that are so far from consensus reality that they can only tenuously function within social norms, and they often live with facts and truths that cause severe pain.

Let's note, however, that the spiritual yearning that drives a personal religion is alive in all people, including those whose inner facts and truths are far different from those of the majority. Indeed, the spiritual hunger of psychologically troubled people is often stronger and more articulate than it is for that majority. An unusually powerful spiritual hunger can produce atypical psychology. Some of history's greatest religious and artistic mystics developed unusual personal religious pathways that we might readily label highly neurotic or psychotic, only to arrive at profoundly resonant deeper truths. Saint Simeon Stylites spent the last thirty-seven years of his life atop a column to find greater solitude.

I claim above that all people have this universal spiritual yearning. In my experience, this perennial truth is suppressed more by materialism than neurosis. I find it hardest to detect the vital spark, or see it manifested in action, within those who are most consumed by consumer culture. Perhaps that bit of light has been snuffed out in some, but it seems more like it has been buried like an ember in ash, able to flare again in the right conditions. I have seen hardened life-sentence prisoners come alight spiritually in music, and I have seen flashes of spiritual aliveness in cold-hearted businessmen and lawyers when encountering a grandchild or approaching death.

There are a few people who come close to full congruence between inner facts and truths and the realities of the world. They are heroes to me. Those are the spiritually enlightened individuals who are sometimes connected to religions and spiritual practices, and sometimes not. I have encountered a few—Adyashanti (the teacher I most admire), Krishnamurti, Byron Katie, Eckhart Tolle— and I have brushed up against a few less well-known individuals who seemed that wise and clear.

Here are three essential reminders about the continuous flux of inner experience:

WE PRODUCE THOSE INNER FACTS—WHETHER WE NOTICE THEM OR NOT.

No human is able to notice all the inner facts speeding across the ticker tape of moment-by-moment experience. Some religions, especially Eastern religions with developed meditative practices, train people to notice the inner facts adeptly, and to hold them lightly as the ephemeral phenomena they are. I know many people with superb skills of awareness who can follow the hectic inner action well; they can slow it down and make things quiet in there for a time, escaping the gravity of grounded minds.

Most of us overlook this inner activity. In workshops, I offer exercises that help us notice "experiences"; some participants are amazed to realize they are having experiences at all, because they are so fish-unaware-of-water blind to them. Other participants are astonished to discover that there is so much going on all the time outside their usual awareness. One woman in a workshop in Nashville refused to admit that she had inner experiences. She said it wasn't "Christian." After a time, she pursed her lips and said she was getting angry. I asked her how she knew that; she said she *felt* it and started to continue, stopped short, looked surprised, nodded at me, and the workshop went on. It took only that little bit of distance inside her, a little step back with her awareness, to see the feeling of anger as an experience, rather than being so identified with it that it was invisible. The separation of that little step back made her anxious, and she felt it was threatening to her religion and her identity. But just a pause to sense that a part of her she trusts was still present when she took that little step back, that observing experiences as apart from identity wasn't a denial of her religious faith, allowed her to proceed with exploration.

Awareness of this nexus of artistic, religious and spiritual understandings is common in my work in the arts. It can be surprising to participants in the moment because it is a new "fact" in their experience, even though a quiet wisdom in them knew it all along.

The fish becomes aware of water. The wary evangelical woman notices that things she feels are facts of transitory experience and not attacks on her religious faith. The separation of that "little step back" is crucial, separating "I" from the persona, the Greek mask we wear so much that we come to think of it as ourselves. In that gap, we begin to disidentify from the inner facts—they are things that occur, feelings, thoughts, plans, etc.—but they come and go, and are not who we are. Inquiring into who and what we are is the path of a personal religion.

WHATEVER THOSE INNER EXPERIENCES ARE, THEY HAVE
A TRUTH, WHICH MAY OR MAY NOT BE "THE TRUTH."

If you daydream yourself stranded on a desert island with a favorite movie star, the story may not be true in the way that a tax deadline on April 15 is true, but there is truth in your fantasy. It holds something genuine about your longings, about your taste and imagination, about your preferences in people, island landscapes and ways you like to spend your time. It tells the same truth the arts tell. A self-portrait in older age by Rembrandt may or may not show exactly what he looked like (a mundane ambition that now manifests in billions of photographs), but it does capture deep verities about aging, hard living and earned wisdom. And it says these things in a way nothing else can say as exactly.

Any feeling holds some truth for that individual, even if it is surprising or inappropriate or disconnected from the truths of others. Emotional responses may not adhere to logical sense, but they always come from somewhere, and there is a truth in the connection to that source. As an actor, I had to find why Hamlet said precisely the words he said, if they were to ring true to me and to an audience. Finding that truth made the difference between a merely well-spoken performance and a creatively truthful one. (Some years ago, I had the actor's delight of meeting someone who told me her life had been changed by seeing me play Hamlet twenty-seven years earlier. She stammered to describe why it had such impact, and she said, "It was just so, so … true.")

If you have inner events that seem odd—irritation with a very nice person, an inexplicable intuition about an environment, a yen to eat something unusual—attend to the truth in that fact of inner life. You may be responding to something less than nice under the smooth surface of that nice person (perhaps he is a control freak or a secret sexist); your intuition may be based on something not visible but very real, like a change in humidity, a triggered memory or some sort of extra-sensory data; your craving for bananas may be your body's way of getting the potassium it needs.

Even bizarre connections can hold rich truths. When Picasso connected African masks with prostitutes' faces in "Demoiselles d'Avignon," the images upset and confused people, but many decades later, we still feel a rightness that we cannot name.

Even lies hold a truth under their surface.


TRY THIS.

*Get a piece of paper and a pen. Make up a whopping lie about yourself. Anything. Write it down. Now look at that lie, and write down any truths you can spot buried in it. For example, I might write down: I am an Olympic Gold Medalist in the high jump. Within that lie, I can recognize the truths: I admire great athletes; I sometimes*

*fantasize about being an athletic star; I hold something
about leaping, aspiring to overcome earthly limitations,
as a metaphor inside me; I like to go it alone.*

Lies hold truths. And truths also contain falsehoods. At least
great truths do. The theory of complementarity of the great
physicist Niels Bohr states that opposites are actually two different
aspects of a higher unity that exist beyond our capacity to perceive.
The distinguishing feature of a small truth is that its opposite is
false, while the feature of a great truth is that its opposite is also
true. The flip side of Bohr's Theory comes from the physicist David
Bohm, whose insight is one of the reliable guidelines of my life:
anytime you see seeming opposites, look for the greater truth that
contains them both. Bohr and Bohm, two of the greatest physicists
of the 20th century, providing powerful guidance for philosophy
and personal religion—science and spirit meet in new ways in the
era of quantum mechanics.

Holding an inner fact as if it might also be false provides that
little step back of disidentifying spiritual distance. The oxygen of
aliveness rushes into that gap.

INNER EXPERIENCES DON'T JUST HAPPEN TO US; WE ARE NOT
PASSIVE RECEIVERS OF EXPERIENCES—WE MAKE THEM.

This fact is hard to accept because we don't feel in control of
most of what happens in there. Indeed, we are in conscious control
of only a modest part of our experiential three-ring circus. Whatever
the jumble of actions happening under the small top, we create
everything that happens in our experience, whether unconsciously
or intentionally. We see a tulip; our brain has translated the cell
activations of a surprisingly small percentage of the retina to fit
the gestalt expectation of "tulip," and we respond to the particular
set of neuron connections to create a experiential sense of its
beauty. We see that our child has drawn a tulip on the bedroom
wall in lipstick, and we go through similar inner processes, and end

up creating a response of anger or amusement. We are confused when we hear something that doesn't match with known sets in the experiential library—for example, listening to the atonal music of Webern or the quasi-logical sentences of a psychotic—and our neurons cobble together a response to that particular uncertainty. We create an irritated feeling, or curiosity, or appreciation of its inventiveness. As many philosophers have pointed out, we form our own experiential heavens and hells.

We create our own experiences, and we can change the kinds of experiences we have. This is not some esoteric mumbo-jumbo; we do this all the time. For example, we take actions to provide ourselves with certain kinds of experience: we eat when we are experiencing hunger; we call a particular friend when we want to reminisce; we watch particular TV shows to get particular predictable kinds of experience. There are subtler ways we manipulate our experience: we actually do not see or hear things that do not fit into our expectations and intentions. You probably know of the famous social science experiment "The Invisible Gorilla" by Christopher Chabris and Daniel Simons. When assigned to count the number of basketball passes in a videotaped group of people, observers fail to notice that a person in a gorilla costume enters the scene, pauses in the center of the circle and exits. We miss the gorillas moving through our habituated attention all the time. When we are about to move to a new area, we notice all kinds of new things about the current neighborhood in the final days before we leave.

Even more dramatically, we sometimes bring about the very experiences we fear. You have probably dropped something moments after you thought about not dropping it; you probably know people who have started dating exactly the same kind of person who recently broke their heart. Sometimes, we even create "accidents" or crises to bring about certain inner necessities. We *do* all of that.

This is not to imply that we always use this experience-creating mechanism healthily or effectively. Disorders provoke us to create strange and counterproductive experiences. The neuroses all of us share, at least a little, give an idiosyncratic, illogical and inefficient shape to many of our inner creations. We keep psychotherapists in business trying to deal with the ramifications of this reality.

As we develop as people, we bring more awareness and intentionality to that inner art studio of experience. Maturity recognizes that those inner experiences determine the quality of our lives. More than the stuff we own, the experience of the stuff we own is what rewards us. The experiences that reward us, the best things in life, are as free as the old saying tells us, but fulfillment is not entirely free. We have to pay attention, spend time and be willing to invest in experiencing things differently.

Personal religion relies on these three experiential realities— their constant flow, their inherent partial truth, their self-made origin and the value of noticing them. Here they are again:

WE PRODUCE OUR INNER FACTS—WHETHER WE NOTICE THEM OR NOT.

WHATEVER OUR INNER EXPERIENCES ARE, THEY HAVE A TRUTH, WHICH MAY OR MAY NOT BE "THE TRUTH."

INNER EXPERIENCES DON'T JUST HAPPEN TO US— WE MAKE THEM.

The source of the word *experience* is the same as that for *experiment*. An experimenter is curious to discover more about reality, is a good observer, takes that "little step back" of awareness to see more clearly. As experience-experimenters, we attend to the play of inner facts, and we need that little remove to witness it well.

That little step back in awareness provides the crucial shift that wakes up the spirit or soul. For example, that little step back focuses not on the ideas on this page but on a reader sitting with this book in a particular location doing some delicate inner work in response to things written on the page.

Most (perhaps all) spiritual traditions address this "witness consciousness," using different terms but emphasizing its crucial importance. This is the step back in which someone who is worrying about how he looks becomes someone who compassionately witnesses the one who is worrying about how he looks. With a step back, anxiety becomes awareness, our personal story transforms into a human story. We are looking for the one who is looking, as St. Francis said. Who is looking is the conscious, creative experimenter in us.

TRY THIS.

*Identify some specific aspect of yourself that led you to read this book. Name it. For example, it might be "the part that knows there is something deeper than coping all the time." Looking at just that aspect, locate three places in your life where that aspiration expresses itself. The inner work you did to accomplish that last step requires you to take a witnessing step, at least to some degree.*

*Or maybe your answer was, "I liked the cover." In that case, step back and notice where else in your life you 'judge books by their covers', and how that tends to work out. You have to take the same objective observer's perspective.*

When people describe the experience of this "little step back," they make the same physical gesture with uncanny frequency. Placing hands side by side, palms down, they lift one hand as if the upper palm were looking down on the lower hand. It captures the sense of pulling back, removing ourselves from the action in order to look "down" on it. We feel "higher" with this shift in awareness. No wonder we point up to indicate heaven or God; the divine part of us can separate and observe, as if from a higher place. It is a gesture you will see in many statues of The Buddha.

In Buddhist, Hindu, and other Eastern religious traditions, the distancing step back becomes the central capacity in spiritual development. With practice and time, it leads to dis-identification with our persona. Who or what is that entity that sees the bundle of things we take ourselves to be? It has no name or gender, no identity or judgment. As some Buddhists say, "it is the part of you that doesn't get upset even when you get upset." We come to see that who we truly are is not our body nor the tangle of stories of our history and personality attached to it. Over time, this disidentified awareness leads us to recognize the dreamlike illusion of the way the whole world works. This realization—that most everything we have accepted as true is a delusion—disorients us on the deepest levels. In that uncertain state, new kinds of experiences and discoveries can arise.

The clarity about the illusory world contains a paradox within it—the paradox that concurrently, the world does have real things in it. It is no illusion that it hurts when we stub a toe. Indeed, that hurts as much in an enlightened person's foot as it does for yours or mine. What enlightened awareness demands of us is the recognition that the stubbed toe and its resulting pain are "real" in that some kind of experience is occurring, but that experience doesn't mean anything. The same way that the "inner facts" of our experience are there and then they are gone.

Humans are meaning-making machines. Adam's first assignment on Earth was not to experience things but to name them. But full awareness requires us to hold concurrently that we make meaning in response to life's events—and that the meaning doesn't really mean anything. That's the sublime poignancy of life. And of art. The little statue that means so much to us, and that was shaped out of a lump of river clay by a sculptor, also holds our humanness. Eastern enlightenment knows that we are also more than human. We are an embodiment of divine aliveness that doesn't have any meaning; it just is. We are made of this perennial consciousness at least as much as we are made of human ways. Humans are made of clay, as the Bible says, and also made of that which is beyond clay, as all the wisdom and mystic traditions say. We are both human and divine, and the journey of a personal religion is for the human to access direct experience of the divine. We yearn for this.

# · CHAPTER 4 ·

# YEARNING FOR *THE MORE*

THE ARTS AND RELIGIONS spring from the same spiritual source. Throughout human history, religious and artistic clans have developed different names to refer to that source. The different terms have led tribes to believe they are talking about different sources. Tribes come to believe they have different gods, different artistic motivations; just as different generations of teenagers believe they discover what is wrong with their parent's generation. Of course there are differences between understandings of God, artistic motivations and teenage rebellion, but there are also enormous similarities that tribally minded humans tend to overlook.

Imagine an archetypal old-fashioned Brooklyn cabbie listening to a debate between an abstract impressionist and a neo-romantic painter in the back seat. At some point he might interrupt with something like, "You crazy? You are both painters. You both put dabs of oil paint on canvas and talk a lot of PBS." His next fare brings a debate between clerics about their different religions. He listens and responds with some version of, "Come off it. The way you practice your religions is the practically the same; your people troop off to a particular building once a week, you say and sing the same stuff, you pray and wear funny costumes, and you make such a big deal about the differences."

The cabbie and I agree: established religions are not different inquiries, just different styles of inquiry, as are different schools of art. Islam and Catholicism—different styles. Raku pottery and cool jazz—different styles. And further: different artistic disciplines can be seen as different denominations of spiritual inquiry. Conversely, different religious denominations can be different media for artistic inquiry. Protestantism, pointillism, prayer, paint—different styles of creatively inquiring into that which lies beyond ourselves. The etymology of the word *discipline* means *knowledge*—a discipline is a way of gathering wisdom, and a disciple is a learner. Art and religion are different media for disciples to inquire into the same mysteries.

In *The Varieties of Religious Experience*, William James distinguishes between two aspects of religion: the "external arts" that seek to influence God and the "internal arts" that arise within individuals, apart from institutional affiliation. This distinction maps closely with religious scholarship, which refers to exoteric vs. esoteric spiritual practices. This book pursues the latter, and it is those esoteric "internal arts" that engage artistic endeavor. James describes personal religion as "the hot place in a person's consciousness" and "the habitual center of personal energy." That place was essential at the beginning of the 20th century when James named it, as it was seven centuries before when Rumi sang it, and centuries before that when ancient Greek and Chinese philosophers were describing it in slightly different terms. It is alive and essential today, feeling new, even though it is perennial.

James introduced a term for the source of spiritual endeavor: he proposed that religion, the studio of those inner arts, is about *the more*.

What is this *more*? It is that which lies beyond the ordinary, beyond our mundane daily lives and understandings. James could not precisely define it; shelves of books try too. *The more* is the divine, the Absolute, God, Ultimate Reality… it is the wholeness beyond any way of describing it.

*The more* lies beyond ourselves, beyond our current understandings, outside our grasp. The moment when self-centeredness is no longer sufficient, we awake to *the more*. Our hunger to experience *the more* grows the more we know of it. We might say that we all seek the land of more, while we each have a sense of different destinations within it. This is why, in creative spiritual practice, the inquiry into *the more* can only be an individual path. You can engage in religious practices together, but you undertake the spiritual journey alone. You often attend artworks with others, but the journey of connection is yours alone.

Artistic and spiritual experiences are the indicators of our efforts to gain a firmer personal grasp on *the more*. At the heart of the process lies the word yearning, another term for the reach toward *the more*. Yearning is our natural impulse for more of whatever kind of experience we value deeply. We yearn toward experiences we cannot describe, although we get flashes, images, symbols that express aspects of them. Works of art are documents of an artist's yearning—a Rilke poem, an El Greco portrait, a song by Kendrick Lamar.

It is important to distinguish yearning from desire. They both have *upward energy* in their linguistic lineage—desire comes from the Latin for *star* and *constellation*, as in coming from the stars; and when yearning first appeared in English it meant *the baying of hounds at the moon*. But in current usage, desire attaches to specific things—a Maserati, a pair of expensive shoes, an attractive person. Pursuing desires is a hunt, a power game of acquisition. Yearning draws us toward an aspiration, and we follow its suggestion as a direction, not a destination.

One person may yearn for a more visceral sense of being alive, another toward feeling unconditionally loved or loving the world unconditionally; another may yearn to experience freedom. Yearnings can be multiple and mixed. It can be frustrating to talk about our yearnings because, as opposed to naming our particular desires, we sound vague and unsure. Yearning does not lend itself to simple verbal description as desire does, but the language of spiritual yearning can become explicit in the hands of dedicated masters of art, philosophy and spirituality—novelists, gurus, religious scholars, mystics, poets and composers who have created masterpieces of specific clarity. I have my favorites; you have yours. We owe them such a debt of gratitude for their dedication to clarifying the unnamable to help us; discovering a truth you knew but didn't know you knew, whether in a book or artwork or conversation, is a resonant moment in our spirit and a bonding moment with that other person. (Most would insist they were mostly serving themselves, the call to follow their own particular star, during their years of exploring the expression of their yearning.)

Great seekers usually develop more concrete language, more eloquent metaphors, over years as they discover the deeper nature of their yearnings. Many seekers, adept and exploratory, turn to the languages of the arts to capture their inquiries and discoveries. The arts approximate the ineffable dialect of yearning most closely and provide humanity's best documents of the yearning experience. In the language of lifestyle, the evidence of yearning is scrawled all over us: in our habits, our relationships, our possessions, our time allocations, our conversational metaphors.

Yearning is a universal human energy. Yearning well requires skill, *the* fundamental skill set of art and religion, with three aspects: becoming aware of our yearning, keeping it alive and investing it in good problems. I've known people who succeed in all three aspects. I admire and respect them, and have a strong tendency to love them, even when their personalities don't jibe with mine. I've known people who have failed or given up in all three aspects. I don't have real friendships with them, and pleasantries are all we've got.

We all yearn, especially as children. But as adults, it is not so easy to keep our yearning muscles in good condition. America loves desire but dislikes yearning. The natural yearning we have as children, and that we harbor inside as adults, gets trained into desire, reifying it into wanting *things* and into gratifying those desires as quickly as possible. In the U.S., people are referred to as consumers; omnipresent advertising brilliantly transubstantiates ineffable yearnings into images for sale; we are trained to want-and-get and not to yearn. This is an enormous difficulty we fight, surrounded by incessant pressure to literalize *the more* into *more stuff*. (We will delve into this cultural pressure in a later chapter.) An actual *Vogue* advertisement read, "spiritual equanimity ... is only a credit card receipt away." The average American encounters four to ten thousand advertising messages a day. Two centuries ago William Wordsworth saw this: "Getting and spending, we lay waste our powers…"

The impulse of yearning is easily overwhelmed, as Sam Keen argues:

> We are creatures of longing, every religious tradition has told us that. But the great change in the modern world came as mass advertising began to creep inside our desire system and say, "Look, I know what you want. This is what you want. This will really satisfy you." We are bombarded by images that literally colonize our desire system. The advertising industry tells us that our deepest longings are going to be satisfied by a Rolex, or by a new Buick or by a Range Rover. And when we get those things and we're still not satisfied, we're hooked into trying again, like addicts. We're hooked on getting the next fix instead of going back to those deep, deep questions: What is it that has real meaning for me? What is it that I really desire?[8]

The U.S. is a literal place; we tend to lean away from things that cannot quite be named. We resist experiences that are slow, subtle, indefinite and deep—which happen to be the experiences that matter, that promote growth, that change us. Americans usually have little patience for the slow process of describing something that is hard to grasp. Americans are uncomfortable with issues that preclude correct answers, and with objects (like art works) that require our participation to understand.

Consequently, as natural as the instinct is, in this society it takes courage to yearn. It takes *the full spectrum of the human heart* (the etymological sense of the word *courage*) to overcome the reifying pressures of our culture and the demands of our institutions—often even our religious and artistic institutions—to hear and follow yearning's delicate insistence. Even within lives that have been voluntarily simplified, within active religious practice, within an artist's career, the skill of yearning must be at play or those structures become as anesthetic as any others.

The skill of yearning keeps the hot place in our consciousness actively grappling toward *the more*. To create fulfillment in daily life, our yearning must be alive, aware, and aligned with what we do. Those whose yearning is alive but is not exercised through their daily lives get depressed. Those with limited access to their yearning live small, no matter the abundance of their material lives. Yearning fuels our making things that matter to us, be those things paintings, new understandings or new ways of experiencing the divine.

Healthy yearning instinctively practices the work of art in ordinary, everyday ways that philosopher Arthur Danto called "the transfiguration of the commonplace." Suppose we tell a friend about an important insight. Without engaging *the more*, the factual report of the insight will get filed, but the impact of it, the possibility it holds and the creative achievement it represents, will be lost. For example, I might relate the facts of the story in the Introduction, about my finding a solo site in the wild. If I were not yearning to share its deeper truths, I could tell the tale, and we might both say, "wow, that's really something" before bobbing along to my friend's story of getting caught in heavy rain while hiking. If I sought *the more* through the telling, we would explore by the implications, be creatively unsettled by the unnamable truths it suggests.

Yearning similarly provides the critical difference in religious practice. In a church service, we can sing the Doxology either as a pleasant step toward the conclusion of the service as we remind ourselves to get milk on the way home, or wholeheartedly in gratitude. Either way, the service will end, and we will buy the milk, but the experiential difference and life consequence are enormous. The issue becomes whether a religious service has experiential impact or not.

As expressions for this universal yearning, the media of art and religion are not as separate as they seem. Is singing a hymn art or religion? Is grasping the significance of a parable art or religion? Is visceral understanding of a stanza of Whitman art or religion? Is the ability to rejoice in the "Ode to Joy" artistic or religious? Is making a powerful connection with another person a creative act or a spiritual act? Who cares how it gets labeled?

Institutions care. Existing systems and networks care. Those who have a stake in those systems and institutions care. The part of you I am speaking to doesn't care. The yearning part of all of us couldn't care less what you call it. The place where we meet is beyond institutions, labels, and separate bodies.

Of course, the practice of personal religion also occurs outside religious locations; we pray at home in the easy chair. In the La-Z-Boy, we can pray for a salary raise, or for positive results on a health test, or for a teenager not to take drugs—all decent things to want, yet none yearn toward *the more*. This is reification in the form of a prayer. To pray creatively, anywhere we sit, we pray in a different way. We tap the yearnings that lie under the surface of those three requests, which might be: release from the grip of worry about material sufficiency, complete vitality to experience life fully, and love of the vulnerability in all of us.

In such praying, we release (rather than cling or try), we open to a sense of aliveness (underneath any action in our medical situation), we invite and receive the deep goodness of others (regardless of their current life circumstances). In such prayer, we take a small step back from the psycho-mechanics of desire and allow ourselves to relax into its opposite. Instead of efforting our way out of some scarcity, we rest in the larger truth of sufficiency.

We yearn individually, but somehow most yearnings lead in the same direction. As Hindu philosophy says, "There are many paths to the same summit." This summit is described by many names, such as the perennial philosophy, or the universal religion, or the wisdom tradition. If humankind is going to survive, the force of this aligned yearning will be the reason.

# CHAPTER 5

# WONDERFUL PROBLEMS

IT IS THE FIRST DAY in this year's wilderness circle, and I am seething with anger, fed up with myself—why must I go to such ridiculous lengths to find peace. Why not set up in my backyard, or in the easy chair in my study? The anger spills into rages about social injustices, annoyance at colleagues in my work, indignities past. I plan solutions and withering rejoinders I wish I had barked. It begins to rain. As usual out there, I am not wearing clothes, so I let it drench me. It feels good and makes me even madder. A few flashes of lightning and thunder. I am getting chilled and King Lear-like.

Then the sun breaks through while the rain continues; both drench me. There is a partial rainbow. It's almost too much perfection to appreciate. I soak in as much as I can, feeling grateful for the physical delights and for the sudden respite from anger that had puffed me full of righteous indignation. I recognize the problem underneath my anger: I am out of touch with the gifts I receive. I set myself a specific challenge: identify a thousand things I am grateful for in my life. I take the rest of the day, into the night, to do it. Some of the very things I had raged about become objects of gratitude. By the end, I am so high from gratitude that I sleep in peace.

*A Thousand Gratitudes* has become an annual wilderness ritual for me. I dedicate a day (it takes six to eight hours) to recalling and visiting briefly with a thousand things in my life that I am thankful for. I count with fingers and sticks. Remembering comes in waves, and I have learned to trust that fresh memories will rise when I seem to run out at 639. I confess I sometimes reach a bit far to, say, gratitude for the efficient working of my spleen, and thanks to the incompetent border guard who didn't find the barely hidden marijuana in my car when I stupidly drove across the Canadian border at age 19. A thousand gratitudes packed into a day makes one very grateful. It is a habit of mind that, over years, has spilled into and colored my daily life. I find I now naturally say "thank you" at the end of business phone calls, instead of goodbye.

In the previous chapter, we looked at the first two skills of yearning: noticing its promptings and keeping it alive despite the suffocating pressures we face. The third skill of yearning is to invest its energy well. Desire wants to possess specific things. But yearning wants to inquire into things—yearning loves great problems. In the wilderness incident described above, my anger sprang from frustrated yearnings that I did not have a way to focus and express. As soon as I found a good problem to creatively pour those energies into, my experience transformed. In this section we redefine what a problem is—not just something that is wrong, but also an opportunity to create something new, right and more alive.

Yearning is attracted to problems as lightning seeks the ground through tall objects. All work in religion, all work in art, all creative work begins with and sustains itself by engaging a problem. Something is not right, is incomplete, in the hot place in our consciousness, and we set out to resolve it. That sense of "not-rightness" can be subtle, hidden, hard to articulate—sometimes no more than an itch or tilt in the soul.

These are not practical problems like realizing we left the shopping list at home. Good problems niggle deeply and require the skills of art and religion to address. Sometimes seemingly mundane problems tap the deeper vein. Children do this often, as when losing a favorite blanket becomes a soul-shaking tragedy, or later, in teenage-hood, when wearing the right clothes becomes an identity crisis. Each of us indicates our sacred concerns in everyday ways—in overreactions to a comment; in a strong loving or hating response to a film or TV show; in our daydreams; in the song that sticks in our heads.

Let's return to the parallels between spirituality and art. All artmaking starts with a problem. Our creative impulse is launched by deficiencies that interest us. We discover or feel the problem (a quintessential act of creation in itself) and we are drawn to work on it. (Genius in art, as well as science, is as least as much the result of great problem identification as it is about great problem solving.) The work in an artistic medium helps us clarify, resolve or put together that which can be said in no other way.

The same pattern applies to artworks we encounter. If we do not find interesting problems in a work of art, we may enjoy the entertainment it provides, but it is not an artistic experience for us because we do not engage ourselves artistically. Entertainment happens within the realm of what we already know, and art happens outside what we know. The entertainment experience confirms; the artistic experience expands. One person's artwork may be the next person's entertainment, which may be the next person's big yawn. It becomes an artistic experience only when the artist is activated in a spectator or listener, enabling them to make a connection to something beyond their previous experience. Encounter the "thing" (be it an "art" object or something else); and *make* a connection. This is perhaps the world's most modest yet frequent creative act. When you match something in your own life experience to something beyond what you've known before, that is a completely original creative act; no one has ever made exactly that connection before. The energy that fuels this small (and hopefully frequent) act of creation is yearning.

All spiritual work starts with a problem. There is some kind of failure in life's status quo; something is deficient at the heart of something. We discover it (usually we cannot name it), and if we yearn to address it, we get spiritual. This is likely not a problem like a car that won't start on a rainy night. (Although it might be: if we find ourselves weeping as we turn the useless key, pounding the steering wheel, and raging at the situation—that dead battery might be a symbol, tapping a reservoir of unaddressed need, a resonant spiritual problem demanding creative attention.)

In fact, all creative work is launched by a problem. Psychologists who study creativity agree that we do not suddenly, out of the blue, discover ourselves involved in creative work. Under the surface of our conscious awareness, we continuously work on many almost-issues, proto-questions and half-thoughts called endocepts. These are the incomplete, creative raw materials oozing around in the primordial soup of our unconscious. Sometimes, as if we were struck by lightning, an idea, question, image or clarification will pop into consciousness. It seems brand new, but the breakthrough is the result of preparatory work under the surface. We go to work on the intriguing problems of clarifying, extending and creating the expression of that emerging notion.

TRY THIS.

*Take out paper and pen. Think of something you have made, recently or not so recently, that you are proud of, that holds some meaning for you. Jot down what that thing is. Under the name of it, jot down some things you were working on in that project. Now rephrase those last jottings as questions you were asking that the work provided answers for. And under those questions, note some other times you have addressed those same questions in other projects. And a final bonus reflection—are these questions somehow connected to bigger questions in your life? If so, you have identified a yearning, and its multiple expressions in your life.*

Creative work appears anywhere we pour ourselves into a problem. We align our inner resources and seek the same fruition: to make something new and meaningful out of already-existing stuff. This fruition may be a brilliant solution—how satisfying to conclude with such a bang. However, most creative breakthroughs are not the dramatic "Eureka" type, upon which our capital-C expectations of Creativity are based. They are the modest "eurekettes," of a perfect phrase, a clearer question, another way to go about something. Isaac Asimov writes, "The most exciting phrase to hear in science, the one that heralds new discoveries, is not "Eureka!" but "Hmm. That's funny..."

Creative people (potentially all of us) actually like some problems. We respond by finding them interesting, sometimes irresistible. We typically think that creativity lives in the way we solve a problem, especially in the dramatic breakthrough moment. That can be true, but creativity researchers confirm that selecting the problem to work on is at least as creatively significant as the way we go about solving it. Notably creative Nobel Prize–winning scientists attest that there is little difference between the way they go about their experimental work and the way most scientists do; the differences lie in the problems they select to address and the ongoing questions they ask. We might take this clue from all scientists. They are fascinated by anomalies—that which does not fit sparks their best attention.

More generally, scientists can teach us about yearning— though they probably wouldn't put it that way. A good problem is one in which yearning is continually engaged, sparked and renewed. In this way we sustain our countless wranglings with little challenges and small achievements, until we achieve the welcome boost of "now I am really getting somewhere." Each of those small-c creative accomplishments sparks a fresh burst of energy to carry on; we enjoy a little insight in the middle of a process and feel a small surge of energy to dig back in. This tiny blip of energy is one of our human evolutionary greatnesses, a hardwired impulse for renewed application sparked by creative accomplishment, even on a tiny scale. I see this in myself and in my work. When people *make* a connection, they usually feel a tiny burst of curiosity—a minuscule surge of yearning toward "more." Success breeds success, even on this instinctive human level.

Unskillful yearners pour themselves into problems that don't provide rewards in the process, and that peter out as a result. They may invest themselves in problems that are too large or too paltry to feed a sustainable inquiry. Skillful yearners are drawn to the best problems, those likeliest to yield rewarding results, including frequent small rewards along the way.

The importance of problem selection applies in art and personal religion too. A problem taps into and organizes our foggy yearning, and we use the practices of art and religion to proceed. I call this an inquiry. The philosopher John Dewey defined an inquiry as the combination of action and reflection. An inquiry is a meaning-making project, an experience experiment. Personal religion is made of inquiries. There is an endless supply of worthwhile problems to inquire into and satisfying ways to proceed. Our yearning skills guide us toward the problems that matter to us and keep us sustained along the way.

Inquiries begin before we can clearly identify or name them. Indeed, the moment when we can articulate the driving question or problem is a major accomplishment in an inquiry process. We have all had the insight that comes with thoughts like, "Ohhh, so that's what has been going on with me." In the example of rage when the car wouldn't start, it would be an achievement to discover the spiritual problem at the heart of that incident—possibly frustration with obstacles keeps that driver from getting "home."

Problems addressed in artistic or spiritual engagements are not "solved" in the conclusive way we hope most problems in life will be solved. The problems that attract our yearning extend over time, across multiple projects; they yield many good solutions. The blessing of a well selected problem is that *any* work we do in relation to it takes us deeper. We can't lose, even if a project is "unsuccessful"; if it is connected to our yearning and we are attentive along the way, we succeed. As an actor, I loved the artistic problems of stylized language. I delighted in Shakespeare, Noel Coward and Sam Shepard because they gave me a chance to address that lifelong problem of making a reality in which intensified language was natural, a world that was both richer and real. Entertainment dialed up to art through poetry. This was not a problem to solve, but one to work on and enjoy. There was no "getting it right," only a lifetime's worth of fascinating practice and improvement. I still practice Hamlet's soliloquies by myself, and am sure they are getting better.

## Picking Good Problems

WHAT ARE GOOD PROBLEMS to work on in a personal religion, and how do we go about solving them? We already know the answers to those questions, even when we don't know we know them. We need only attend to what is under, way inside.

Let's begin with problem identification—remember, that's the skill that makes for Nobel Prizes! Here are some ways you might uncover what you already know about good spiritual problems to attend to. Start by noticing the questions that repeatedly arise in you. Watch for moments when your expectations are surprised. Notice the things you complain and lie to people about. Notice where you lie to yourself. Notice what you fantasize about, what public figures you admire—particularly those you secretly admire but don't admit to others. Notice where you spin out of control. Notice the metaphors you use. Awareness of what is going on under the surface of daily life identifies the problems to inquire into, because you are already dealing with them. Provide them with some awareness-oxygen and the embers can begin to glow. Take that little step back of spiritual perspective to see what you can see about the subsurface issues at play in your life. Your best problems are there, actively present.

Once, after I had given a university convocation speech, I encountered a student who had waited a long time to catch me afterwards. He was clearly upset. He had been training all his life to be a concert pianist, he told me. But two years prior, he had developed a wrist injury from playing that kept him from practicing for many months, and now that he was back, everything felt wrong. He now had to play carefully to protect his wrist. But his joy had always been in passionate abandon. He asked me what he should do to make his practicing go better.

He was in a spiritual and artistic crisis, and he was working on the wrong problem. I told him his sole task was to fall back in love with music. Forget disciplined practice, forget the aching desire for Carnegie Hall; it was time to compose, to teach an excited beginner, to write a score for a student film, to work with dancers. Perhaps his composing might be guided by the limitations of his fragile wrist (as Stephen Sondheim's composing "Send in the Clowns"—his greatest hit song—was guided by the limited vocal range of the actress singing the part).

We kept in occasional contact, and he told me over the ensuing months that his singular lifelong focus on the piano had shifted; the piano problem had really been a symptom of change. He had been desperately trying to reclaim what worked in his past, fearful to move on. His experimentation led him to give piano lessons, through which he discovered a passion for teaching. He is now running a small social service agency he started and loves, and the world now has a joyful amateur pianist rather than a miserable professional.

We tend to deal with the same issues over and over. This happens when we do not inquire into them but let them swirl around and through us, unaddressed. The young pianist needed to solve the problem of finding a creative investment for his displaced passion. We are all working on such problems whether we like it or not. If we have a meaning problem in life (and the scope of life's mysteries guarantees that we do), we may flail as the young pianist had been doing, instead of inquiring into them. Some of us have seemingly irrelevant outbursts; some go numb and function mechanically; some drink or take drugs or continually distract themselves. Indeed, addictions are extreme (and almost never effective) strategies for addressing good spiritual problems. I often wonder if the self-destructive path of an addiction—if it leads one to bottom out and survive—might provide a better start for a personal religion than a path of unconscious compliance-into-numbness.

There are fundamental perennial problems humans have always addressed. Organized as well as personal religions continually deal with these problems, sometimes well, sometimes not so well. Most of our individual yearnings are rooted in these enduring human problems, and tracing those roots helps focus our inquiries. These meta-issues contribute to the problems on your personal radar screen: the anxiety about death (the foremost problem for all religions); the sense of meaninglessness; the experience of aloneness; the overwhelming complexity of society with its appalling range of unfairnesses; the reality of human evil; the elusiveness of the divine; the inexplicability of bad things happening; the paradoxes and impossible contradictions of life; the belief that something is wrong with us. "Good" problems to address in your life are likely to resonate with some of these perennial panhuman challenges.

RELIGIONS ARE THE DESIGNATED PLACES for humans to focus on those big problems. However, religious practice often does not take on the challenge. The fallible humans who lead and practice religions get focused on other, more practical issues. Whether solved or not, weak problems lead to discouragement; they dissipate our spiritual energy. One might argue that the long positive history of religions derives from their investment in the good problems the human spirit faces, and that the long history of religions' horrors—from materialism to slaughter and cruelty beyond imagining—derives from dedication to the wrong problems, problems of institutions and power, rather than the human perennials.

To work well with problems, we must give up the expectation that there will be a tidy solution—a clean, definite, precisely communicable answer. That expectation is one of the heavy costs of our literal, legalistic culture. A healthier expectation appears in the metaphor of a "solution" itself. Think of a solution as a *dissolving* (which is indeed its etymological meaning) rather than a single answer. There are answers along the way, but there is also the loosening—the relaxing *into* the problem that is part of successful problem-solving. Part of effective complex problem–"solving" is changing one's relationship to the problem.

The capacity to step back from identifying with the problem is essential to an evolving, fulfilling personal religion. In truth, it isn't *your* problem; it is *a* problem. *You* aren't the problem, and you don't *have* the problem. It isn't necessarily even *a problem*; it's a set of circumstances, or a set of feelings and thoughts, that you grip as your story. As you let go of the grip, the story loosens into the larger truth. Say the problem is caring for a difficult, depressed octogenarian father. Part of solving the problem includes stepping back to see there is a sad old man you have chosen to take responsibility for, and the pain is coming from somewhere else. Possibly from anger at the amount of time it takes, and the hit that other parts of your life take because of it. With a step back, you can see a part of the solution is an opportunity to learn how to derive more fulfillment from the time-constrained parts of your day that you value.

When I am leading a series of fourteen-hour workshop days that drain my spiritual reserve, I remember to recharge on bathroom breaks. I need to step back from my tiredness and pragmatic urgency to refine the plan for the next workshop segment, even though both are real, and touch base with the peaceful core inside. I may only have two minutes, and it is enough, and the next section of the workshop goes better too. Peeing my way to equanimity. My favorite spiritual teacher is Adyashanti, and he often talks about his Zen teacher. She attained her own enlightenment while she was raising five children. A problem! Asked when she had time to meditate, she answered that there was plenty of opportunity—at stop lights, in supermarket checkout lines, while brushing teeth. She psychically stepped back from the grip of concern about time scarcity, and found plenitude.

The student pianist mentioned above made spiritual progress when he let the love he had focused exclusively on piano-playing become more diffuse, so it could find other fulfilling expressions. Our real problems do not go away, as every reformed addict, every functional neurotic, every self-aware person knows. We get better at dealing with the underlying pressure and dissolve the harmful expressions into other kinds of response, into other kinds of inquiry that can be called a personal religion.

Another expectation we must set aside is getting clear signs. How do we know if we are on the right track? On some level, we expect the divine to speak directly. Divine responses do appear, but not in the child-with-parent directness of the Moses or Bernadette scenarios we know from the movies. Those romantic illusions mislead, like so many other romantic illusions a mature person must outgrow. It all depends on how we look at things; it all depends on the quality of our listening—and these require the perspective we get with little steps back in our awareness. We can discover signs regularly if we are looking and listening from a clear place in us; our prayers are potentially answered every day. Having a prayer answered does not mean we get what we want, like the unspoken Christmas contract we encourage in children toward Santa. Sometimes the answer we hear in that truthful place in us is no, and sometimes the answer is a quiet yes we don't expect. We will not see a burning bush, but there are blazes on the trail if we are looking.

We must bring our best intelligence and attention to the inquiry of the moment, with confidence (remember its etymological meaning *with faith*) that we are spiritually competent. To hear the voice of the divine, we must hear in the way a good parent attends to a child. We listen totally, slowing down, taking the child's thoughts and ideas very seriously, enjoying them for the original and wonder-filled content they contain, even when they are not expressed clearly in adult terms. That is the way to attend to inner experience and find the best problems to work on. Not condescendingly, but with wholehearted belief that those tiny inner impulses and pieces of ideas we hear when we are quiet are enough. These whisper the voice of the divine. Those truths themselves are basically indifferent as to whether we attend or not; they are simply truths; they don't care what happens to them. (Half-truths and ideas connected to our personality identity *do* care what happens to them; you can watch for this indicator. If you find yourself advocating inside for a perspective or arguing for its validity, pause, take that step back in awareness, and you are likely to find they are not really your yearned-for truth.) If we care enough to attend to those whispers, they serve us well. We can practice such hearing with our children, and with works of art that beckon us. Works of art serve us well in this regard, and have since the Paleolithic caves.

To know if we are succeeding spiritually, we need to use the etymological definition of *success*, which means *to have a follow-through*. By this definition, we become successful disciples (etymologically *learners*) not by adhering to a set of behavioral requirements or becoming spiritually materialistic to attain certain inner states, but by remaining unattached-but-curious about dealing with our life problems. Similarly, artists, whether struggling and not, must remember that they are successful artists if they continue to delve into interesting problems and make stuff they love.

# · CHAPTER 6 ·

# TENDING THE PERENNIALS

ONE OF THE GREAT overlooked subtexts of the human adventure is the similarity of the feelings, the messages, and even the responsive behavior of most saints and spiritual innovators. It seems that all were inspired by strikingly alike core impulses and arrived at common spiritual conclusions and commitments. I believe they all shared the same kernel of enlightenment experience in their breakthroughs. Our shared set of human spiritual truths. Many paths, one summit.

After finding their new clarity, each of these creative individuals pursued a spiritual path, a personal religion, for the rest of their lives. They made new discoveries that informed their daily lives and about which they were quite certain, with that wordlessly intimate assurance that comes from direct discovery. They all had an instinct for teaching and exploring the ways their approaches worked for others. They all became wiser and more compassionate as a result of their teaching practice—one of the best ways to deepen what you know (about anything) is to teach it. Through experience, they learned as teachers and developed good ways to draw others into their understandings. The differences in religions emerged mostly later, after the lifetime of each innovator. I can imagine a dinner party of the dozen greatest religious innovators: they would find so much agreement, it would be a splendid evening. I imagine they'd laugh a lot, even though they were not exactly comics in life. I wish I had a da Vinci-like painting of it, "*The First Supper.*"

Various sects and religions arise when followers deal with pressures the inspired originator did not address. But the spark at the heart of every religion is breathtakingly alike around the world. Religions share many goals and underlying beliefs. Generations of followers develop the practices that become the physiognomy of a religion, and so different religions look different. But under the skin, they share anatomical features, essential organs and skeleton. For example, some version of the Golden Rule has appeared in every major religion. Why? Because it is such an elegant guideline toward a universal human goal.

It follows that the religions we know about have developed common elements. These religious universals, sometimes called "the perennial religion," have arisen naturally every time *Homo religiens* has set about organizing the work of a new spiritual innovator to pass them along. The following shared elements have found expression in a madhouse-variety of ways. However, being common to all, they hold a special place in spiritual history. Any actions that have succeeded for all our religious millennia, appearing in so many religious styles, must be addressing true essentials—no matter how wrong some of the expressions become when distorted. These perennials also provide the reliable foundations for constructing a personal religion.

### 1) CREATIVE PRAYER OR MEDITATIVE PRACTICE

Prayer connects us to something greater than our everyday selves. A direct address to divine or ultimate sources, it requires spiritual openness, particular kinds of reaching-out, and exquisite listening. While meditation is not the same as prayer, the experiential goals and residual effects of successful practice are so similar that it makes no sense to separate them in this perennial view. The most adept practices of prayer and meditation become more and more similar in their central experiences. Prayer and meditation arise from many of the same needs, and emphasize the same things: opening out of mundane thought, attending to minute inner experience, relaxing, "listening" for contact with another kind of reality, seeking to fill with something divine. Religions seek to foster such experiences and to extend them beyond the dedicated acts of prayer and meditation. Every religion aspires to a suffusion of the prayer or meditative experience into the rest of conscious life. As usual, William James defines it well:

> Prayer is no vain exercise of words, no mere repetition of certain sacred formulae, but the very movement itself of the soul, putting itself in a personal relation of contact with the mysterious power of which it feels the presence ... wherever this interior prayer is lacking, there is no religion; wherever, on the other hand, this prayer rises and stirs the soul, even in the absence of forms or doctrines, we have living religion.[9]

Almost all Americans (from 90 to 97 percent, depending on the survey) say they pray. People say they pray more often than they have sex. Half admit that they pray to get things rather than worshipping through prayer.[10]

Of the many different kinds of prayer, let us draw one basic distinction here: the difference between creative and formal prayer ("formulaic" in James' terms). Formal prayers (the external art) require only that we perform certain formulae, say the words, or go through the steps—its definition of success is not concerned with the personal experience during the performance (although performance of the form is intended to influence the inner state, and usually does). For example, the Lord's Prayer is repeated millions of times a day by individuals asking for things from their Christian deity; in how many cases are they truly embracing divine will over their own, as one phrase claims? How often are they considering what the words of the prayer require of their egos and petitions?

In creative prayer (the internal art), we make it up as we go— yearning to make contact, dealing with the experiences and ideas that arise, and then yearning toward the goal of that prayer. The distinction between creative and formal prayer is not so clear as it may seem. Formal prayer certainly can include creative involvement under its surface; some people get high as a kite saying the rosary.

TENDING THE PERENNIALS

Most religions invite and expect formal prayers to be filled with creative intent, yet they accept the formal practice as adequate.

Any time we try to reach beyond what we know to make contact with some source beyond ourselves, we begin to pray. We may pray with two hands pressed together or with one holding a pen. We may pray as we reflectively walk a deserted beach on a winter morning, or notice the beauty of the carrot we just cut. As the writer-philosopher Simone Weil said, "Full attention is prayer."

In creative prayer, we engage in the work of art to create a connection to something greater than ourselves. We make new things in creative prayer, including new connections to things and even new forms of prayer. Prayer is a way of extending the mind, opening to the full range of perception, wherever and whenever we do it. Creative prayer is serious play in the medium of spirit.

There is a special significance in the prayer of a child. Not the memorized formulaic prayer, even though that child may well be filling the experience with an un-institutionalized essence. Not the wanting prayer that can range in intent from Christmas materialism to genuine need to altruism. But the invented prayer, the created form that holds a direct connection between the child's sense of the way things should work here on earth and that which lies beyond her understanding. It is one of the earliest vessels shaped by suffused artistic and spiritual impulses. Did you create such a prayer? Do you remember anything about it?

I remember mine, mostly because I offered that prayer every night, without fail, for so many years. It was a secret; I never told anyone about it until my forties. The format developed over time, but by age eight it had achieved a satisfying enough shape that I did not make substantial changes until it fell out of my life in college. I let go of this security blanket in 1969, when a combination of life experiences released my grip. I was facing decisions about the military draft that intended send me to Vietnam. I had been in a car accident in which I should have died and didn't, saved by implausible luck that didn't feel connected to prayer. I'd experimented with hallucinogens, which changed my relationship to those things that lay beyond my understanding.

There was no parental pressure on me to say a nightly prayer growing up—quite the contrary. It arose from an innate impulse. Looking back on it now, I see it as more ethical than spiritual, emphasizing hard work and personal responsibility, with an elaborate sense of accountability. That child, and then teenager, and then young adult believed that the outcomes of daily life on a personal and global scale were shaped by a mix of our personal efforts as well as by forces beyond human size. I still believe that.

I stopped believing in and praying to a monotheistic all-powerful male around my early teens. I was a practicing Quaker by then, and their metaphor of "inner light" became "the other" to which I offered my prayer, replacing Michelangelo's grizzled elder. Inner light isn't a bad metaphor for the state of heart and mind that comes closest to my now–old man's sense of prayer.

My every-night prayer began with a short invocation before its three main sections. There was a formal entry phrase I can't remember, something I had made up that sounded vaguely King James–biblical, which served as a greeting. Then there were some casual improvised thanks for the best things in the just-finished day, much the way you might quickly share positive highlights of a day with a sibling or spouse while setting the dinner table.

This led nicely into part one, a more formal review of the day just passed. I evaluated highlight experiences, bad things I had done and things I was unsure about. Most importantly, this section included an assessment of how I had fared in my previous night's intentions, promises and hopes. This accounting was the longest section of the prayer, and only when I sensed I had considered things fully could I move on. If I had "been good" and fulfilled my promises, especially if they had been difficult or undesirable ones, this gave extra power to the subsequent sections of the prayer, which gave shape to tomorrow. I was infantile Puritan—if I had suffered in being good, I would earn rewards.

The second section was an allocation of divine intention for the next day. I allowed myself 100 percent of wishes for the next day and had to divvy up the portions. The zero-sum challenge was that my wishes for other people, for the world, and for myself came from the same 100 percent. Every night I had to weigh my own personal desires with my concerns for others. If my sister had a big test the next day, I gave her some percentage points; if my cousin was sick, I gave him some. Along with such obligations, I wished that a classmate would invite me to her birthday party, and invested some wish-points for a bike speedometer for Christmas in two months (I didn't get that wish and had to buy one with my savings). It was further complicated by my vague sense of the larger world. If I heard that children were starving in Bangladesh, I wanted to give them some percentage points too; I wanted to provide divine support for Jackie, Caroline and John-John Kennedy after the assassination, and for the safety of an orbiting astronaut. Remarkably, this responsibility did not feel like pressure or strain. It was just a task I assumed and performed with seriousness and without guilt. I know I hogged the goodies sometimes, taking 20 percent to prevent my making errors at second base the next day, while giving flood victims only three or four points. There were no entitlement programs—every point was up for grabs every night. To this day I am good at adding to one hundred.

The final section of the prayer was the commitments. If I really wanted those things I had just tallied, I had to promise to do certain things the following day—things of the sort "God" would want, and I might not. The deal was that if I kept my promises, I got the percentages of grace delivered the way I had doled them out. I believed in inherent fairness: if I did my part, God would do "his." Somehow the fact that I was more likely to fulfill my part of the deal than was God never seemed to deplete the intent in prayer. Cynicism and doubt didn't appear until I was sleeping in a college dorm. There were usually two or three promises made every night, but a single one was enough if it were a biggie. Then, of course, the first part of the next night's prayer included an assessment of my promise-keeping. I recall feeling bad when I had blown my promise (and expected diminished fulfillment of the next day's wishes as recompense; the kids in Bangladesh were not going to eat much the next day). I recall dreading some acknowledgments of abject failure, but I always copped to the full truth, and somehow I never felt ashamed before the divine, even though I was subject to shame with people.

I developed a closing phrase that I can no longer recall. It had something of the solemnity of "for thine is the kingdom and the power and the glory for ever and ever; amen," but the feel was more along the lines of "thanks for working with me on this."

TRY THIS.
*Imagine you were going to create a nightly prayer format. It is designed to express the relationship you want between your daily self in the world and the ultimate truths you believe. What are some things you'd want to reflect on before sleep to support the best possible outcomes the next day? Jot down some kinds of reflecting or thinking or feeling you would want to include as an every night practice to deepen the alignment between your beliefs and actions. Can you make it positive and not punitive? Can you shape the protocol so that it includes interesting and productively challenging stages? Can you design it to be pleasurable to do?*

## 2) Rituals

Human beings danced religion before they were able to discuss it. We might define rituals as patterned activities through which a community accomplishes its greatest tasks—necessities like marking life and death passages, connecting to essential sources beyond the quotidian, altering everyday consciousness, binding the group, addressing fears and threats, getting right with God, making it rain or stop raining.

TENDING THE PERENNIALS

Yearning makes the ritual impulse so strong that it appears outside religious settings, in all situations that affect people deeply. We tend to devise rituals as part of secular observances when we wish to acknowledge the presence of something larger than the individuals involved: legal proceedings, political gatherings, the World Series, the start of the school day. On a deep level, humans believe that the group that performs rituals together stays together. Rituals are fundamentally conservative; they evolve at the pace of glaciers. Perhaps that glacier metaphor isn't accurate anymore in this climate change era.

Rituals are deliberately set apart from daily life and often performed in particular places. (Biologist Rupert Sheldrake and others who believe in the theory of morphic resonance propose that the locations themselves contain particular force, and that is why the rituals live there.) The actions in rituals intentionally appear different than those in daily life. Rituals are jam-packed with symbols; like works of art, they are designed for emotional impact and ensure that the rational mind cannot control them. Rituals are highly structured, and the religious anthropologist Van Gennep points out that they share a basic tripartite foundation: separation from the daily world, participation in a non-ordinary state (sometimes called "the liminal") and reintegration to life with a change.[11]

Rituals often include artistic expression and use artistic media, especially music and patterned movement. These are are central to many rituals, not merely as a decoration but as the ritual act itself. Within ritual, individuals who are absolutely sure they are not artistic are able to sing, move gracefully in choreographed ways, and invest in metaphor-making—quintessential actions in the work of art. Rituals rely on repetition and metaphor, two basic tools of all artistic media. The arts are not frills in perennial religion; they are the most efficient, effective way to get the job done. Rituals invite the presence of mystery and require imaginative participation to have impact. Like prayer, like art, rituals defy logic; they seek to change our consciousness, to bring us out of the literal and into the liminal.

Rituals are an obvious feature of organized religions, and they also appear in personal rituals. They may appear as candle lighting before a bathtub relaxation or in preparations before and during lovemaking. Many people have a pattern of mental preparations they undertake before they pray or meditate. Rituals mark and facilitate the transition between one kind of consciousness and another, between the everyday and *the more*. Organized religions accept perfunctory participation in rituals (and generally frown on divergent interpretations), but the perennial human need is answered by the experience of full participation in a ritual, not by the ritual's form. The personal investment in the ritual *is* the ritual. The creation of a personal ritual, and the ability to experience its intent, is artistry in the medium of the spirit.


### 3) TRADITIONS

Traditions are informal rituals. They hold essential information that is learned and held in the heart differently than formal practice or direct instruction. There are white dresses and parties around Confirmation; there is the Seder day of preparation, apart from its evening formalities. Traditions teach behavior, teach how the practices of a formal religion should be thought about and used. Like rituals, traditions provide informal bonds between generations; they place us in a time continuum beyond the duration of our own lives.

Traditions are not limited to the special times and places of ritual; they are taught in the home, in the Sunday school room (rather than in the sanctuary), at social gatherings, at the dining room table. Traditions are taught by any faithful individual with natural authority, often someone within the family, rather than by a designated religious authority. Loving instruction in family traditions becomes a powerful marker in a child's life. For many people, traditions learned in childhood remain the most positive part of their religious training, even after they have left a family church. Traditions are also conservative, but they welcome personal flair and invention.

As beavers make dams by instinct, so we make traditions. We create traditions in our cultures (around holidays and national events), our workplaces, our religions and our personal lives: we make New Year's resolutions; go to high school reunions; wear something borrowed and something blue at a wedding.

Personal traditions are rich with personal meaning, just as formal religious traditions are packed with metaphor and message. The traditions we sustain hold volumes of personal religious text that are available to read at any time. In my workshops, I often ask people to study a tradition they keep, be it a family reunion or a visit to a gravesite. We rediscover the meaning of the event and each of the parts; we attend to it as a work of art.

TRY THIS.

*Identify a tradition you keep. Imagine your way through it, from its pre-beginning through its finish. Write down the stages or steps, or make a map of it. Now imagine this tradition being performed on a stage with you in the audience. Viewing this presentation as a carefully constructed statement, what would you say are the main purposes and themes of this tradition? What would you want the actors to be feeling at each stage of the sequence?*

Traditions must be rediscovered, reinterpreted, reinvented, re-invested in the present tense to stay alive; slavish repetition is the slow death of tradition. As Jaroslav Pelikan said, "Tradition is the living faith of the dead; traditionalism is the dead faith of the living."[12]

## 4) SEEKING ANSWERS

There are big questions out there, about everything: death, God, the purposes of life, the beginnings and endings of the universe, evil, truth, bad occurrences, what we should want and what responsibilities we have to one another. Our inquisitive species has no universal answers to any of those questions, but religions raise their hands to offer suggestions. They often do more than make suggestions, they bellow, demand, threaten, shame and punish. Questions and answers, questioning and answering—these occupy a central place in the practice of personal and institutional religions, but they live differently in each.

Religions rarely explain things convincingly. Explaining is a logical exchange, while religions trade best in questions beyond logic. But they invariably try. Religions try to make problems binary to help the answering—life/death, God/man. They also trade in threes, developing inherent trinities to explain things that are more complex: heaven/earth (or purgatory)/hell, Father/Son/Holy Ghost, the Three Bodies of the Buddha, and Shiva/Vishnu/Brahma for Hindus. These metaphors, like all metaphors, evoke and require artistic rather than logical involvement. But that doesn't deter the irrepressible impulse to logically affirm and argue the knowledge held in the metaphor, for centuries at a time.

Religions answer questions in various ways, using dogma to clarify purposes, great tales to teach us how to be, and direct instruction to suggest how to interpret and think about both. Practices that point in the direction of possible answers, catchphrases to comfort, and sayings, images, poems and songs repeated from our earliest years subtly shape the way we think for the rest of our lives. But religions offer their richest answers when they reach beyond logic, providing myths (of creation and what happens after death, for example), parables, mysterious symbols and images.

A friend of mine once passed a farmer while walking down an Irish country lane, and asked the farmer how he was doing. The farmer replied, "Oh, you know, the usual...stumbling among the immensities." Those big, jaw-dropping life questions, the ones we tend to avoid as adults, are not the only issues we stumble among. A personal religion is packed with the tension of paradoxes and incomprehensibles: the temporal vs. the lasting, dualistic thinking vs. holism, aloneness vs. love, our sense of puniness vs. our expansive potential, eternity vs. the world in a grain of sand in a mortal hand and poem.

Like good arts education, religions wisely offer multiple levels of instruction and practice that offer kinds of inquiry into important questions, including a track for the most passionately curious. The ambitions of this "most dedicated" group, including the monks and nuns of many faiths, are strikingly similar. The fervent converge toward the same experiential goals as they seek wisdom through various traditions. The inquiry processes of the most dedicated non-institutional seekers converge to closely resemble the inquiry processes of the most dedicated institutional seekers. Perhaps all paths lead to the same summit most directly for the most dedicated climbers.

Our personal religion idiosyncratically uses many of the same tools that religions use to seek answers. We turn stories into parables as we imbue them with meaning and tell them again and again, especially when the family or close friends gather. The etymology of *parable* is *to put beside*; we turn a story into a parable when it serves as an analogy, when one meaning is placed beside another. (Analogical thinking is a cornerstone of the work of art.) Our lives are filled with potential parables; the news is filled with them.

I intend the stories in this book as parables; and then you transform them into working parables when you investigate them for their meaning to you. Take the story I told in the Introduction about finding my way to the right wilderness site even as I botched the plan for the hike and got frantic. That story becomes a parable when you begin to connect it to your own life experience, when you find the relevance for yourself. Perhaps the story becomes a reminder of the ways you are doing this all the time. Perhaps it suggests a reason that you are reading this book.

Like religions, individuals instinctively develop their own dogma, and offer it frequently. Many get as bound up in opinions and beliefs as dogmatic religions tend to get in theirs. Many souls get lost in the opine forest. Listen to the dogma of another's religion—it sounds demanding, restrictive, inflexible, set in its ways, maybe even preposterous. That is how we sound when we let fly with our streams of opinion about the ways things should be. As religious dogma is the codification of once-live spiritual exploration, so religious opinions become the tombstones that mark where personal religious inquiry once lived. The way back to life is to detach from identification with the answers, to take that little step back in spiritual awareness to observe those opinions as creations that are partly true and partly not, partly yours and partly not, and get back to live inquiry.

## 5) SYMBOLS

All religions use symbols. There are cups and cupolas, rug patterns and stars, fish and lambs, bitter herbs and water, dances and hand gestures. (My nephew, when young, thought third-base coaches were very religious because they made all those gestures like Catholic priests to tell the batter to bunt.) Religions use symbols because they work. They draw us in to active participation, into repeated and deepening creative engagement. Symbols can hold more information than microchips. Ask a thousand people what a cross means to them, and see how much information that symbol holds.

Symbolization thwarts the logical mind, something the microchip struggles to do. You cannot come up with a single correct answer to the meaning of a symbol, and if you can, it won't stay long in the face of ongoing curiosity. (A symbol that has a single meaning is not a symbol at all; it is a sign. Symbols refer to something more abstract than themselves; signs refer to something more literal.) This is especially important for addressing life's unanswerable mysteries.

Penetrating mysteries requires artistic work, which engages many kinds of thinking, including the logical mind's valuable contribution. Symbolization defies the arrival at final meanings because we continually remake our understanding of a symbol every time we engage with it. Rediscovery, changed meaning, is the status quo with symbols.

Symbols don't have to sit still on an altar or wall. Myths are also religious symbols, a flipbook of symbols that tell profound truths. As Carl Jung taught us, myths like those of Parsifal or Persephone are so rich with resonant symbols that we can spend productive lifetimes discovering and applying their implications. All religions use metaphors—in some kind of creation myth, in the levels or hierarchies demonstrated by light and the sky, in conjuring a sense of an afterlife. Symbols appear throughout religious texts and tales; we hang them around our necks, place them on our walls and rely on them in our speech. Religions use music symbolically to say things that can be said in no other way, to say things that lie beyond words. Religions use enactments and dance, use masks and liturgical costumes as symbols.

In our personal religions, we instinctively symbolize in the same ways. We deal with hierarchies because we experience higher and lower functions in ourselves. We get high, and feel low. We instinctively gesture up in reference to the divine, and look down when dispirited. We gesture toward our hearts when we refer to ourselves. We create our own myths about our beginnings.

If you doubt this, try this exercise by writer Natalie Goldberg in her book *Writing Down the Bones*.

TRY THIS.

*Take out a piece of paper and a pen. You are going to write for three straight minutes without stopping to pause or think. The whole point is to just keep putting down words. If you get stuck, just write down gibberish until the next idea appears. (If you have done this activity before, do it again now; you will discover different answers.) Start by writing these three words and then continue for three minutes. Ready? Write: "I come from..." and keep going. When you have finished, reread what you wrote, and you will find the beginnings of a personal religious myth.*

Our spiritual impulse creates symbols because we engage in the work of art whenever we try to find meaning. In ancient Greece, the word "symbolon" (root of the word "symbol") referred to a tradition. At the end of a fulfilling occasion, like a visit or memorable feast, a host would take a coin or ring and break it, giving a piece to to each departing guest. This piece represented the pleasurable "wholeness" of their experience together. The piece was the symbolon, the tangible, present part that represented the intangible, absent whole being recalled through artistic imagination. This is how symbols work when we invest our attention. They are real bits that connect us to larger, more indescribable, whole experiences of personal meaning. *Whole* is the source of the word *holy*.

## 6) GRACE

All religions provide a sense that things can be well with the Absolute, that the divine is present, appeasable and willing to work with us. (In most religions, that willingness is highly conditional.) Grace brings a sense of sanctity; it sometimes manifests as the experience of beauty, or the experience of flow—being "in the zone." Grace is an awareness of the divine flowing through us. Some religions see grace as direct intervention by God; personal religion sees it as a state we experience when in close alignment with the divine.

We can also get out of whack: dis-grace. Shakespeare's "Sonnet 29" begins, "When in disgrace with fortune and men's eyes..." I notice I get less physically coordinated when I am in that state. I bump into things, drop things; I become graceless when I am feeling low. Indeed, this connection is so reliable that when my hands start getting clumsy, I look for what is amiss in my heart. I notice that I move more gracefully when I am in sync with the divine. When I am using my chainsaw because I "have to" get some cutting done, I am herky-jerky in my movements (and feel stiff as an oak the next morning.) But when I cut because I feel like cleaning up the forest floor and preparing firewood for my house, I gracefully guide that noisy knife as if through butter, and roll out of bed easily the next day. The same pattern holds true spiritually for projects I take on for money or out of obligation versus those that spring from my heart.

The word *grace* comes from the Latin *gratus*, which means *pleasing*; grace is the deep pleasure of things being right with the world. Etymologically, grace is a sister word to *grateful* and *agree*; the experience of grace is life's deepest "yes" and universally evokes the response of gratitude.

Many people hold the sense of grace as the goal of personal religion. They know things are right when they feel it, and they sense things are off when they don't. Grace is certainly a wonderful state to experience—all the time if that were possible—but making the experience of grace the goal of religious practice is a misalignment. Grace is a gift, not a goal.

Grace appears in this way: we inquire into the issues that engage us; we invest ourselves in the challenge; and then at some point, we may get lucky and experience grace. To seek a steady diet of grace is spiritual materialism, and it will lead us away from the divine as surely as the store-bought kind. It is a catch-22 of spirituality that you get an experience of grace only when you don't seek it.

The experience of grace lets us know where we should be headed. Where in your life do you tend to experience grace? What yearning guides those experiences? The answers to those two questions provide spiritual and practical direction.

Do not seek grace in your personal religion, or you deter its appearance. Be grateful for the gift if it arises. The processes of a personal religion can shape the kind of inner and outer life in which grace may arise, without expecting or waiting for the gift.

## 7) Sacred Texts

Across all religions, sacred texts have rewarded generations of the faithful with insights and inspiration. They are not always written in words—some are written as visual artworks, some are written in music. These texts provide a tangible presence of the divine, touchstones of the holy to which we can return endlessly to make fresh connections to *the more*.

Sacred texts are rich. I performed Alec McCowen's one-man play *St. Mark's Gospel.* The play is the Gospel of Mark, King James Version, word for word, told as a story on a bare stage. Two hours of nothing but Bible-speak—I feared that audiences would not just be bored, but need a concession stand renting sleeping bags. McCowen created the piece and made it a hit on Broadway, and I performed the American tour for a year. He told me to "trust the text," not to act up a storm. I discovered McCowen's wisdom (an ancient wisdom of theater) that simply sharing the words gave the sacred text a freshness, a universality and power that drew audiences in because they joined the work of making personal connections. (This is the mystery of the actor's art: The less you do, the more the audience does—but you have to do that *less* just right, or it doesn't work.)

The Gospel took me six months to memorize, and another four months to rehearse, before I went out on the road to perform it onstage hundreds of times. In those hundreds and hundreds of recitations, I found new discoveries in that sacred text every single time. My most significant discoveries came toward the end of the tour; I was investing less psychic energy in the mere task of memory and performance, and that greater surface relaxation allowed me to find deeper connections in the moment. Hundreds of repetitions, and continual fresh insights—and St. Mark is merely one small part of one sacred book.

The secret of sacred texts is that we, as individuals, give them their sanctity through the way we respond. Some in the audience found my telling of the Gospel as a story illuminating; others may have found it dull. Many Christian friends admit they usually listen to the Bible reading in a service and think, "What the heck is that all about?" And even after it is "explained," they understand intellectually but have no gut response. (Research affirms that explaining usually diminishes curiosity; and curiosity is an early indicator of yearning.) They find more spiritual connection in an ocean view at dawn. A sacred text itself is not an automatic revelation, just as a poem never is. The sacredness arises in an improvisation between the text and the individual reader/listener. If we engage with any of the great texts with our skills of art and spirit, we create personal religious responses. If we don't, we can doze through the holiest passage ever penned.

Outside of formal religions, we create and discover our own sacred texts. We write, make or discover something, and then we sanctify it in the way we experience it—we transform it by finding the divine aspects in it. Such hallowed texts rest on our desks and nightstands, are framed on our walls, lie in shoe boxes under children's beds, in drawers and attic collections of family stuff. The books we loved as a child may be sacred; the *Boy Scout Handbook* or the Tao Te Ching, *The Little Prince*, the family photo album, the aging pages of a diary, the story of a friend long gone—potential sacred texts all. Favorite poems we discover can become texts as divine as any biblical verse. As I settled my father's financial matters after his death, the checkbook, the ledger, the history of stock transactions felt like sacred documents, authentic texts of my father's lived life.

The word *sacred* derives from the Latin *sancire* which means to consecrate, or more specifically *set apart for special noticing*. The word *text* goes back to the Latin *texere, to weave* (as in texture) and originally *to build*. We can put those word histories together to see the that power of sacred texts lies in the way we construct meaning, weave things together, with that special kind of attention. Throughout our lives we select texts to invest with that special noticing, and we create the connection that feels divine. The tangible documents that remind us of those connections, many of which are rich enough to provide deeper discoveries when we attend to them fully again, become the sacred texts of our personal religion.

### 8) COMMUNITY

Religions are composed of and sustained by communities. The word *community* originally meant *duties performed together*, and religions have always thrived when observed by groups of the faithful acting upon a particular set of shared beliefs. Whether religion was practiced by a whole village in the veldt, by a small group of aging Anglicans gathered in a cavernous cathedral, or by a secret outlawed sect in a musty basement, religion has not been a solo act. Even religious founders, who created new spiritual understandings on their own, usually in a retreat from society, soon attracted followers and began to teach.

How does this community imperative square with the focus on individual religious experience in these pages? Should we practice a personal religion on our own, ignoring the ancient imperative to gather together? As happens so often in a post-adolescent worldview, the solution is not "either/or"; it is "both/and." As with institutional religions, the practice is both entirely personal *and* necessarily collective.

On one level, we *must* address personal religion on our own, because we alone construct our inner experience. Religious experience of any kind eventually comes down to the action and abilities of the individual spirit. (Similarly, aesthetic education prepares groups of people to experience works of art. But when the final moment comes, when the curtain goes up, each person must meet the artwork alone in the dark. Connections will be created one-on-one, or not at all. Paradoxically, this solo encounter happens in an auditorium full of individuals doing the same thing at the same time.) Spiritual experience happens between each of us and the world, no matter how many co-believers sit in the same room or how much stained glass beautifies the light. Each individual constructs a temple of religious experience in an inner clearing.

Community is also essential. The right network of people sustains a personal religion; the lack thereof can deplete one. A group of people who share beliefs and priorities, who engage in good dialog and experiment together, can stimulate new inquiries, support the pursuit of fledgling yearnings, and comfort when the going gets tough. Try singing alone in the living room and then try singing with a skillful chorus. Try meditating alone and then in a roomful of advanced practitioners. Try thinking through deep spiritual issues on your own, and then in dialog with a committed fellow seeker. It is not that the shared endeavor is better, but that it is essential to support our solo pursuits.

Personal religion does not recuse us from community; it invites us to create the group that works for us. We must find like-yearning people and work our way to a level of commitment that supports the ongoing work of each. We have to create the traditions and the symbols with them—which is what we do with real friends anyway. Basically, we need to do what every new religion has done: follow our own discoveries and gather a supportive group of explorers to carry on. We need not set up small, huddled, nameless meetings in basements throughout the town; this kind of community is less literal. Envision a web of connections to various soul mates, with you gathering and sustaining this network in ways that support the development for all involved.

We may find these individuals within the larger community of an organized religion we practice. Some of our friends are spiritual colleagues, even if we practice different religions. I make a piecemeal community. I have had a spouse whose spiritual seeking was her primary life goal, and now have a partner whose interest responds to my lead. I have friends I turn to for particular kinds of dialog. Those friends don't necessarily know they are part of my religion; in fact, I imagine a dozen readers of this paragraph wondering if they are unannounced participants in my personal religious community. They know we have intense talks, that I am enthusiastic in pursuing certain topics with them, that I raise issues they didn't expect. They comprise my religious community, and I love the occasions when we gather in twos or threes for dinner or a hike and discover what we share. Those services advance my practice, feed and challenge my yearning.

I call them in to a disorganized service when I need their help—the meeting can look like email exchanges or questions I raise with them over lunch. The communion is usually less about the specifics of their advice and more about time spent in close connection with them. If I am really focused on some troubling issue, I find I raise it with my entire disparate congregation over time. It is a kind of group prayer; a kind of singing in multi-part harmony.

When I read a book that addresses concerns I grapple with, the author becomes part of my community. Buying a copy of a great book for a friend at just the right time is an act of religious fellowship. When a student asks me a question that resonates with my own life concerns, I welcome her to my community, even though all she knows is that the teacher seemed to care about the answer. When I hear about a great arts project in another town or of a great spiritual teacher or of a wonderful church, I celebrate the expansion of my religion, pleased to know of affiliates everywhere. When I am able to gather teaching artists (as at the International Teaching Artist Conferences), it feels like a secular-spiritual revival; and many of the delegates describe its impact in phrases you hear after religious convenings. When you make a connection to some idea in this book, I gratefully greet you in my community.

This is heroic, world-making creative work. We each assume the role of religious innovators. We become Jesus and Gautama Buddha, Mohammed and Abraham, in our own humble ways. We admit what we are: the creators of our own religion. We assume the tasks those individuals did too, drawing in others who evolve with us toward greater wholeness, as individuals and together.

Perennial plants grow anew each year; it is their nature to come back. They can be ignored and still survive for years. But to produce their best blooms and fruits, they require care; they need the right nutrients and space to thrive within the uncertain and sometimes difficult conditions they face. It's up to us to tend our own perennials.

# CHAPTER 7

# OH, LORDY

*It is easy to understand why there are some who propose a period of silence about "the last things" so that the misused words may be redeemed. But this is not the way to redeem them. We cannot clean up the term "God" and we cannot make it whole; but, stained and mauled as it is, we can raise it from the ground and set it above in an hour of great sorrow.[13]*

MARTIN BUBER

WE MUST TALK ABOUT GOD. Not all people or religions believe in God (which is why I have not included that belief among the perennials), but the idea of God is pervasive. Like Martin Buber, I find the word "God" troubling because it evokes particular images and reactions—a specific entity, usually male, with the motivations and thinking of a magnified human. To conceive of God requires imagination (the capacity to make images), and most of us are notably unimaginative regarding God. We resort to images we absorbed when young. We do not use the same playful multiplicity of ideas, metaphors and willingness to reinvent our understandings that we bring to our most creative work. Carl Jung wrote:

> I cannot define for you what God is. I cannot tell you even *that* God is, but what I can say is that all my work has scientifically proved that the pattern of God exists in every man, and that this pattern has at its disposal the greatest transforming energies of which mankind is capable.[14]

In this book, the term *the divine* covers the ground the term God usually occupies. I use *the divine* because it evokes fewer picture-book images and suggests a state that is more than a particular being with a beard. Please accept the term *divine* as an allowable reference to your particular sense of God, Allah, Jehovah, Ultimate Order, Almighty, Truth, Great Spirit, the Absolute or whatever symbol you use in your spiritual imagination. Scholars tell us that the word *God* probably derived from an ancient Sanskrit word meaning *call*, which gives it an etymological meaning of *that which is invoked*. As Martin Buber suggests, each of us conjures God no matter what we believe in. When we get lost in the woods at dusk, when we are diagnosed with cancer, when we send our mind out into the night sky, we invoke the same "whatever"—which is what we call God.

In *A History of God*, the British scholar Karen Armstrong catches this universal necessity: "Jews, Christians and Muslims have developed remarkably similar ideas of God, which also resemble other conceptions of the Absolute. When people try to find an ultimate meaning and value in human life, their minds seem to go in a certain direction. They have not been coerced to do this; it is something that seems natural to humanity."[15]

In my own earlier years, I vacillated, sometimes believing in a God and sometimes not. No longer. The need or sense of a singular divine entity has simply fallen away. I confess that even when I did at times believe in a particular God, it was with less certainty than the visceral faith I feel for other beliefs like the personal benefits of the creative process, the power of beauty, and the universality of artistic ability. I believe in an active cosmic order (which science helps us understand and appreciate), an energy or wholeness that applies universally. I respond to symbols that express that wholeness, and God is a compelling symbol; but relating to a symbol and insisting on a factual reality are two different things. Religious practitioners tend to mistake the symbol for the referent—worshipping the idol as the deity, turning an evocative story into a literal fact—exactly as the Old Testament Yahweh commanded against, and other sacred texts remind the faithful not to do. (Perhaps this literalization arises so often within religions precisely because the sacred texts are written down and require interpretation. Concrete interpretations are easier to grasp and hold than the continual rediscovery of interpretations that rich symbols require.) Believing in a deity as a literal fact transforms that deity into an idol, as soon as we stop inquiring into the mystery God represents. Without our active yearning for *the more*, God becomes the less.

We can all be the chosen people if we live our lives in tune with the divine. One need not even believe in God to gain the benefits of engaging with the divine. At least that is true in my experience. I gain more wisdom and aliveness from taking a little step back in spiritual awareness than I ever got from reverence for an imagined deity.

Binary questions about the existence of God "out there" spark an unrewarding inquiry. However, when we recognize the divinity in a tree or a person—and are able to feel and act in harmony with that feeling—we slip inside the experience of the divine, no matter what our vote on God might be. That is the goal of personal religion: awakening the direct experience of the divine and applying it in the best ways.

"Is there a God or not?" is a weak question. There are more useful questions for us to explore: "What do I get from the belief that there is or isn't a God, and what would change in my life without that belief?" "How does the experience of the divine come about in me?" "Where does God-like experience appear in my daily life?" "What do I praise?" "If I were a little more aware of the divine in my life today, how would the day be different?" Or even, "What is God like?" Such thoughts are hardly original. They were clear to the ancient Greek philosopher Hippolytus:

Abandon the search for God and the creation and other matters of a similar sort. Look for him by making yourself as the starting point. Learn who it is within you makes everything his own and says, my God, my mind, my thought, my soul, my body. Learn the sources of sorrow, joy, love, hate. Learn how it happens that one watches without willing, loves without willing. If you carefully investigate these matters, you will find him yourself.[16]

TENDING THE PERENNIALS

A person's stated belief or disbelief in God tells little about the quality of that individual's spiritual vitality; actions often belie stated beliefs. We can't even assert that belief in God means a person is more spiritual—many "believers" and "faithful churchgoers" live depressed, ungenerous, narrow lives, and many atheists and agnostics and "I don't deal with religion"-ists live lives brimming with spiritual fullness.

I believe in God the verb. We can argue about the noun or nouns of God at length and get nowhere slowly. But the debate about the existence of God misses the difference the divine makes in the world. The difference lies in inner facts and outer acts—how we look at things, what actions we take, what experiences we make for ourselves and what we give to others. A God alive and moving, not caught in the aspic of opinion.

I want to meet your understanding of God in the experience I have of you rather than in the words you say. God exists or doesn't exist, is alive or dead, is present or long gone, in the way we function as humans moment to moment. God speaks or is mute in our actions of spirit—not just in our occasional heroic actions or weekly response in a service, but in our minute internal choices now and now and now. When we create satisfying religious experiences, thank God we can participate with the divine so personally. We experience God-the-verb every time we invest our best (call it heart or soul or spirit or essence) to create something we care about.

Physicists remind us the universe is *all* built of "verbs." The rock in our hand is almost entirely composed of space, is whirring with motion, and is changing slowly into something else. The road-killed possum is busily engaged in becoming earth. From the slow-changing stone in the stream to the speedy flow of changes in our thoughts, perhaps there are no nouns, just verbs of differing speed.

IS GOD DEAD? Many brilliant theologians have argued this issue— and the world certainly feels God-abandoned sometimes. The arguments range from elaborate intellectual analyses to a simple belief that there cannot be a God in a world that created the Nazi Holocaust. God is no deader or livelier today than when those arguments began to appear hundreds of years ago. What has deadened is our capacity to imagine and create a divinity that provides for our experiential needs.

I recognize two main reasons why people have difficulty in finding God, and literalize the struggle with the headline claim that God has kicked the holy bucket. First, God rarely speaks to us unequivocally from baritone bushes. The experiential sensors that enable us to hear, recognize and connect with the divine are subtle, and the surrounding noise and distracting busyness of our lives are so loud that we assume God is dead because the presence is so faint. In the interesting field called psychophysics, there is a common-sense principle called the Weber-Fechner law that relates external stimulation to personal experience. The law sensibly proposes that our sensitivity to phenomena diminishes in proportion to the amount of stimulation. If there are two flashlights lit in a dark room, we readily notice the addition of a third; however, we do not notice the addition of a hundredth flashlight into a room with ninety-nine. The gentle evidence of the divine, the subtle hundredth flashlight of divine light, cannot be noticed or attended to among all the flashing that surrounds us, inside and out—so we assume it is gone. Little wonder that seekers throughout time, intuiting the Weber-Fechner effect, have retreated from the busy world when they needed to do serious spiritual work—to reduce input so that divine light becomes more perceptible.

Second, our requests of God are so helter-skelter, and our expectations of God's answers are so askew, that we preclude the subtler experience of the divine. There is much we ask of God, on a given day, often in a single prayer: everything from inner peace to health for a loved one, more money, food for children starving in an African famine, food for children hungry in one's own household, help with a particular project at work or for a loved one with an addiction, or simply to win the lottery. With such a jumble of needs, we cannot notice the delicate inner experience that begins to offer answers to those prayers.

Usually, we don't really want a divine response; we want results. But presenting a wish list with the expectation of overnight delivery is hardly the humble practice attuned to receive the quiet answer of divine experience. Our expectations of God are shaped by our cultural training, and we expect a parental presence that delivers the goods or a clearly recognizable answer. We have all yearned for a sign that God exists—one unambiguous signal would do. Our preconceptions set us up to ignore the abundant evidence of divinity. It all depends on how you look at things.

Americans' attitude toward Santa serves as an interesting metaphor. We expect *stuff* from Santa, not a vague sense of connection to a mystery that Father Christmas once symbolized. I have played the role a number of times in school and public-event settings. The younger children are terrified; they sometimes cry no matter how genial the ho ho–ing becomes. They are fully invested in the symbolic potential of this figure: in their experience, this is God. Even more terrifying, he is wearing a weird outfit; he is continually laughing for not-very-good reasons; he is a big stranger who wants to touch them; he knows their secrets and is reportedly judgmental. (I would cry too, if I were coerced next Christmas to tell my most heartfelt wishes to a twenty-foot-tall bearded stranger in a ridiculous outfit who is laughing falsely, who knows everything about me, is judging me, and wants me to sit on his lap.) The older kids have got the game down; they come to see Santa as a transactional means to desired ends. Some go through the bizarre Santa rituals knowing the fakeness of the guy in the get-up, but still willing to perform the rites in hopes it will somehow dispose the situation to be more favorable on their behalf. Angry theologians describe sometimes churchgoing in such terms.

There is the story of a terrible flood rising in a town. A state trooper knocks on a door and asks the very religious man to come with him to safety. "No, thank you, sir, I believe in God, and I put all my trust in Him." The water keeps rising, and the man moves up to the second floor. A neighbor in a little boat offers to take him to higher land. The man says, "No, thank you, my friend, I trust in the Lord to take care of me." The water rises till the man clings to the roof of his house. A helicopter bullhorn barks a demand to grab the harness to be brought aboard. The man shouts, "No, thank you, I have trust in God." That night the man is swept away and drowns. He meets St. Peter at the pearly gates and, in telling his story, lets on that he is annoyed with God for letting him down when he needed Him. Saint Peter says, "God let you down? He sent you a cop, a boat and a helicopter. What more do you want?"

The capacity to hear, to see, and to experience the quiet presence of the divine is the crucial skill of personal religion. These actions with their specific skills are largely the same as those with which we germinate the seed a poem, commune with the composer during the symphony, or discover answers to life's big questions while perusing the hardware store.

HEAVY PACK, HOT AUGUST DAY, I struggle up a mountain again, but this time under a high canopy of Adirondack trees. Flash forward from my first wilderness retreat: now an experienced wilderness soloist, I no longer need a support organization to help arrange my weeklong retreat in the woods. I just get the right map, dust off the compass, load my pack and go.

Bushwhacking my way up the third small mountain of the day, I scope for a retreat site, at least four sweaty miles from the nearest path. I am frustrated to be tired and still unable to find a workable location for my wilderness week. I think about the weight of the pack, considering what I can leave home next time. Suddenly I realize I have forgotten to pack my whistle; it is still hanging on the peg at home. A whistle is a safety device in the wild, one last-resort way one might attract help if one got into serious trouble. As far out as I am, it is a pretty thin lifeline in the case of a broken ankle or bear attack, but it's something. I feel a cold wash of fear pass over me—a safety mistake. Not a good way to start. I trudge on, angry at myself, irritated with the local topography and map, worried that my week of solitude was going to be stuck in a lousy site.

Less than a minute later, I see a glint in the undergrowth. I have not seen a single evidence of humans, no scrap of windblown litter, no boot-bent stalk, for hours. What could it be? Too bright a reflection to be mica, it has to be man-made. I head over to it and push aside the fern it hides beneath. It is a whistle. I pick it up and try it quietly. It works.

That whistle sits on my desk today. What guided me to that spot? Did God have something to do with this? I don't know—and my knowing or not doesn't make a whistle of difference. What mattered was the experience of fear; the discovery of a simple miracle; the superb jump-start to a week of divine experience in the wild.

We are surrounded by such whistles. Sacred, divine objects and opportunities. Simple answers to our needs and fears. It all depends on how we look at things. It comes down to wonder.

Wonder. Perhaps the quintessential capacity in a personal religion. One of the few words I have ever studied that has no agreement about its etymological origin. It has reverence and mystery in its DNA. The philosopher Immanuel Kant noted that wonder includes astonishment that does not disappear when novelty wears off. We will come back to wonder, the experience of shedding our conditioned selves to enter that which is greater than us.

Rabbi David Cooper's book entitled *God is a Verb: Kabbalah and the Practice of Mystical Judaism* appeared in my local bookstore just as I was finishing a new essay entitled "God is a Verb." It happens. I thought I was onto something important and original—and it was important, but it wasn't original. I have no expertise about the Kabbalah; I arrived at the same conclusion through the arts. Many paths lead to the same clearing.

I know what *I* meant. I had settled my uncertainty about the existence of a divine being with a quiet knowing there was no such singular entity. My clarity about something "divine" was coming into focus too. If the "something" we yearned to connect with "out there" didn't exist, what was going on in nearly all humans? The divine was the yearning; there was nothing more. The reach was the only arrival.

# PART II
# SKILLS AND TOOLS

## · CHAPTER 8 ·

# COMING TO ATTENTION

*Attention is an intentional, unapologetic discriminator. It asks
what is relevant right now, and gears us up to notice only that.*

ALEXANDRA HOROWITZ

ONE YEAR'S WILDERNESS SOLO SITE lay within earshot of a lively
brook. The stream ran a hundred yards from my circle-world, and I
briefly violated my 104-foot boundary once a day to get water. But
its sound provided company the rest of the day and night. One afternoon I decided to take some time and listen to the stream; that may
not sound thrilling, but when there is absolutely nothing else to do...

Normally listening to a stream means hearing its sounds,
enjoying the soothing white noise for a pleasant minute till the mind
snaps to something else. This time, however, I give the sound of the
stream my full attention, for many minutes. I distinguish four different
tones within the general babble and follow their interplay. There are
patterns and unexpected changes—a quartet improvising a Philip
Glass-like piece. The more I give my attention, the more I hear, and
the more I fill with a kind of delight that grows toward ecstasy. I know
this is the best thing on Earth I can be doing at this moment, and I
am not doing anything special. The noise doesn't "mean" anything,
just water over rocks. Yet, with my full creative attention, I create
something beautiful with that brook. I participate in the divine order
by adding the thing that humans can do, perceiving, appreciating,
participating, and then if wise enough, going beyond even that to
what lies beyond.

Certainly, the experience felt great. But feeling good was not
the point—I might feel bad the next moment when I focused on
my stiff back. There was a deeper resonance: I had co-created with
nature, more fully realizing something beautiful that is always there

but grows richer when perceived. I brought joy to the natural world the way a particularly lively audience would reward me as a performer. It was more than appreciating nature as if it were art; it was using my arts skills to grasp a divine creation more beautiful than any human artist could create.

The cartoonist Jim Borgman tells the story of his young son's benediction as they sat down to draw together once: "Okay, Dad, let's make some paper happy." I understood his son's impulse; I had made the divine happy by applying the best of what I, one flawed human, could bring.

In this part of the book, we will explore the skills and tools we use to create spiritual and artistic experience. We begin with attention, a center point to which we will endlessly return. The attention I use in my solo circle is the attention many religious traditions place at the heart of their training. It is the attention Cézanne turned toward Mt. Saint Victoire, and the attention many turn to his paintings of that mountain. We cannot find or follow a spiritual inquiry without using attention well. How we attend is how we live; and what we attend to determines who we are.

Full attention to one thing at a time—a spiritual foundation with an experiential reward. For the rest of that wilderness retreat, I experimented by applying that same full attention to other opportunities. Sure enough, with full attention, even the tiny challenges of tooth brushing became fascinating. The improvisation in the small theater of my mouth was full of rhythms and choreography; its subtle music resonated inside my head; it became sensual and hilarious. I came to look forward to toothbrushing every morning and evening. Every activity I touched with that attention became delightful. My 104-foot circle became a spiritual amusement park, with attractions like walking across the circle to get a drink of water, feeling the breeze on my chest and thinking about the people I love. Every action became a creative improvisation. With enough attention, anything becomes profound. Any act can deliver delights.

Some psychiatrists, and some parents, listen in this way. Orchestral conductors and lovers listen that attentively, and feel the same rapture I did with the brook. The feminist theologian Nelle Morton states an aspiration I live by: "We can hear one another into being." Martin Buber describes this universal partnership. "No encounter with a being or thing in the course of our life lacks a hidden significance. The people we live with or meet with, the animals that help us with our farm work, the soil we till, the materials we shape, the tools we use, they all contain a mysterious spiritual substance which depends on us for helping it towards its pure form, its perfection."[17]

There is a Zen story of a man who seeks wisdom. Having studied Zen for many years, he makes a pilgrimage to meet the master he reveres and learn the final secrets that will take him to full enlightenment. He walks for years to reach the remote location. After days of purification, he is brought in to meet the great teacher and says, "I have studied long and traveled far to reach you and receive the ultimate wisdom. I am ready." The master nods gravely and says only, "Attention." The seeker waits for more, but that is it. He gets mad and says, "Master, I have dedicated my entire life to this study, I have gone to extraordinary lengths to come here; you could give me something more than that." The master looks serious, nods again and says, "Yes, you are right. Attention, attention, attention."

Attention leads us toward the truth. Attention constructs our sense of reality by connecting inner experience with tangible reality. Full attention accomplishes an astonishing feat: we simultaneously stretch out with our senses while we stay aware of what is happening at experiential home base at the same time.

Full attention is the kernel of consciousness. The word *consciousness* (from the Latin *conscire*) etymologically meant *to know something with oneself*, which aptly describes what we do when we attend well. Inherent in the word is the witnessing, the little step back in awareness, that marks the beginning of spirituality. As St.

Francis reminds us, we are looking for the one who is looking—and who is looking is the part of us that pays attention.

The idiom "pay attention" reminds us that it costs us something: we make adjustments in mind and heart to "invest" psychic energy in a chosen encounter. We can attend fully to just one thing at a time, so we gamble that the experiential results will be worth the cost in energy and sacrifice of the other things we might have done with our attention. We apply intuitive criteria to determine our attention investments, and we expect to get something worthwhile back, experientially or materially, for the attention we pay. No matter how tiny the action arena of attention, resonant issues are involved.

These "decisions" about attention allocation occur in milliseconds. We think of these processes as fully autonomic, like a peristalsis of the mind. They are not. Brain neuroscience is teaching us that there are indeed habituated patterns of synaptic connection in our seeing, but they are not locked in. They are disruptable and redirectable. We all have the skills for guiding attention intentionally; they are more developed in some than in others, and need further development in all.

Generally, people are pretty stingy with their full attention, spending it for familiar or advertised rewards, withholding it out of habit, fear or laziness, rarely giving anything full attention. Our upbringing and culture in the U.S. do not develop faith in the experiential rewards of exploring the new, apart from new sensations in arenas we already know. With new ideas, people who are different, and new phenomena, we tend to be inattentive, judgmental, cautious or even cynical.

It seems fair to say that at one time in the U.S., our greatest scarcity was basic commodities; then it became money; then it became time; and now it is full attention. Multi-attending has become an American norm, with several demands for our attention active at most times. The problem is that there is no such thing as multi-attending in the human brain—there is only quicker shifting between the one thing your conscious attention can manage at a time. This habitual jangling of attention has subtle but profound consequences in the human animal, not least of which is increased difficulty in reflecting and feeling spiritual aspiration.

Young children who have not yet been conditioned into focus-fragmenting habits attend wholeheartedly, in a way that skillfully discovers the value in new things. "Whosoever does not receive the Kingdom of God as a little child shall not enter into it" [Mark 10:15]. In my wilderness circle, I rediscover the innate skills of attention that are so often poorly applied, and there no longer seems to be a scarcity of marvels in the world.

A quick distinction between attention and awareness, even though the words are often used synonymously: we attend by investing ourselves, by reaching out to encounter and make a connection. Awareness opens wide to see everything that is happening; it witnesses. Attention has a particular focus and a thrust; awareness takes in. Attention seeks; awareness simply is. Experienced meditators recognize the difference between attention to breathing (dedicating focus to the specific experience of each breath) and awareness of breath (following breathing as it lives in the wider context of consciousness).

Generally, the arts are more concerned with issues of attention, and religions with issues of awareness—but the fullness of experience in art and spirituality alike depends on both attention and awareness. All religions, all arts, all spiritual traditions need us to attend in particular ways to get the rewards they offer. They all require the same kind of attention, the same kind of awareness.

To develop these skills of attention and awareness, religions offer exercises and practices. Few Western religions directly address the fundamental skills of attention and awareness in general practice, relying on religious events themselves, with their dramatic structure and theatrical elements, to direct our attention. Throughout the centuries, most organized religions have spent so much energy on other (often secular) issues that they have not grown in these most essential skill areas. If one-quarter of the energy that has been expended on minor points of dogma, on squabbles within the faithful and against those of other faiths, or on issues of money and control were dedicated to developing better ways for the faithful to attend and become aware, we would enjoy a much more enlightened world.

However, every religion attracts a subset of particularly enthusiastic faithful. This crucial core group finds ways to pursue intensive study, which includes practices to develop attention and awareness. Ramana Maharshi, for example, is just one of many Hindu sages whose idiosyncratic personal journey to enlightenment inspired legions of followers. The Abbess Hildegard von Bingen (12th century) translated her ecstatic visions into music and poetry that invited an aesthetic attention to spiritual devotion, as did the poetry of the priest St. John of the Cross (16th century). The exceedingly detailed training practices of Tibetan Buddhism, including the guidebook *The Tibetan Book of the Dead*, were refined over centuries of accrued expertise by monks cloistered in esoteric study.

Theologian Karen Armstrong describes a challenge we all face:

> One of the reasons why religion seems irrelevant to us today is that many of us no longer have the sense that we are surrounded by the unseen. Our scientific culture educates us to focus our attention on the physical and material world in front of us. This method of looking at the world has achieved great results. One of its consequences, however, is that we have, as it were, edited out the sense of the "spiritual," of the "holy," which pervades the lives of people in more traditional societies at every level and which was once an essential component of our human experience of the world.[18]

The stretching out of the self (the etymological meaning of *attend*) is the transitional moment when profane experience can begin to turn sacred. In that moment, we awake spiritual potential by forgetting ourselves and giving over to discovery. The improvisatory act of attending always happens in the present tense; it lives in the moment, the time frame of spiritual experience. The sign on the wall at the bingo parlor says, "You must be present to win"—in life-bingo, more than your body must be present.

Attention as a spiritual touchstone is hardly a modern discovery; inquirers have focused on this skill for millennia. The Stoics in the Golden Age of Greece were not a bedsheet-wearing philosophy club that tested their resolve to "stoically" resist pleasures so they could be more productive. (Those were Puritans, except for the sheets.) The Stoics believed individuals are part of a connected whole, that each individual person had an absolute value, and that fully concentrated attention on the present moment was the way to gain access to the totality of the world. We could all do with being more of that kind of stoical.

> *The wise Rabbi of Kotzk was visited by a group of very learned men. He surprised them with the question, 'Where is the dwelling of God?' They laughed at him, saying, 'What a thing to ask! Is not the whole world full of his glory?' Then he answered his own question, 'God dwells wherever man lets him in.' This is the ultimate purpose in life: to let God in.*[19]
>
> MARTIN BUBER

# CHAPTER 9

# PUTTING US ON NOTICE

AN ENCOUNTER WITH THE NEW begins in noticing, which is the tip of the attention iceberg. Noticing is so ordinary an event that we might not even register its occurence, but it is an act of consequence. Its parent word (the Latin *notus*) signified *knowledge*, and indeed, what we notice provides the building blocks of what we know.

Here are two important, overlooked aspects of noticing: 1) we rarely notice what we notice (which takes awareness); and 2) we can choose a great deal of what we notice. Noticing can be trained; it is a skill of attention.[20]

If noticing is the tip of the attention iceberg, then the awareness that notices what we notice is the nine-tenths of importance below the surface. Noticing is usually a spotlight we wave erratically, illuminating this and then that, inside our minds and out in the world. In noticing what we notice, we take that "little step back" in our psyche; we shift perspective to see what our noticing choices illuminate. That little step back of awareness brings spiritual potential to profane experience. The spiritual exercises of great religions seek to train attention to noticing in students through meditation, contemplation, prayer, yoga, tantra and martial arts.

TRY THIS.

*When you have read these directions, put down the book. Take thirty seconds and do nothing but notice what you notice. It's hard to do. See how quickly your attention shifts, notice everything you can of what your attention touches on. It is only thirty seconds, so try to stay with it. Those who have tried to meditate know the scene in there—how relentlessly the different items arise, and how challenging it is to take that little step back to notice them rather than be grabbed by them.*

It is difficult to follow the fast, erratic noticing. Meditators know this aspect of the human condition well. Humans seem to have no choice about what arises in there; attention races around like a manic child. Buddhists call it the "monkey mind," and it is difficult to quiet. We also do not have a reliable ability to simply notice what arises, rather than being caught and pulled into the thinking, feeling, planning, daydreaming and so on.

However, noticing is not as anarchic as it may seem. If we were to collect our noticings for a day and study them, we would see clear themes and patterns. Chaos Theory in action—under the surface pandemonium, there are unifying principles at play. There are relatively few *types* of things we notice in a day, and they correspond to our active life issues. If fear is an active issue, we notice things to be wary of or things that are safe; if we are food-absorbed, we notice edibles everywhere; if we are lonely, we notice people and their contact potential, or the contacts they have that we don't. Noticing shifts with changing life issues: if we decide to get a new car, and are interested in a Camry, suddenly the world is filled by Toyota ads and dealerships, the streets are filled with Camrys, and other cars are noticed as Camry comparisons.

By noticing what we notice, we can discover our active yearnings and interests. A poet mulls a particular phrase, even though a hundred others ticker-taped through her mind in an hour; a father ponders a look he saw on his daughter's face; an adult daughter catches herself using a tone of voice she often heard from her mother. Such noticings brim with potential.

The thousands of bits we choose to notice in a day comprise a profoundly accurate collage of us as individuals. We are what we notice. We notice things for many different reasons, including instinct, safety, upbringing, social conditioning, desire, habit—as well as to satisfy our own idiosyncratic interests.

## "Clean" Noticing

WE DEVELOP INNER TEMPLATES that cover almost all of the noticing opportunities of the day. We expect certain things and notice within those expectations, and we especially notice anomalies that jump out as dangerous or dramatically different. This efficiency of expectations is necessary, of course; no one could cope with the madhouse that a day of full noticing would provide. We naturally edit out 99 percent of what we might notice because our unconscious attention, with its templates of normalcy, tells us something is not worth the attention investment. Think how differently we attend on the first day of a new job, because we have not yet developed normalcy filters for the new context. Psychologists also confirm how much we do not notice because we find it painful to admit to our consciousness. Our defense systems can prevent us from noticing even blatant realities in front of us—a loved one with a serious problem, a medical warning sign, how similar to a bad previous boyfriend the new one is.

If we rely too heavily on those expectations and noticing filters, life begins to seem boring, predictable, routine. We say, "Nothing new ever happens," because nothing new is happening in our experience. I have heard people who have been on previous safaris in Africa say, "We never see anything new," as giraffes and elephants graze in their view. I have heard many people say they are bored in an art museum.

To counteract this natural tendency, we must develop the skill of noticing cleanly. It enables us to perceive what is present afresh, not muddied with our presuppositions, instant judgments, and snap interpretations. It resists the strong tendency to skew what we see in the direction of what we know.

HERE IS A SIMPLE PRACTICE:
*to help you to notice cleanly, separating observation from interpretation and judgement. Wherever you are sitting, look at something on a wall. (A painting of a tree*

*in a meadow, for example.) Take a full minute just to observe it. Do you notice how quickly judgments start to creep in about whether you like it or not, or what is good and bad about it? Slow down that process. Speaking aloud, make statement after statement about aspects of that object you actually see. What else do you see, what other features does it have? (There is a main tree, two others in the background, and then a distant forest. There are shadows of the branches, etc.) When you have pretty much exhausted all the observable aspects, start to draw some conclusions or interpretations about how those elements fit together. (It seems to be morning. The artist was interested in the spring-like quality of the leaves. The painting is divided into roughly four quarters, each with a mood. Etc.) And only after offering as many interpretations as possible, give in to judgments about it. (The tension between the grass and leaves gives the scene vitality. The artist was fascinated by the tree's shadow, but perhaps it is too intense.)*

Observe first. Just attend to what is present, before allowing opinions, judgments and conclusions to appear. This is difficult. We zip in with our opinions, likes and dislikes, comparisons and critiques before we have bothered to see what is there—even when we try not to. The pause to merely observe sets aside the judgmental impulse for a few moments and opens a world of new seeing.

When we develop this as a habit, our generalizations and prejudices lose their control. Curiosity and optimism increase. We can support this habit of mind by regularly following the process described above, asking simple questions like: What do I really see there? What other features are present? What specifically is provoking the response I feel? We find that our usual interpretations and judgments change when we base them in what is there, freshly noticed. Teaching artists use the guideline "observation before interpretation" to help learners internalize this habit. For those who are pedagogically inclined, the work of Visual Thinking Strategies has honed and researched this work to such a degree that it has been widely adopted throughout the fields of arts learning and beyond.

Another necessary habit is "noticing in and out." We must balance and connect our observation of things in the world (outer facts) with what is going on inside us (inner facts). Individuals tend to rely on one of those inclinations more than the other. There may even be some influence from the extrovert-introvert continuum—extreme "innies" incline toward overreliance on the inner facts, extreme "exies" lean toward outer facts, and most of us are arrayed across that spectrum. Which is your natural tendency?

Newness attracts attention. We notice many things when we drive a new car for the first time; we notice nothing about the car when we drive it for the thousandth time. An advanced skill of attention is experiencing the not-so-new as if it were new. Call it naiveté-on-demand, or fresh eyes. It is the capacity to rediscover within the known.

This capacity enables us to go deeper, rather than stay addicted to novelty. We set aside known elements, accrued attitudes and expectations in order to attend afresh to familiar things like the words of a prayer, the routines of a task, the contours of a still-life painting or the face of a spouse. This is more difficult than attending to novelty or to obstacles. Zen Buddhists call this "the beginner's mind," a mental state of openness and curiosity, and they follow a rigorous training to reach this beginning. If we can perceive the unseen in the familiar—if we can create new improvisations of connection with the well known—we transform the ordinary into the extraordinary. Long-term relationships require naiveté-on-demand to stay alive and grow.

*Look at something familiar in your home, say the surface of your desk or a bookshelf. Notice your way through a rediscovery of it, as we did in the previous exercise. As you are observing, also ask: what is something about this place I have never noticed before? What would someone else notice who has never seen this before? Ask: if this were in a photograph composed by an artist, why might she have placed things exactly as they are; what might she be trying to say? Ask yourself: if this were in a historical museum, what might an astute observer come to understand by looking at this? See if you can answer: what is wonderful about this? Where might the divine be present in this?*

## Choosing Our Noticing

WE CAN INFLUENCE OUR NOTICING. While many of our noticings are determined by demands beyond our easy control, like fear and neurosis, habits of mind or evolutionary demands, our attention has time for discretionary noticing. If we are in touch with our yearnings, we notice things that interest us; if we are closely aligned with our yearnings, we experience a steady stream of relevant, rewarding, raw material in daily life. This is not some esoteric practice—we sometimes experience it without even trying. Another example, similar to the "buying a Camry" example from a few pages back: you make the big decision to remodel your kitchen, and suddenly kitchen supply stores appear out of nowhere, and ads with kitchens appear in magazines. They did not spring up overnight; you begin to notice them because your yearning is activated, and your sub-liminal skills of attention serve up a supply of raw material for you to work with.

This pattern is familiar to artists: the choreographer engaged in a dance of duets suddenly starts to see pairs of people dancing throughout the city. The workings of internet commerce calculate algorithms that serve up advertising messages most attuned to your interests. Social psychologists and commentators are becoming aware of how insidiously these algorithms affect us—not just to channel what we buy, but to influence what we read and think and do. However sophisticated the manipulations of internet may become, they are simplistic compared to the deep, incalculable, non-binary workings of your psyche to accomplish a similar end. Thank heavens for the mystery.

This works with our spiritual yearnings too. As spiritual yearnings come closer to the surface, we notice what we usually overlook. This experience—noticing things that answer our questions, life delivering up what we are curious to learn about—is the beautiful feeling that it all fits together. It is a state of grace. This is the experience of spiritual inquiry, with the world (inner and outer) as an abundant personal resource center. As Derrida writes, "From the moment that there is meaning, there are nothing but signs."[21]

We can't fool noticing with pretension—we notice what our true impulses prompt. Let's say you want to have more spirituality in your life. You can say the right things and hang ancient symbols around your neck, but if you are still caught in anger and money-concerns, you are going to notice things that irritate you, things you obsess about having, and all the things that are wrong with you and everyone else. There is nothing wrong with "negative" emotions, but if you yearn to experience more spirituality, you can't pretend your way out of them. We must notice what we are noticing, even if it isn't pretty. What we notice is always a flashlight toward a truth. Want to test this theory?

TRY THIS...
*but you must fully invest yourself to give it a fair trial. Following are several metaphoric ideas to choose from, any of which might be relevant to a spiritual inquiry. Pick one that appeals to you. You are going to carry this metaphor with you throughout a normal day, and try to*

*apply it to situations as often as you can. (For example, if you pick "about to bloom," it might apply to a young assistant, to an idea you are working on, a pimple on someone's chin, the part of a song on the radio when it modulates to a different key, or—poignantly—to a near-dead flower on a desk.) The challenge will be not in finding applicable situations, but in remembering to do it. Perhaps you might write it on a little paper you carry to help remind yourself. Perhaps tuck the reminder paper under your watchband, and every time you notice the paper, try to apply it. Find as many places you can apply it as possible; people frequently discover twenty or more relevant appearances (some are examples, some variations, contradictions, ironic comments) of that metaphor in a day. At the end of the day, review the metaphors you recall making during the day. Ready? Choose one of these and play with its appearance throughout the day:*

- *In a cage*
- *About to bloom*
- *Painted-over surface*
- *New skin under the scab*
- *Pattern within a pattern*

This activity demonstrates that 1) despite the heavy demands on our noticing, we have plenty of discretionary attention if we choose to take advantage of it; 2) we can influence the flow of our noticing to enrich the issues we care about; 3) our yearnings appear when we attend fully; and 4) there is a personal truth held in those metaphors, awaiting your attention.

## Active Receptivity

FULL ATTENTION delicately balances effort and relaxation. The relaxation is general; the effort is specific. And the relaxation is more than remembering to drop the shoulders and breathe deeply every now and again. Good attention is open and active; let's call it active receptivity.

Our typical attention is passive and narrow-gauge. We are too busy to notice much. We wait for things to grab us, and our culture obliges with brilliantly crafted attention-grabbers designed to fulfill many agendas (primarily commercial) other than our own. Or we attend through the lenses of preconception: we overlook the bright, playful twinkle in a young relative's eye because we see only trash-talking teen. The skill is to have open perceiving ready when yearning's subtle tickle of interest says, "Attend."

It takes skill to identify the most productive occasions within which to open wide into noticing. Most spiritual practices develop this capacity to open the heart; most highly developed spiritual people can be distinguished by their open availability to the world. All paths lead to the same summit, and reaching that universal summit requires a courageous, eager openness to experience. This openness in adept practitioners is universally described as childlike, because it is so filled with curiosity and wonder. Remember: "Whosoever does not receive the Kingdom of God as a little child shall not enter into it" [Mark 10:15].

Active receptivity, as distinguished from passive, has an energy in it, an eagerness to welcome whatever may be. It is poised to receive, with "yes" waiting on the lips. When actors are in training, they focus on the capacity to detach from the past and future so they can be "in the moment," receptive to whatever happens in the scene. This state of mind can be called the "energized zero"—zero preconceptions of what will happen, but alive to receive. Different schools of actor training, different teachers within those different schools, have specific training techniques to develop this spiritual capacity. They are gurus of a kind, developing spiritual capacity necessary to elevate performance into art.

Research on creativity asserts that active receptivity is associated with highly creative people. These people lean into experience, with a taste for novel experiences, new ideas, disruptions in patterns, the unexpected. That subtle difference in attitude, two degrees of inclination, makes all the difference in the world. As we lean forward, eager to discover whatever may arise, we say yes to the world and sign a contract to participate in it.

In a workshop with division managers at a large corporation, I placed an oddly abstract African sculpture on the table and gave them a problem. "Imagine the company president called you in and told you this piece was just donated by the chairman of the board. The president needs to butter up the chairman by putting an article on this gift in the company newsletter; you have been selected to write the article. No one knows anything about the sculpture—and the problem is that the newsletter goes to press in twenty minutes." I asked the managers to brainstorm ways they might solve the problem. They had ready ideas (they were used to unpredictable crises). They began with negative jokes about their real CEO. The first twelve ideas were all different ways of getting information quickly. And then they ran out of ideas.

I pointed out three things: 1) as a group they had had only one single idea—get information quickly; 2) the one strategy they had was not going to work, so they had no viable solution to the newsletter problem; 3) no one had bothered to really look at the sculpture. I then had them take one minute to speak aloud observations about the sculpture. "It seems to be made of wood." "It shows a human figure but with only one eye." Then we took one minute to ask questions about it, without answering any of the questions. "Why are there no feet?" "What purpose did it serve for the artist's community?" After those two minutes of noticing cleanly, we returned to the newsletter problem. Now they were brimming with great ways to write the newsletter article. "I could write about how art stimulates productive thinking in a business environment." "I could write 'Notes from an Inadvertent Art Critic.'" "What about, 'Why Art in Healthcare?'" The good use of attention woke them up, made things fun, and produced a better bottom-line solution to the problem.

## The Importance of Not Knowing

ACTIVE RECEPTIVITY requires that we be able to "not know." Not knowing (as opposed to ignorance) is a skill—we need to know a lot in order to know how to not-know well. (There is a sentence you don't see every day!) Not knowing requires a willingness to be vulnerable, which we naturally resist—and of course we resist it; it goes against our evolutionary instincts. Not knowing makes us anxious, and we avoid it in a hundred opportunities a day. Not knowing taps the great uncertainties of being alive, and rather than courageously staying open when we catch a whiff of the void, many become terrified, even phobic, about moments of not knowing.

The opportunity to not know rarely comes in a high-drama, cataclysmic moment, like those live televised moments when a public figure gets stumped or caught out. In the everyday-variety opportunities to not know, we usually chicken out and settle for half-knowing or fig-leaf responses that cover the exposure, relying on a sudden opinion, a preconception or a quick-fix choice. For example, the spouse who does the cooking says she (or he) doesn't want to cook for a while. The partner can respond reactively, or snap to solutions about how they are going to eat, or can pause in uncertainty to sense if this means something. It may mean something, maybe something the partner doesn't like or maybe something potentially positive. Maybe. So, stay open, wait, talk and see what emerges. The more skillfully we can hold off the pressures to end uncertainty—by reacting, judging, kicking into action—the more fully we can discover the new. Basically, the better we can "not know," the better we can see what is present, the better we can learn, because we are open to new possibilities.

Artists are often heroes of not knowing. They are familiar with the state and its anxieties; they know it is the starting point of all significant creative work. They secretly love it. We rarely salute the courage of artists and spiritual seekers; they deserve recognition for the fortitude it takes to not know every day, the strength to wait and see what appears in the void, and the savvy to navigate the process, whatever its anxieties, often finding pleasure all along the way.

The implications of this skill are enormous in our spiritual lives. The divine is all about the unknown, so uncertainty colors the divine. (Religious dogma is designed to provide handholds that reduce, eliminate or cover that uncertainty.) We are steeped in so many social and religious guidelines that we have a reflexive range of ways to deal with the spiritual unknowns and invisibles we meet. We readily name, explain or deny, rather than wonder and see. However, our spiritual capacity grows only to the degree that we can relax at those moments of uncertainty, stay open to discovery and allow the slow creative process of new knowing to unfold. This is a discipline, and a good disciple of any practice must be a skillful not-knower—a good learner. Not knowing is different from not caring. Not knowing sustains our attentive participation. Not caring entrenches the status quo, and worse.

As we learn to relax in that moment of uncertainty, we practice what John Keats called "negative capability"—"when a man is capable of being in uncertainties, mysteries, doubts, without any irritable reaching after fact and fiction."[22] At the moment of uncertainty or frustration in any spiritual inquiry, we must apply our negative capability to allow nothing, or something unexpected, to appear. Zen koans ingeniously frustrate the grasping impulse and tickle out our negative capability.

The arts provide good ambiguity-tolerance training. A poetic image—"Life, like a dome of many-colored glass, / Stains the white radiance of Eternity"[23]—doesn't mean any one thing. A concerto movement means many things, few of which can be captured in words. The arts draw us into uncertainties; only by using negative capabilities can we discover what they offer us. Artistic and spiritual experiences require the same negative capability. Art and religion are uniquely important because they are two main arenas where vitality requires us to tolerate the discomfort of ambiguity and uncertainty. Mainstream culture, unfortunately, aims to disrupt that tolerance by providing the easier comfort of certainty, via entertainment (instead of art) and dogma (instead of religion).

MY NIECE ALEXA MILLER is a teaching artist. She was the lead teaching artist in a new course at Harvard Medical School in collaboration with the Museum of Fine Arts, Boston and the Isabella Stewart Gardner Museum. Researchers from Harvard launched a two-year, double-blinded, scientifically sound study of the course's impact that confirmed the significant changes in students' thinking, seeing and language that Alexa had observed. The research team published the results in a major medical journal, which was picked up and reported in major media. Alexa taught in that course for ten years and launched a consulting career with her company ArtsPractica, providing workshops that enable physicians to be more effective and mindful in uncertainty with patients through immersive and interactive experiences with visual art. Alexa believes that the habits of mind at the core of arts engagement are one and the same with great clinical work. Talking with Alexa about this work over the years, I have always been struck at how she leads doctors (from those-in-training, to the faculty who teach them, to the leaders who drive the systems in which they work) through workshops on how to look at artworks: studying the paintings, the doctors learn how to not-know for a longer time, how to tolerate ambiguity, and how to discover and consider more bits of information before coming to interpretation. The developing body of research increasingly affirms that there is a direct transfer of those observation skills to making more accurate medical diagnosis. Alexa's work with leaders across the healthcare professions proves that ambiguity tolerance saves lives, not only metaphorically but also literally. My summary of that body of work? Art saves lives, proven. Proven in this carefully researched instance, and merely true in millions of others.

Let's also note that being able to not know does something wonderful to the ego. It lets us renounce the ego's demand for control; it eases the spirit; it opens a rusty tired old door to brand-new discoveries. Living amid discoveries is more alive than living amid settled certainties.

# CHAPTER 10

# RESPONSE-ABILITY AND MAKING CONNECTIONS

WE DO NOT CREATE SPIRITUAL EXPERIENCES through clean noticing, active receptivity and negative capability alone. They are the essential yin, the receptive side of creativity. The yang aspect—the positive capability, we might say—responds. This skill is response-ability, the capacity to have an authentic response to something new. It is the fundamental creative act.

Responding is not a mechanical act—not simply what you say when the person opposite you has stopped talking, as do poor conversationalists and terrible actors who listen only enough to hear their cue. An authentic response is not the response we are supposed to have, were trained to have, or have had in the past; it is the spark of *particular* response that springs from who we really are in a particular moment. Carl Jung draws this distinction: "Any reaction to a stimulus may be causally explained, but the creative act, which is the absolute antithesis of mere reaction, will forever elude the human understanding."[24]

From the Latin *respondere*, to respond etymologically means *to promise back*, and a real response is indeed a giving of oneself. The skill takes us beneath personality and social training to quickly touch base with our soul or spirit. Response-ability offers a personal commitment to the moment; it honors the world's offerings to us. If we are response-able in life, we treat ordinary experiences as fresh opportunities to invest in. Response-ability engages us in the work of art, as we take the moments seriously enough to attend well and give back a genuine response—not a pre-fabricated opinion but a discovery. Such *authenticity* (etymologically *self-made*) changes the quality of the ensuing experience. We feel the difference between an automatic response and an original one, and the difference is often enormous.

Artists and spiritual creators are skillful responders. They touch down into their own understandings readily and come forth with a unique, surprising, sometimes profound and beautiful response. Both artists and spiritually creative people dip into that well constantly in their work. Every formal prayer offers new opportunities to respond and discover anew, opportunities we usually miss with our attention aimed elsewhere. Similarly, good stage actors will tell you a performance is different every night, because the responses come out afresh. (This is not always the case. Actors can get automatic, responding with bits that "always work," and entirely miss the experience of the work of art. For example, Alfred Lunt was troubled one night when he did not get an expected laugh after his character abruptly turns to the servant during a serious moment. He asked his acting partner [who was also his wife] what had happened. She responded, "Of course it wasn't funny, Alfred, you were asking for a laugh instead of asking for tea.")

Response-ability seeks to make connections; we promise back in order to form a bond with something. The idiom "to make a connection" underscores response-ability as the atomic level of creative action. When we are relaxed, awake and curious, we are inherently creative, inspired to make connections. Humans have evolved to function this way; this is our work on earth: to create worlds small and large, as the divine has done and continues to do. Making connections is a holy act.

Artists and spiritually creative people (the same people in my view, just wearing different name tags) apply their response-ability often, making connections everywhere. They live to make worlds, using many of the same inner tools, and feel fully alive when they do. It begins in the moment of response, and in each moment of response.

Our society, and consequently our schooling, prize logical connections above all others. Logical connections are powerful and essential, obviously, but humans also make emotional connections, associative connections (when we connect a previous experience to a new one), physical, visual and intuitive connections, plus a host of subtle kinds that we lack names to describe—as that quotation from Carl Jung states. We need this range of ways to respond because there are so many different kinds of opportunities in life. The psychologist Abraham Maslow pointed out what happens when we have few ways to connect: "If the only tool you have is a hammer, every problem comes to resemble a nail." Much of the depression we see in society today results from having too few ways to connect to the abundant and urgent world. To make sense out of the complex mix of our daily lives, we need to be able to make many kinds of connections.

The greater our range of skills as connectors, the greater our ability to make multiple kinds of meaning in life—which is the central goal of art and religion. Making personal connections is the first step of making meaning. Jean Houston, one of the leaders of the human potential movement, tells us that all religions believe every individual contains a God-seed, a bit of the divine to be developed through practice. Response-ability is the God-seed to be planted in any given moment.

All art, all learning, all dialogue, all love, all satisfactions, all complex understandings—all the best things in life—are born of simple connections. In making a connection, we link something we know with something new. Even if a connection has been previously discovered by others, it is still a creative accomplishment each time it is made, because our unique personal histories give every discovery a different shading. There *are* new things under the sun, and they are us!

We get into spiritual trouble when we lose touch with our basics. Just as the Dalai Lama meditates and soprano Dawn Upshaw does her vocal warmups every day, so must we attend to our modest occasions of attending and responding, creating new connections a hundred times a day. It is humble work; spiritual inquiry never stops being humble work—the etymological meaning of humble is *close to the ground*. One of the paradoxes we must tolerate is that in order to "go high" (reach new summits of spirituality), we must stay low (practice the basic skills that take us step by step).

## Bouncing Into Inquiries

CONNECTIONS SPARK FURTHER CONNECTIONS. I prepare a group to hear a Shakespearean sonnet, which I recite after preparatory activities. (Teaching artist at work.) They relate to it strongly. I am swamped with questions about sonnets, about why the form has such power, about resources to find out more, about Shakespeare. Six minutes prior, they had no interest in sonnets and cringed at the thought of Shakespeare.

I have seen it a thousand times: a person has an insight, comes up with an idea, discovers something—in other words, creates a connection—and the very next thing that happens is a small burst of forward energy. I call it "the bounce," and it is a distinguishing feature of humans. Being inherently creative, we do not flop into satiation in response to a creative accomplishment large or small; we naturally seek more. (Well, maybe we do take a rest on the seventh day for the biggies.)

Through this spark plug of yearning, one connection leads to another connection, and so on. We do not need to apply the "getting-started" energy (that all still bodies must apply) each time we give ourselves to a challenge; rather, we follow the bouncing ball of interest, using the creative momentum that artists and mystics know well. This human trait defies the second law of thermodynamics; energy does *not* run down when we are creatively engaged—it feeds itself.

Making a connection and bouncing forward is almost like stitching a new garment; each connection provides a "yes" and each bounce says "and." Together they create a rhythm of "yes, and," "yes, and." This is the rhythm of inquiry, be it artistic or religious (or scientific). Subtle as it may be, we must feel that spark and follow it, because it sews our connections together to produce the garments of art and religion.

"Yes, and" is the most basic rule of artistic improvisation. Whatever your partner introduces, you say "yes" to it (no matter what it is, and even if you don't much like it), and then add to it. The rule is that once it has been offered, it has become a part of the reality and so cannot be denied. For example, say you are improvising a scene with a partner about going out for a romantic dinner. If in the middle, your partner says, "but the doctor told me I shouldn't eat too much before my hemorrhoid operation in the morning." The operation now exists, and you must work with it—how you do that is the creative part. Find and follow the bounce. Do you suggest defying the medical establishment? Do you gently try to help your partner with this instance of a recurrent hallucination problem? The answer depends on what your character "wants"—the theatrical version of yearning. The attitude of "yes, and" activates our receptivity and develops a playful attitude toward whatever comes down the pike.

When I imagine a divine being making the universe, I hear a colossal "yes" after each new aspect of the universe appears, plus the "and" impulse to add more. It is our job to take over that role in our small corner of the cosmos, to "yes, and" our contributions in the ongoing improvisation.

That bounce leads to satisfaction in the small improvisations that comprise our days. It sustains our ongoing creative work in art or religious inquiry; if we lose touch with it, we stall in the quality of our praying or piano playing. The experience of this bounce manifests as curiosity, as attraction to something, as interest. We must nurture every curiosity, follow our attractions, feed our interests. That easily disregarded blip of curiosity is the indicator that a greater yearning is present; it is a gift of grace from the divine.

To sustain the inquiries sparked by curiosity, we must attend to the subtlest, most tentative "and."

*Look back to a section in this book that caught your interest. Any bit. Read slowly, very slowly, sentence by sentence, thought by thought, taking pauses, staying attuned to the tiny moments when you take in an idea, and it sparks a further thought. Follow that process of taking in a thought, responding to it, and following your thought either to a next thought or to return to the page to catch my next sentence. This natural practice of "yes, and" happens all the time. When you and I are working well together in these pages, we are bouncing along in a creative jazz improvisation.*

How does a series of little connections turn into a sustained inquiry? Are they coherent? Wouldn't the sequence of connections become directionless without a master plan? Two answers: there *is* a master plan, and yearning does provide a direction. Some religious people refer to this as God's plan for us. I see it as our particular step-by-unpredictable-step path toward the spiritual summit. You don't know the master plan in the early going, so you find the path rather than choosing one pre-trodden by others. To the degree that we allow our yearning to actively inform our lives, it provides a guidance for the "and" that comes after each connection we make. The overview, the master plan, emerges over time as we learn our way forward.

Yearning guides the ongoing improvisation of our personal religion. Let's say you yearn to read more in daily life, but can't seem to get to it. One day you notice you have a half hour free for reading, but you notice the inner fact that you don't feel like reading. Instead of taking the half hour to accomplish some other necessity, or to give your attention to a distraction, you say "yes" and take that opportunity to inquire into the inner fact, not knowing what it means. You realize that you don't hunger for reading, but something reading represents, or a feeling you associate with it;

you have launched a new inquiry into that empty place you are feeling in your life. Perhaps you discover that reading was a symbol for large unbroken chunks of time in your day, which widens the inquiry into the way you allocate your daily time. I have often seen people pursue this particular inquiry into the dead end of "there is not enough time," and shut down. They get to the hard part and say "no." There is no ensuing "and." That dead end is where the inquiry gets difficult, as we address the priorities of our lives and have to make some choices.

Every creative process requires choices. Choice is an act of consequence; the commitment of "yes" says "no" to other options. Picasso famously said that every act of creation is first an act of destruction. The work of art builds up our choosing muscles, so we can apply that strength wisely throughout the choices that fill our lives. Some people get stuck on the difficulty of saying no. It can shut artists down; it can cause us to postpone creative progress in any field. In *The Instruction Manual for Receiving God,* Jason Shulman writes: "Choosing is not about saying no—it's about a resounding yes to life, yes to the fiery chariot that takes us Home [to the divine]!"

Attending, using what we notice, responding, making connections, following inquiries and making choices comprise the basic set of artistic-spiritual skills that support the creative growth of a personal religion. Let's look into some of the work-of-art tools we naturally employ with those skills.

# • CHAPTER 11 •

# SYMBOLS, METAPHORS, AND MYTHS

BECAUSE OUR INNER EXPERIENCE is invisible and ineffable, the mind makes symbols to hold and share what it knows. Symbols are to art and religion what numbers (and mathematical symbols) are to math and science. Symbols are a bridge between more and less tangible things, just as the piece of coin, the symbolon, connected the Roman guest to the experience with his former host. A symbol is a kind of shorthand, a distillation process in which one specific something stands for many less specific things.

The whistle I found in the wilderness sits on my desk. The ash tree shoot grows out of the diseased century-old tree I had to cut down right outside my study window. We all have such symbols in our lives—knick-knacks on the shelf, photos on the desk, plants growing in eloquent ways in the yard—that hold an unnamable complex of memory and experience, available to us anytime we choose to reconnect. We also carry a trove of personal symbols etched within us: images of childhood pets, travel sites that impressed us. These objects that connect to our yearnings are religious symbols. The bronzed baby booties, the rocks in my lawn, the image of the Virgin Mary.

Symbols require attention. Like Tinkerbell, they lose their vitality unless we pour our belief, or at least our fresh discovery, into them. We create the experience of a symbol, and recreate it every time we reconnect. We use symbols to go deeper, to build on previous understandings. Similarly, art works are tombstones that mark locations where significant acts of consciousness once took place. They await fresh attention to bring them back to life.

Symbols wait for us to attend. It is up to us to bring them to life, to discover and rediscover the "wholeness" they represent for us—a wholeness we cannot name or describe, but know and recall through the symbol. In this minuscule act of symbolization rests a kernel of spiritual fulfillment. As Aldous Huxley reminds us, "The man who has learned to regard things as symbols, persons as temples of the Holy Spirit, and actions as sacraments, is a man who has learned constantly to remind himself who he is, where he stands in relation to the universe and its Ground, how he should behave towards his fellows and what he must do to come to his final end."[25]

I end this section on symbols (and foreshadow the next on metaphors) with observations I sent to friends in a holiday letter last year.

The rocks are rising in my yard. Slowly, over years. But they are emerging as inexorably as a baby's crowning head. It isn't erosion, or any subtractive process; I can tell. It is some force, defying gravity, bellying up the substrate toward the sky. It's all in flux, of course—the lawn, the rocks, the trees, and us. Those rising stones themselves are changing, just more slowly than anything else in the yard.

It turns out that heat causes the rise. Stones conduct the heat from deeper soil more quickly than they do the surrounding earth, so the soil freezes under a rock first, nudging it up just a little before the surrounding soil freezes. It is delicate ice crystals that lift the heavy rocks. So there's a plausible explanation to ponder as I fill the red wheelbarrow with the spring's harvest of rocks. But, laws of physics are not what make me pause as I toss them from the wheelbarrow into the rock garden area; rather, it is the realization that I am relocating them for the first time in hundreds of millions of years. Talk about speed variation. And then I fill in the lawn holes with compost born at its own pace from decay of the kitchen scraps.

TENDING THE PERENNIALS

I am left, as so often in life, with a metaphor exposed on the surface of my thoughts. Some invisible, perhaps delicate, but certain force, be it physics or psychology, compels the hidden, harder, buried things to rise. They will be, must be, seen and tended to or eventually they break a blade or cause a fall. Hard things, long buried, will appear. We must lift and carry them to a new open place in the wild garden.

## Metaphor

SYMBOLIZATION TAPS an important, elusive function of the mind. It can be called the metaphoric mind, and it awakes an alternative sense of reality that escapes the flat literalism of our social environment. It uses the mind's "other abilities," those beyond logic. Metaphors are not merely linguistic devices we struggled to identify in ninth grade; they are cognitive tools with which we order our experiences. Scholars of metaphor tell us that "we draw inferences, set goals, make commitments, and execute plans all on the basis of how we structure our experience, consciously and unconsciously, by metaphor."[26]

The etymology of *metaphor* (from the Greek *metaphora*) means "to transfer" or "to transform." We transform one thing into another in the metaphoric moment: when we see a lion as king of the jungle, we transform our vague sense of an animal ecosystem through our understanding of a known human hierarchical system. Our big concepts like love, time, governance, power and death *require* metaphoric definition because they are not understandable by any other means. Making a metaphor is a fundamental creative act; it grasps *the more* in things.

Metaphors gain power by confounding logic; they are extra-logical. They demand that we grapple with other kinds of truth because they are untrue by logical standards. The familiar trope that the "lion is king of the jungle" is not literally true—there are no coronations, with gorillas placing crowns on leonine heads. The metaphor is untruthful in that literal sense, but it captures a larger truth: there is something apt in the comparison of jungle mammalian systems and human social hierarchies. And this metaphoric truth is more interesting, more valuable, than the literal truth it disrupts. (Not to mention the odd mistake in the common metaphor—lions don't live in jungles.) Metaphors extend the reach of our understanding brilliantly, elegantly, playfully. Without frequent play in the non-literal truths of experience, we feel flat or depleted, get depressed, become less than human.

Metaphors are small works of art. They require the work of art to create, and they require the work of art to grasp the truth in metaphors made by others. Artists and spiritual creators are metaphor masters; they live and trade in work in the metaphoric mind. This is just one of the many reasons artists are valuable contributors (when assigned well) in other sectors of the economy— they bring metaphoric capacity to the flattening force of literalism. There is a good reason that eleven New York City government agencies have hired teaching artists (the program is called PAIR, Public Artists in Residence) to improve their effectiveness.

Many Americans are metaphor-averse. Metaphors are challenging and elusive; they can feel sloppy because they mean different things to different people. They require that we play seriously with "other kinds of truth." In workshops, participants are comfortable with similes ("this workshop is like a wolf pack") because it is safely amusing to consider. However, the group is awkward with metaphors ("this workshop is a pack of wolves") because it is not literally true; it challenges, inviting more complex thought and exploration.

This discomfort around metaphors is paradoxical, because we utterly rely on them. Our conversation is filled with distilled metaphors: we catch the train or the flu; we strike out on a date; we bomb in a presentation. We base and communicate many understandings on metaphoric assumptions, for example: time as currency; understanding as light; relationships as journeys; justice as a system; the mind as a machine; people as specific animals;

more as better. We would be completely hobbled as communicators without metaphors. Even science requires metaphor; good luck finding an article in a scientific journal that does not use metaphor to communicate a key idea.

Religions are packed with metaphoric premises: a male, parental, hirsute God; angels with wings; the snake in Eden; hierarchies in the divine order; complex things divided into dualities and threes; "up" connected to goodness, light and holiness, and "down" connected to evil, darkness and death. Metaphors are easier to recognize outside our own belief system; we comfortably see Apollo as a metaphor for the sun, but are much less comfortable viewing Michelangelo's Sistine Chapel image of God as a metaphor for a deity.

The examples above are called "base metaphors" because they hold our beliefs as an unquestioned foundation upon which we build ideas and opinions. Like fused-through-repeated-usage neural patterns in the brain, base metaphors efficiently bypass the necessity of conscious consideration of phenomena. Organized religions, institutions of every kind, rely on metaphors to bind the community. "The Lord is my shepherd." Such a metaphor provides an efficient way to manage the infinite complexity of that subject matter while bringing people together; we can describe the meanings of the metaphor even when we can't describe the abstract enormity it refers to.

In accepting base metaphors, we create what we cling to—what we deem to be true. These metaphors hold our belief systems. They detect danger, providing an early warning when an experience jars against a long-held metaphoric template. (Suggest the divine as a female, for example, and many people's personal alarms start ringing.) The alarm almost always activates defend-and-attack mechanisms rather than deeper consideration of the issue; those occasions when we do slip into reconsideration of a bias, for whatever reasons, are significant moments in a spiritual journey. We tend to use metaphors as hard facts rather than aesthetic propositions. Yet they are artistic creations, which by definition require regular rediscovery and reinterpretation of the truths they hold.

Metaphors require re-exploration to stay alive. For example, in the U.S. we routinely accept the metaphor that "George Washington is the father of our country" as the truth. How do we inquire into the truth of that accepted belief? First, transform it from a fact back to a proposition. Pose questions: what does it means to be a father to a complex thing like a country? Which aspects of fatherhood apply? There are some pretty dreadful fathers out there, and also various ways of fulfilling the role well. What do I know about George, and what more do I need to know, to evaluate this belief properly? He had wooden teeth and possibly died of syphilis; how does that fit in? The unquestioned fact now becomes an inquiry.

A great metaphor—"in the beginning was the Word"—can serve us for a lifetime. Every time we return to it, our understanding shifts. Changing our sense of a metaphor, or creating a new one, is a significant occasion. As author Lynda Sexson writes: "Changes in metaphor are changes in religion."[27]

TRY THIS.

*Identify a metaphor in your belief system, like "time is money"; or experiment with a belief as if it were a metaphor like "Jesus is the Son of God." In either case, give it the "father of our country" treatment we just practiced, by looking at it as a proposition and asking questions of the proposition. (In what ways is my time not like money? In what ways did Jesus behave like a son and not behave like a son; what kind of son was he? Aspects of what other kinds of relationships appear?) As your questions develop, whatever the metaphor under study, inquire into the notions that catch your interest. In so doing, you use the work of art to go deeper in your understanding. Metaphors evolve as we evolve.*

Cultural metaphors change as we grow. In the short span of our lifetimes, the cherished metaphor of America as a melting pot has transformed into that of a salad bowl; research reveals that ethnic populations actually tend to retain aspects of their ethnic identity even when able to contribute to a multi-ethnic mix, rather than fully melt into the American alloy.

It is also useful to play with the notion of our routines and habits as metaphors. Apply the metaphoric mind and imagine them as if they were constructed rituals. For example, I make a cup of tea before writing in the morning. Not a big deal. But as a metaphor, it becomes a tea ceremony in which the stages of preparation—heating fresh water that comes from the area's water table under the earth in my yard, giving it flavor from leaves that grew in an exotic overseas locale, waiting for it to cool to the narrow temperature range that suits a human body—suggest the life under the surface of life. As I play with the metaphoric implications, I slip into the work of art and re-energize my ordinary daily actions.

TRY THIS.

*Pick a habit of yours. Describe it simply aloud. Then describe it again metaphorically, as if it were an intentional ritual practice. What might it be about? What is the beginning, middle and end of the ritual? Name the ritual. What would be different if you attended metaphorically to some of these possible sub-surface connections as you perform that ritual today?*

# Mythology

*The task of our times is to de-literalize*
*and re-mythologize our minds.*[28]
— LINDA SEXSON

*The universe is made of stories, not of atoms.*
— MURIEL RUKEYSER

SO WE AMBLE ALONG in our naturally creative lives, making a symbol here and a metaphor there whenever our attention is drawn to make a little meaning. Our yearning says, "Great. Now more." The metaphoric mind loves movies as much as snapshots— it spins metaphors into narratives large and small. And when the metaphoric mind meets the narrative mind, mytho-logic begins and mythology appears. Myths are the true stories of *the more*, our tales of yearning. They are sometimes called "tall tales"—not just because they share truths beyond literal but because they loom large in the psyche, rising above quotidian facts into internal prominence. A report tells factually what happens; a myth is a metaphoric story, developed within a tradition, that captures a transpersonal truth.

The word myth is also used (*abused* in my view) to mean "falsehood." While myths are not literally true, they hold a deeper kind of truth our lives require. To live fully, we need both reports *and* myths, logic *and* mytho-logic.

It is not disrespectful to say that cherished teachings of a religion are myths. All organized religions are constructed of myths. Even with stories based in historical events, the retelling over time engages the work of art and transforms the details into coherent, compelling, rich truths of *the more*. Moses is both a historical and mythical figure, and the mythical Moses is more important to our lives. This holds true for all religious and spiritual heroes. The myths of Gilgamesh, Jesus, Mohammed and Dionysus are works of art that hold deep truths of faith, regardless of their historical sources.

Religions need us to deal with their central myths the way painters want us to deal with their masterworks: have a strong first encounter that provokes lingering reflection, find personal connections to the creator's intent, return to it periodically to rediscover its richness, and maintain an ever-deepening lifelong relationship with it.

ALMOST EVERY RELIGION HAS a creation myth; Judaism and Christianity present more than one in The Old Testament. Most religions offer myths to help us grapple with death and afterlife—myths that tell stories of heaven and hell, of the cycle of karma and rebirth, of travel through the after-death stages. All are works of art that hold truths for essential human fears and yearnings, whether they are literally true or not.

Some religious believers deny that their treasured beliefs are myths. Indeed, Joseph Campbell's favorite definition of religion was "the misinterpretation of myth." The literalization of myth into fact depletes the vitality of the underlying truths, makes less of *the more*. It is easy to recognize the myths of other religions for their imaginative, poetic, sometimes bizarrely creative aspects; it is easy to appreciate them as works of art without accepting them as literal truth. It can be more difficult to take that perspective with the myths of one's own culture or religion. One of the hallmarks of fundamentalism in any religion is shunning the metaphoric and clinging to the literal interpretation of key symbols, stories and figures. Most "creationists" would snort with derision at an insistence that the tale of a giant turtle holding up the world (an image in a Hindu creation myth) be taught alongside Darwin in an Indian classroom. The battle over creationism being taught in U.S. schools shows how firmly some people insist on a literal interpretation of a myth. Stephen Hawking told the story of an eminent scientist confronted by an outraged elderly woman who dismisses his theories as nonsense, because everyone knows the universe is held up by a giant turtle. When the scientist inquires as to what's holding up the turtle, she replies, "It's turtles all the way down."

Personal religion thrives on myths as much as organized religions do. We explore myths created in our own and other cultures to discover the truths that resonate. A good inquirer will find resonance in Hanuman, Wotan and Persephone, as well as Moses. We also embrace the mythological worlds created by artists in the same way: Faust, *The Hobbit*, Harry Potter.

Our mytho-logic urges us to create our own personal myths of explorations into *the more*. It might be said that discovering, creating and making good use of personal myths is a key goal in the practice of personal religion.

**TRY THIS.**

*Tell the two-minute version of a story of an important occasion in your life. You report facts, but you create myth as you select and shape them into a story of significance. I'll go first.*

WHEN I WAS NINETEEN, I attended a party at which Buckminster Fuller was present. I loved the two books of his I had read; he was a hero for me. He was an old man, surrounded by a group of fawning adults. I wanted to meet him and wondered if I should try. Finally I gathered all the courage a shy teen can manage and joined the unofficial line that had formed to talk with him. I waited a long time for my turn. I stepped up to him, and before I could launch my prepared bit of admiration, he said, "Who are you and what do you have to say to me?" I immediately picked up his sense of having his time wasted and understood my bland offerings were not of use. I stammered out my name and said I had nothing of value to tell him but that his books had meant a lot to me. He thanked me and turned to the next person. His cut-to-the-chase directness taught me a new lesson about the preciousness of time, the value of sharp truth and the waste that social politeness can be.

Can you feel the mythical elements in that story? A larger-than-life character. A personal challenge. An unexpected entry of another world. A transformation. To frame it through a more traditional mythological style: a young warrior leaves home and sees a great older warrior at a tribal celebration. The young man decides to overcome the protocol and directly address the great hero. He approaches humbly. As his moment comes, the great man cuts off his explanations, saying, "What wisdom do you bring that makes you disrupt this gathering?" The young man realizes he has love but no wisdom, that his intrusion is not helpful to the great man, so he graciously withdraws. The warrior sees his learning and nods. The young warrior gains a little piece of wisdom.

**NOW IT'S YOUR TURN.**

*Try the same with a personal myth of yours. Pick a story of significant learning in your life. Tell the two-minute version; then tell it again in a more mythic style. (If you ever have an urge to write a short story, this activity might get you started.)*

Carl Jung illuminated mythological constants inherent across all people and cultures. As human beings, we share some mythic elements so deeply that we tend to apply and re-create them endlessly. We rely on them so innately that they work in our unconscious, producing the models and archetypes that appear in our own personal myths, the myths of religions and cultures, and in the mythic elements of our dreams. *Archetype* etymologically means *original pattern*, and we all relate to stories or individuals who resonate as heros, innocents, explorers, rebels, sages, magicians and so on. We all have aspects of these archetypes in us, and they appear in our dreams, our aspirations and our affinities; we have holy fool–ish actions, heroic aspirations, jester impulses—all within our life experience.

The etymology of myth (from the Greek *mythos*) is *a story of unknown origin*. Myths come from a mysterious place beyond the certainty of the logical mind; myths come from the divine. Who is it in us who can step back and see the unfolding story of our lives; who can name the forces that are moving in and around us? Who sees and tells that mythological story? Remembering that St. Francis thought that we look for the one who is looking, I believe it is "the self" or "the soul" that finds and tells our unfolding myth. It is said that we are made of many stories, and the self or soul is a center of narrative gravity.

> *The symbols of mythology are not manufactured; they cannot be ordered, invented, or permanently suppressed. They are spontaneous productions of the psyche, and each bears within it, unchanged, the germ power of its source.*[29]
> — JOSEPH CAMPBELL

# CHAPTER 12

# BELIEVE-ABILITY
# AND SATISFACTION

WHEN I WAS 14, my impending 15th birthday loomed as an event of consequence. I decided to mark the occasion by writing down everything I believed. Over several days, I wrote my beliefs into a little notebook I bought for the purpose at Woolworth's. My resulting six pages were a hodgepodge of moral directives (it is better to give than receive), earned insights (lying is bad and gets you into trouble) and religious tenets (God knows what we do). They added up to the optimistic, humanistic, no-nonsense cosmology that children often report when asked. These were not beliefs I had developed through experience, but I didn't know that. Feeling good about this birthday practice, with the profound solemnity a child can muster, I self-proclaimed a commitment to undertake the same challenge every five years for the rest of my life. I never shared this plan or the documents it produced with anyone.

I kept that vow at 19, but produced a very different document. During the countdown days before 20, I blurted down all my beliefs on a notepad. The ideas of 15 were mostly gone, and the '60s had sparked beliefs about art, sex, drugs and free choice. The jumbled thirty pages of political, personal, religious, philosophical and hippie beliefs emerged in no particular order; sometimes I wrote pages on one belief. Mostly I was trying on beliefs to see how they fit. I read them through on my birthday in my first apartment, in a dicey district of Boston, surprised that they fell into two main categories, new beliefs and old beliefs. I was much more excited by the new beliefs, but couldn't rule out many of the old—although, it being 1970, I did delete "When in trouble, ask a policeman."

At 24, I believed in art and human potential. I was by then a professional actor, living with a powerful woman in a relationship that I knew was "the big one," as indeed it became for some thirty-four years. I was following my bliss, and the omens were good. The document, in the back pages of my journal, took weeks to prepare because the busy young professional was running between rehearsals and performances. My statements got right to the point: I had new beliefs about living a life in the arts, about love and money, about ways you build relationships, and a little about the ultimate questions of being alive. This document was basically "How to Make a Good Life." There was no mention of reincarnation or drugs. I proposed (originally, I thought) that heaven and hell were internal states; that we were all Adam and Eve, and that God was not dead but busy elsewhere.

At 29, I tried but couldn't get the belief list together. I started to write things down in a blank book I bought for the purpose, but each belief seemed so complicated that I wasn't sure if I believed it or not. I ended with several pages of scratchings so incomplete, so unsatisfying, that I gave up. I turned 30 without a credo. I had begun the exploration into what I really believed. Indeed, I think that is about the age most of us begin to find our own beliefs—not the ones we were taught to believe, or believe in reaction against what we were taught. It's no coincidence that Jesus left town to figure things out in the local wilderness around that age. It is ironic that as soon as I got to the first really original work in my "beliefs project," I failed in documenting it. For a time. I wrote the first tendrils of this book in the years leading up to my 50th birthday. I used a computer this time. I didn't finish it till eighteen years later.

WE USE THE SKILLS OF ART and religion to create myths, which tell the true stories of journeying in the invisible landscape. We carry old maps and make new ones to help guide our travel. The markers on the maps, the places named through experience, are our beliefs. Both organized and disorganized personal religions depend on beliefs and believing, as links to the divine and as a compass to guide us among the myriad choices with which we make a life.

We have all been hurt by beliefs. We have had cherished beliefs (people are good) challenged by harsh experience. We have confronted hateful beliefs (women are inferior, Muslims are dangerous). We have encountered hypocrisy in ourselves and in others. We hear of wars and atrocities committed on the basis of beliefs about divine intention. We live in a world so complex that almost anything we believe encounters contradictory evidence. It seems that perverse beliefs underlie much of the world's ugliness: lining one's pockets is more important than the environment or anything else; convenience is more important than aesthetic; not all humans deserve the rights we want for ourselves, etc. The perpetrators of such human damage would never admit to those underlying beliefs. The 20th century was a bad one for tenderness, for craftsmanship, for the ways people naturally learn, for subtlety, and for belief.

Some suggest we live in a time when belief itself is passé, that we should base our choices on data and make decisions without the airy hokum of belief. Others insist that we should believe what previous generations have believed, that changing beliefs is the self-serving short-term expediency of ungrounded people, and that old truths are the only ones that count.

Beliefs, like symbols and metaphors, are things we make; and like symbols and metaphors, they can become so embedded that we forget they are little works of art. Beliefs live beyond words, but by stating them, or identifying our own beliefs in statements by others, we bring them into awareness for investigation and conscious application. (It is my hope that several times in these pages, you have thought to yourself "Yes, I believe that" or "No, I don't believe that" in response to something I have proposed.)

A belief is more than a pumped-up opinion. The ancient source of the word *belief* is the Indo-European root *leubh-*, meaning *to love*, whereas the source of the word *opinion* (Latin *opinare*) is *to think*. The capacity to believe is a skill of the heart, not of the head. It is a giving of oneself to something that cannot be verified; it is a willingness to place a heartfelt truth at the center of one's life and make a commitment to it, whether it makes logical sense or not. (I work with hundreds of dedicated artists who *know* the importance of bringing the arts into the lives of young people, and dedicate their lives to that belief, even though the research that confirms that belief is a patchwork of positive indicators.) We can argue the truth of an opinion, but we "just know" the truth of a belief.

What do you believe? It is a strangely difficult question to answer. As we examine the inventory, we see how many different kinds of things we believe, how contradictory some are, and how many sources we have for belief. We inherit beliefs from family and other kinds of instruction. Some are created out of experience, including trauma; others are held simply out of inertia, because they have always been there. We keep them even when they are at odds with experiences we have.

Mostly, what we do with beliefs is just have them—like stuff in a packed basement—and defend them (even before they come under attack). We tend to grip our beliefs, rather than hold them lightly, because our identities are so tied to our beliefs that to dissolve a belief can feel like the dissolution of who we are. We usually go on the offensive to block any situation or person perceived as a threat to the belief status quo. Indeed, we need to adhere to our beliefs, but we must be able to see them, examine them and let them develop healthily. A vibrant personal religion requires that we be able to take that little step back in awareness to detach from our beliefs; we need to recognize them and their influence, examine them compassionately and hold them lightly enough that they are available for change.

Let's focus on the active aspects of belief, the skills of belief, rather than any particular accumulated basement hoard. First, how do we discover what we believe? We can directly ask ourselves, "What do I believe?" as I did when young, and we will get some useful answers.

More reliably, we can discover our beliefs embedded in what we do; the true text of our beliefs is written in our acts. Our beliefs undergird who we are, not who we say or think we are. Our credo is carved in our checkbooks, calendars and conversations. Looking to our lives to discover our beliefs eliminates the range of hypocrisy that stretches from posturing, to overstatements that make us look good, to downright fakery. To discover what we believe, we must look into what we think and do.

TRY THIS DAYLONG EXERCISE.

*Assume a well-intentioned researcher follows you around for a day, observing every action—what you listen to on the radio or through your phone, what you eat, what you say and what you really think. (Yes, this researcher can hear your thoughts, and she notes them down.) At the end of the day, what would she say you believe? Follow your day through her eyes. When you choose what to eat, what belief is active? When you choose how to spend the evening, ask "from what belief does this action arise?" You may feel you are stretching it sometimes, that some actions are not based on belief. Try anyway. This game brings us into the present tense, revealing unexamined beliefs of the past and their projections into the future. I have tried that experiment several times, and been surprised to learn what I believe. My actions sometimes contradict my stated beliefs, sometimes glaringly—showing me discrepancies I need to attend to.*

## Belief Skills

AS FRIVOLOUS AS IT SOUNDS, we must *play with* what we believe. This means we take that small step back in our awareness, allowing us to hold a belief as a personal creation, not a relic. Like sculptor's clay, beliefs require handling and fresh moisture to stay pliable; otherwise they get dry and brittle.

*Take a belief you hold dear; state it simply. (For example, I might experiment with my belief that we are happiest when in tune with the divine order.) Then ask: What would be different if it were not so? (I begin to ponder what would happen to the millions, perhaps billions, of people with spiritual aspirations, if the experience of happiness were not directly connected.) Is its opposite also true? (Are some people at their happiest even when they are disconnected from their spirituality? Maybe the word in my belief should be "fulfilled"? What is the experiential difference between happiness and fulfillment?) The goal is not to confound the belief, but to chip the crust off of it, handle it anew and spark fresh inquiries to take into the world. Your turn to experiment with a belief of yours.*

Another worthwhile game in the serious play of belief is trying on some new beliefs to see how they fit.

TRY THIS.

*Finish the following question by selecting one of the two options, whichever you find more interesting; then follow the train of thought you've selected, imagining the fallout if that new statement were true. Ready? "What would be different if ... a) a deity were personally watching my every thought?" or "... b) someone I don't like were an angel?" The gentle transformative power of "what if" in this exercise leads us to expand possibilities. This kind of experience is the job description of a child—to make believe, to play with possible realities, to discover what new truths and delights they offer. William James followed this advice himself to rediscover meaning in life: "Be not afraid of life. Believe that life is worth living, and your belief will help you create the fact."*

TENDING THE PERENNIALS

Another skill of belief is the appropriate use of disbelief. Inappropriate uses are gullibility (too easily setting aside one's beliefs) or cynicism (being armored against input that might change our beliefs); we avoid the former even more fiercely than the latter. It's a risky world out there, and we don't want to get conned or screwed, so we must skillfully pick the right situations within which to dare to open to the new. Some people are so frightened of the risk that they wear disbelief lenses all the time, finding it hard to drop cynicism to see what is truly there.

The poet Samuel Taylor Coleridge wrote of the "willing suspension of disbelief" as an essential step in entering works of art, a capacity to set aside disbelief mechanisms and fully invest ourselves in an exploration. We need to give ourselves over to an opera during its performance or a poem as we read, setting aside our preconceptions, our ticker tape of judgment, and our everyday ways of thinking, in order to discover what it has to offer us. We must enter its world, discover its reality, and take away whatever we get.

Similarly, we need to do this during encounters with other people, with new experiences, and with other religions. We do not become naïfs if we suspend the instinct to reject the unfamiliar; we are not fluffheads if we can fully encounter the imaginary. On the contrary, we become larger. We experience the divine only in the suspension of disbelief. Our task, then, is to develop our intuition for occasions when suspension will lead to worthwhile new learning.

A FINAL THOUGHT ON BELIEFS. Personal and institutional religions do not propound random lists of disconnected beliefs; we develop belief systems, not belief catalogs. The oxymoronic words "belief system" live at odds—"system" usually implies an organized, detailed, interdependent arrangement, and "belief" requires no logic or evidence. Artistic schools, like Dadaism, twelve-tone composition, and classical ballet are belief systems too—they offer structures within which to see, understand and interpret complex experiences, and upon which to base choices. Deriving from the verb *to love*, belief is an active improvisation in which those truths we love play with the world we encounter. *System* derives from the Greek meaning *to combine, to cause to stand together.* A *belief system* then, etymologically, is *the way we connect things to stand together in love.* Does your current belief system deliver that to you? Does your personal religion provide that for the way you live?

The test of a metaphysical theory (or, by extension, of any religion or philosophy) is the kind of lives it produces when adhered to. The test of a belief system is the way it helps us put things together so we can act with love. Belief systems (institutional or individual) that do not make us more compassionate, more connected to the divine, fail the truest test.

## Satisfaction

THE PHILOSOPHER GEORG HEGEL proposed that we have an empty place in us. We desire things to fill that empty place, so we direct our lives to seek what we desire in order to achieve that end. However, instead of feeling satisfied, we find that the hunger increases. This provokes an escalating cycle of desire, acquisition, the experience of incompleteness, more desire, more acquisition and so on. The experience of satisfaction temporarily dispels the cycle of desire, yet many cannot experience lasting satisfaction.

How do we develop the capacity to feel the fullness that "things" are expected to provide? We must yearn. The desire cycle reifies yearning, taking us toward material objects that provide fleeting pleasure but not true fulfillment. This congealing eliminates the natural play of art and spirit in favor of the drive to get and spend. If we yearn toward *the more*, instead of desiring stuff, we make connections (which produce satisfactions, small and large) instead of purchases. Blaise Pascal is credited (although he never used the exact phrase attributed to him) with the statement that we each have a god-shaped hole in us that we seek to fill. Making meaning begins to fill that hole with the experience of satisfaction, in a way that gratification never can.

Satisfaction doesn't just happen to us like a lucky kiss from a passing angel; it is a skill. We *do* something inside to bring about that little visit with the divine; for a time, amid all the pressures and complexities of life, it is enough. Indeed, the root meaning of the word *satisfy* is *enough*. In the brief but timeless moments of satisfaction, the world is right and experience feels whole. In the experience of satisfaction, we stop. We relax in the present un-tense. For those moments, we do nothing other than bask in the holy. The skill is to allow this experience to arise (amid all the demands, doubts and neurotic pressures that drive us) and to protect it from being cut short.

All people find satisfaction in the experience of beauty. The *experience*—not just the recognition—of beauty. When we perceive the wholeness and/or aesthetic attributes of something, we create the experience of beauty. Yes, beauty too is an act of creation in the perceiver. Its potential waits in the roses and the great paintings with which we collaborate, but its appearance is the result of our active participation. Beauty is our creation, and we can find it at the garbage dump or in the face of an "unattractive" old man. One of its attributes is that we stop doing everything else for a little while, and stay inside the beauty we have recognized—it is a timeless, divine moment of our own creation. The sculptor Edith Rae Brown has a handwritten sign on the wall of her studio, which reads: "In this building there is all the time in the world. Time is not a concern when one loves what one is doing." It is enough. In the moments of satisfaction, everything is perfect for a time. Religious mystics have told us for centuries that everything is perfect just the way it is; the timeless moment of satisfaction provides a glimpse of the perfection, or nirvana, enlightened people have hoped we might see. (I delight in the Zen adage, often attributed to Shunryu Suzuki: "Everything is perfect just as it is, and it could do with a lot of improvement.")

The term *projection* implies that we can only perceive that which is already in us. (For example, if I see you as a kind person, it is only because I have kindness in me that resonates with something I find in you.) The delight in perceiving beauty is a projection of something in us—a celebration of the divine in each of us.

It is natural to experience some satisfaction from the big completions: the opening night, the renovated den, the fruition of a major project at work. The skill lies in experiencing satisfaction often, and in small occasions. A big project need not (had better not) withhold its satisfactions for one big orgasmic "ahhhh" at the end—no books would get written if that were the case. The skill of satisfaction enables us to find satisfaction along the way, in a good image, a nicely revised sentence, a paragraph that is just right. That is a skill we want active throughout our lives, isn't it?

The capacity to experience satisfaction in the process, and not just in the end product, is the capacity to allow the divine to appear. It is not enough to strive to make things better; we need to arrive sometimes, to hang out in wholeness. Many can strive but not arrive. As described in the Bible, the Hebrew God paused in satisfaction at the quality of the work after each step of creation, noting that it was good, not only at the end when he rested on the seventh day.

Satisfaction is not indulgent back-patting. Many of us tend to judge ourselves and our work strictly; like good Puritans, we withhold satisfaction from ourselves, and indulge in it only on special occasions. The mental/emotional ability to allow satisfaction into the creative process enables the artist to sustain the work. The painter must experience satisfaction even as a brush stroke does what she intended and one corner of the canvas begins to look right. Artists (in all disciplines) are satisfaction exemplars, because the experience of satisfaction is so integrated in their process; it is not distinguishable as a separate occasion. No wonder artists love to make their art so much—the art-making experience is suffused with divine experience. It is frustrating and infuriating too, but the holy occasions of "yes" occur regularly, and they are enough to keep the work and the worker going.

Satisfaction is such a powerful experience that sometimes we try to cling to the activities that once produced satisfaction, long after they stop producing experiential rewards. We revisit the same people and kinds of dialogues that once provided satisfaction, even though it has been years since such conversations produced creative rewards. This is a problem in many marriages and relationships, and in jobs, careers and religions—we thwart our yearning by clinging to outgrown routes to satisfaction, to activities in which we no longer invest fresh interest and discovery. We keep going back to dig in the same spot where digging once produced a bone. No wonder the classic midlife crisis includes dramatic disruptions to entrenched patterns, as the forty- or fifty-something-year-old fights to reconnect to the yearnings and satisfactions of being fully alive. To avert such desperate disturbance, we must feed our yearnings consistently and find satisfaction in ongoing ways. This is the true meaning of Joseph Campbell's oft-misunderstood advice to "follow your bliss." He did not advocate a life of indulgent hedonism; rather, he advised that we stay close to our yearnings to sustain a steady diet of satisfaction and ongoing full engagement.

It might be said that consumerism is built on dissatisfaction; art is built on satisfaction. Consumer culture distracts us from the creative challenges that lead to satisfaction, pulling our attention to immediate, expedient, alluring gratifications. We postpone dealing with deeper causes. Gratification is brief and pleasant, as rewarding as secular action can be; satisfaction, however, is a sacred event.

We usually "satisfice," a psychological term for grabbing the first acceptable solution or offering that comes along. This is reasonable in many situations: in the grocery store, in logistical problem-solving. We do not satisfice (I hope) when are selecting a college to attend, whom to go to bed with, what book to read next. If we satisfice, we cut off creative potential; we settle for less than satisfaction. Without the skills of satisfaction, we will never have enough.

· CHAPTER 13 ·

# Skills of Inquiry

*In order to come to the knowledge you have not,*
*you must go by a way you know not.*
— ST. JOHN OF THE CROSS

IF A SATISFYING CONNECTION to *the more* is the promised land, how do we get there? Not by a predetermined path. We blither our way forward, following a trail of choices based on our intuitions, knowledge and learning from experiences along the way. We proceed the way artists proceed toward the completion of a work. We improvise our way, even if we follow the sequential path of a specific artistic, religious or spiritual training. Coming from the Latin *inquirere*, inquire originally meant *to ask into*. We inquire our way into *the more*.

Let's take a "microscopic" view of a moment. The spiritual blip appears on our experience radar, perhaps no more than a ripple of curiosity, an attraction to something, a sense of something beyond the mundane. Our skills of attention catch the potential of the moment, which our yearning urges us to pursue. We follow the impulse, not quite knowing where the journey will lead. We aim toward satisfaction by creating some kind of connection— emotional, intellectual, visceral, associative (connecting it to a previous experience). This is inquiry. The journey may last no more than a few moments, as we follow a new thought or feeling to a realization, or as we encounter something new and make some discoveries about it. The journey may last just those moments, or it may work its way through a day or into a longer process. With skill, the journey becomes a series of explorations that make a life, as it did for the Jesus, Gurdjieff, Matisse, Allen Ginsberg, Joni Mitchell and so many more.

I find five basic kinds of inquiries in personal religion, five different flavors of *the more*, that manifest in short- and longer-term explorations.[30] Take a moment with each kind of inquiry, and note the ways in which you naturally pursue that spiritual end. What is your personal style?

1) SELF-AWARENESS. We inquire into how we function; we seek to become more aware of what is going on inside and in our behavior. We find satisfaction in insights, and in finding concrete evidence of growth, strength and compassion. This kind of inquiry can be pursued in therapy, in artistic processes or journal writing, and even in moments of inquiring into the sources of experience. Such inquiries may begin with questions like: "What is happening in me right now, and why?" "What underlies what I now feel?"

2) CONTACT WITH THE DIVINE. We inquire into the presence of the divine in daily life, or into the big questions and experiences of cosmology and theology. This inquiry may be practiced through prayer or the exercises of spiritual traditions, through an artistic medium, or merely in an attitude that asks where the divine appears in any given moment.

3) CONTACT WITH OTHERS. We seek to make deep interpersonal connections, creating a bond with the divine in others. Such inquiries may be no more than turning a good conversation with a friend into a meaningful, great conversation, or they may be as dramatic as passionate love. Religions seek to be communities of this kind of inquiry.

4) RIGHT ACTION. We seek the divine through what we do in the world. We seek creative flow; we bring spiritual inquiry to our daily activity; we yearn to know what we should do to align ourselves with the divine. Such inquiries may be no more than pondering the deeper implications of an ordinary action like sorting the trash,

or they may seek the merging of our vocation and avocation, the better to serve the divine.

5) DEVELOPING PERSONAL PRACTICES. We seek to develop our own spiritual methods to spark, sustain, and advance the previous four kinds of inquiry. These inquiries may become habits of mind or daily practice, like remembering to pause and experience beauty when we encounter it, or may become personal rituals, rich with meaning and creative reward.

These are not mutually exclusive kinds of inquiry, of course; they overlap and shift. Most people have a preferred style and develop habits that conform to their preferences. There are two things we can do to support those inquiries: 1) document the inquiry experiences in some way, and 2) reflect on our inquiry experiences to glean their content and derive their benefits.

## Documentation

INQUIRIES LEAVE TRAILS of breadcrumbs, symbols we recall and use—that is, if the birds of forgetfulness do not eat them up. Ideas sketched on napkins and phrases jotted down in journals hold the emerging ideas, discoveries and new questions made in the inquiry process. The arts provide articulate markers of past inquiries: paintings and plays are eloquent documents, rich evidence of the artist's discoveries in an inquiry. Religion has always used the arts to document key discoveries, as the arts have always used religion; those artistic documents, like the Venus of Willendorf and the poems of Rumi, become touchstones for renewed inquiries.

In fact, the arts have documented and supported inquiry better than anything else "*Homo inquiriens*" has invented. The dominant four artistic disciplines have had an amazingly successful run ( merely the entire span of human history) atop the hit parade of media for inquiring into *the more*. Think the Parthenon is old? Go back ten times further, and you find music, dance, drama and visual arts. These four media of expression (and then that Johnny-come-lately, the literary arts) provide supremely satisfying ways to inquire into and hold essential truths we cannot describe in any other way.

In the medium of daily life, we most commonly use words to capture the fruits of our artistic-spiritual inquiries. We must set down some of these words, whether artistic or prosaic, to hold their content. Write in a journal, make a voice memo on your phone, jot thoughts on index cards—no matter what medium of inquiry you use, documenting your inquiries will support progress.

When I am out in the wilderness, I have no way to write (this is one of the constraints I voluntarily impose on my retreats). So I devise other ways to document my discoveries, until I get back to the luxurious world of binder and Bic, iPhone and laptop. I make up and memorize small poems, little songs, movement sequences, which I repeat, as cultures have done for so many millennia. My little ditties and dances are definitely not created for audiences; they are working tools I use, as have been tribal dances in native populations around the world for eons. (Have you seen a Native American or Maori ceremonial dance presented in performance, as I have? As well intentioned as the situation may be, it feels wrong, distorting the intent and value by putting it in the wrong frame.)

In a personal religion, the process of documenting an idea in song or dance (or of writing in a journal, or sketching an idea, or storyboarding a process) is far more important than the quality of the result. Documenting the spiritually creative process dignifies and supports it; doing it regularly makes inquiry a habit rather than a fluke. Left in memory, artistic-spiritual accomplishments evanesce; we lose them. When we get them into some stable, documented form, we provide the sustenance that an ongoing creative process requires.

Rachel Ramen, author of *Kitchen Table Wisdom*, tells the story of a cancer surgeon who is deeply depressed by the nature of his practice. She advises him to write three answers in a journal each evening: what surprised me, what moved me and what inspired me today? At first he finds nothing to write. Over time, he begins to realize that he does have observations to record, and eventually he finds the practice of writing each night has transformed the way he attends all day, so that he is noticing many surprising, touching and inspiring moments each day. The inquiry into those questions changed the doctor's life, but the reason the entire exercise worked was that he documented his process in a journal. It is unlikely that the positive chain of events would have gained the momentum necessary to change his mental habits and emotional patterns if he had not developed the nightly documentation practice.

## Reflection

*In consciousness we seek the art and discipline of sustained self-observation coupled with non-judgmental self-acceptance.*[31]

— NATHANIEL BRANDEN

AMERICANS ARE SAID TO BE many things: insecure, belligerent, selfish, over-privileged, hardworking, simplistic, incurious, optimistic, generous, cautious, innovative, prudish, insensitive. We are all those things, and more. One thing Americans are never said to be is reflective.

The anti-reflection training begins early. Young lives are media- and activity-packed; lazy daydreaming and long walks are no longer staples of American youth. Of the many cognitive skills taught in the first thirteen years of schooling, reflecting on our learning experiences is just about at the bottom of the priority list. Yet reflection is one of the absolute essentials of learning. As John Dewey, the American philosopher of education, wrote, "Comprehension means that the various parts of the information acquired are grasped in their relations to one another—a result that is attained only when acquisition is accompanied by constant reflection upon the meaning of what is studied."[32] More colloquially, he is reported to have said, "If we do not reflect on our experiences, we do not learn from them."

TENDING THE PERENNIALS

Our anti-reflection training continues in the action-oriented world of work, where reflection is seen as non-productive time, and staring at the ceiling in an effort to better comprehend is perceived as being slow or goofing off. Our overstuffed lives allow scant time for reflection. The etymology of *reflect* (from the Latin *reflectare*) means *to bend back toward*—we bend back the linear flow of our experience to see the experiential contents with greater clarity. The variety of tools we use in reflection enable us to accomplish many things, such as gestating solutions to problems and questions, remembering, and reviewing. Perhaps the most common endeavor of reflection is to precipitate a few key things—ideas, feelings, questions, images, associations—that we hope to retain from rich experiencing. As Dewey tells us, without the actions of reflection, that nugget of meaning, that bit of potential, is lost. Especially in the crunch of the relentless input-output of American life.

Perhaps many Americans feel lifeless because they do not reflect, and thus cannot grasp the richness of the life experiences they are actually having. Like vampires, we hold the mirror up to our nature and see nothing, having lost the capacity of the living to reflect.

Art and religion are two main places in American life—perhaps the only two—where reflection on personal experience is expected and approved. In fact, the primary purpose of art in America is to provoke a reflective mindset in consideration of certain objects.[33] We may not all accomplish the task particularly well, but we know that is our job when we stand in front of a painting. And in religion, a leading endeavor of clergy in direct address to the faithful is to guide theistic reflection on their lives and actions. The subtext of most religious and spiritual books is, "think about what you are doing with your life."

What do we do inside as we reflect? What natural processes do we engage? Where do we learn the various reflective strategies we use, and how do we know how to use them? Here are a few conclusions:

Reflection is not a single action. It is composed of many different kinds of action (thinking, comparing, feeling, assessing, imagining, symbolizing, etc.) that tap many natural aptitudes we all have.

Reflecting is not the same as worrying, planning, psyching oneself out, obsessing or coping. It may or may not be part of daydreaming or reliving experiences. The distinguishing element of reflection is its purpose: to get closer to the truth as we experience it.

We don't reflect in general, we fulfill specific sub-liminal tasks when we reflect. Reflection introduces a series of short- or longer-term tasks: answering questions (e.g. "Why?" or "How?" if looking for deeper patterns), scanning for evidence, resolving disparities or incongruities, finishing almost-complete connections, and looking for patterns or organizing principles.

We have individual reflective styles, and tend to rely on particular methods that "work" for us. We sometimes get into reflective habits that avoid other ways of reflecting, and yet we often get rewarding results when we do reflect in fresh ways. For example, we may reflect scientifically on challenges at work, but never bring those skills to bear on our personal lives. Bringing some of that analytic mindset to reflection on inner work can open entirely new avenues to pursue. The psychotherapeutic process relies on this, and often provides positive results because of it.

The activity of reflection is inherently creative. Reflective experience is the world's smallest creative workshop. In it we make new connections, make metaphors, put complex things into new organizations, search for and create symbols, and play with personal experience to make meaning.

There is a bounce in the creative work of reflection. A success in the work of reflection (an insight, a sense of resolution or knowing, a clarification), bounces our energy toward further curiosity.

～ Reflection is not separate from active inquiry. We reflect throughout the time we make works of art or write in journals, etc. Then we also reflect on the completed documents to sustain those inquiries and to squeeze the full measure of awareness out of our creative work.

Spiritual people suffuse their actions with a reflective sense of their meaning and origin, without even consciously thinking about it. Mastery of reflective skills is a distinguishing feature of those with natural artistic and spiritual authority (not necessarily those who hold authority positions in art or religious institutions)—those people we turn to and defer to when questions arise. Those who reflect well communicate with a resonance (even those who are not good speakers) that others recognize and respect.

Through my years of consulting, I often observe that in a working group, there will often be one attentive individual who plays an unnoticed but critical role. The person doesn't say much but attentively and reflectively follows the action. Sometimes she offers a few comments that crystallize issues; other times she doesn't offer up the critical clarification, but has it in her head, and enables the rest of us to get there. The group doesn't function as well without this quiet contributor, who doesn't seem important by the superficial professional standards, but who in fact makes the critical difference. I cannot name the mysterious means by which one effective reflector can silently serve as the catalyst for accomplishment by the whole group, but I have witnessed it many times. Perhaps this subtle power has to do with the quality of that individual's listening, the care within which she holds the conversation. Psychotherapists often assist the healing of the client just by reflectively, creatively, lovingly listening.

What does this personally religious journey of inquiry feel like, with its reflection and documentation and so much more? It sounds like work. It feels like play.

## Serious Play

I CALL IT THE "WORK" of art and spirit. This implies effort. I have misled you. This work feels more like play, serious play.

Serious play is an attitude—a quality of life, not a category of life. In serious play, we participate imaginatively; we offer our energy, our creativity, our selves, for no other reason than the doing of it. Any field offers opportunities for serious play, and the same work can be experienced as work or play. The difference lies in the attitude.

Harvard psychologist Ellen Langer cites research about adult subjects who were divided into two groups, given the same task of sorting "Far Side" cartoons, but told in one group that it was a game, and in the other that it was work. They completed the task with similar results (in the same amount of time, with categorization of equal quality), but the "play" group reported more pleasure in the task, and an eagerness to do it again; the other group just wanted to leave. The only difference was that tiny bit—one word, basically—in the instructions.[34] I can imagine a "Far Side" cartoon with two identical panels showing a dog making mess in digging up a garden; one panel is titled "Ginger at work," the other, "Ginger at play."

Serious play is the attitude that fills the work of art. Artists may appear intense in their work, but they are playing with serious intent. Religions tend to evoke seriousness surrounding their practices (you don't crack jokes while the Pope performs Mass), but in fact spiritual work thrives in an atmosphere of serious play: we improvise a prayer; we take an idea from a book and play with it in our minds to see what it means to us. Creative play is closer to the true nature of life than the formal solemnity of ritual practice. Ovid wrote: "In our play we reveal who we are."

The T-shirt philosophy states, "He who dies with the most toys wins." This expresses the American way of play, but in an ironic tone that makes clear the emptiness of this way. In actuality, she wins who logs the greatest number of hours in serious play.

*. . . man is made God's plaything, and that is the best part of him*
*Therefore every man and woman should live life accordingly,*
*and play the noblest games . . . What, then is the right way of living?*
*Life must be lived as play . . .*[35]

PLATO, *LAWS*

# CHAPTER 14

# A Grain of Sand

*To see the world in a grain of sand*
*And heaven in a wildflower*
*Hold infinity in the palm of your hand*
*And eternity in an hour.*

— WILLIAM BLAKE

A LOVELY SERIES OF IMAGES. Blake romantically evokes a metaphoric sense of our remarkable artistic and spiritual capacities. He calls forth the spiritual inquirer in us. If we could actually do that, actually see the world in a grain of sand rather than just appreciate that poetic idea, we could create the sacred experience of *the more*. Let's play with Blake.

Imagine you are standing on a beach. You scoop up a handful of sand and look at it. You may not see the grains at all; you might see a tan blob or a memory-image of a beach you loved at age five, or the hourglass effect of sand slipping through fingers. Let's say you focus your vision to actually notice a single grain of sand left conspicuously on the fingerprint maze of your index finger—big deal, a grain of sand.

For some reason, you choose to observe the particularity of that grain. (For Blake's sake, let's assume you have superb eyesight or happen to have a magnifying glass handy in your hip pouch.) You see the features of that single grain, its color and shape; you observe everything you can about it.

Instead of dropping the grain and leaving it to brag to its friends below about its solo adventure, you choose to persist in this little exploration. You may tilt your head (a natural indicator of someone changing perspective) to perceive the grain in a different way. You notice what this grain brings up in you; you observe your response to this particular grain. For example, do you sense that you are but one grain amid an infinitude of people, yet still unique in all history? Do you marvel that the ocean's power can reduce boulders to grains of sand? You are taking that little step back in awareness as you do this.

Your response now makes a new connection; an idea appears—perhaps a thought about tininess or an appreciation of the toughness of this speck. You stay with and play with the idea until it clarifies as a metaphor—say the grain appears as a new planet amid the swirling solar system of your fingerprint, or you imagine its journey across miles of ocean floor to years of slow life on the beach to this momentary highlight in its journey toward dust or concrete poured in a strip mall sidewalk. In creating those metaphors, you create little works of art, small worlds. In a final step back, you witness yourself creating that particular world.

This imagined play-by-play of Blake's implied process is a microcosmic spiritual inquiry—a series of self-propelled steps that follow creative impulses to make meaning and witness the process. Yearning to experience something *more* in the encounter propels the process; individual creative impulses guide the process toward some satisfaction. This is the work of art, this is the play of the spirit; this is the serious playground of a personal religion.

This work must persist in the face of one monstrous existential challenge: we make meaning of the occasion even though it doesn't intrinsically mean anything. Our creative tango with the grain of sand is just a little mental riff that some lone walker with time and sand on his hands gets into on a beach; it is gone with the first gust of wind or urge for a popsicle.

In the work of art, we engage in creative processes *as if* they held real meaning because we experience a sense of meaning within the process. In the work of the spirit, it is the same—we create experiences because we yearn to connect more intimately to the more. This is how it works in humans, and it's beautiful. The little step back in awareness that comes with a wise personal religious practice adds complexity in the form of a paradox: the creative processes feel meaning-full, while our consciousness must admit that "meaning" is not a real thing. This paradox is uncomfortable, isn't it? Even frustrating. As the physicist Niels Bohr said, "How wonderful that we have met with a paradox. Now we have some hope of making progress."

The meaning-making creative process is profoundly important. It guides our learning, develops our wisdom. (It is said that a Zen master accepts that life is absurd and meaningless and then chooses to live as if it were full of meaning.) Our personal religion is enriched when we do not become too attached to the meaning we have made—when we hold it as a creation whose truth is as much in flux as those of other creations like beliefs, feelings and ideas. Ideally, we invest ourselves fully in the work surrounding meaning-making while taking care to hold our creations lightly, paying particular attention to the process. Artists and spiritual creators do this: they invest themselves in making things with meaning to them (like dances and beliefs), and then they pursue the inquiries that led to those creations in order to make more. They all head toward the same summit where experience is both meaningful and meaningless, paradoxically gigantic and minute, at the same time. The summit we ascend toward is *the more*, and it awaits us in the least of objects. It awaits us in the consciousness that holds all creations large and small, as well as the processes that produce them, in a compassionately dis-identified way.

# PART III
# SKILLS OF ACTION

# CHAPTER 15

# THE TEN COMMENCEMENTS

LIGHTS, CAMERA, ACTION. Skills of attention, skills of attitude, skills of practice. We now turn to practical ways of applying the skills and tools of art and spirit. The goal is to enhance personal experiences of spiritual satisfaction. What do we actually *do* to reach that goal, not just occasionally, but regularly? Following are ten approaches that work for me, for people in my workshops, and for the proud lineage of spiritual inquirers with whom we are privileged to join. As we graduate from old schools of thought, we begin experimenting with these ten commencements. They are not commandments.

Moses had the longest conversation with God on record. Together, they hammered out a summary intended to guide people to act in religiously effective ways. It was a radical moment: the first written down religious system; the first close encounter with a solitary god; a direct one-to-one dialogue with a male god who preferred dictation but made use of the human's ideas. They didn't produce ten suggestions, or ten pretty good notions; they created ten commandments from a generally angry God.

Since coming down the hill with Moses, the words "Thou Shalt Not" have echoed so loudly off the canyon (and canon) walls of Western religions and psyches that for three thousand years we have had difficulty hearing other approaches to religious experience. But "thou shalt not" is in trouble in our time. Its voice is less compelling—people break those commandments with troubling impunity, and a legalistic society parses, fragments and undermines the meaning of commands. Ours is the time to commence a new kind of religious guidance.

Today, we are more widely exposed to other religions than ever before; we are offered many routes to the divine. With typical media hype, this century was dubbed the "Century of the Spirit" before it was two years old, and in spite of some appalling evidence to the contrary, it may yet prove to be so. There is accruing evidence that spiritually etiolated Americans are taking advantage of spiritual resources, finding divine light in new ways. Individuals want to put things together (the etymology of the word *art*) for themselves; we want to bind ourselves (the etymology of the word *religion*) to the divine. That is the spiritual hallmark of our times.

The following ten commencements offer ways to create a sustainable personal religious practice that works. The word *commencement* is one of those delightful contranyms in English, words that mean two opposite things, like handicap, cleave, buckle and finished. Commencement means both a completion and a beginning: a celebratory graduation from that which we have outgrown, and a beginning to explore the wide world of possibility we have the chance to create.

1.  PURSUE THE DEEP PLEASURE PRINCIPLE.

2.  RELAX. SLOW DOWN AND SOMETIMES STOP.

3.  MAKE THINGS WITH PERSONAL MEANING, THINGS WE LOVE, EVERY DAY.

4.  BALANCE ATTENTION TO PROCESS AND PRODUCT.

5.  DEVELOP A CREATIVE PRAYER PRACTICE.

6.  LOOK AT THINGS IN DIFFERENT WAYS.

7.  PLAY WITH THE WAY WE KNOW.

8.  DELVE INTO EXISTING TRADITIONS.

9.  PRACTICE CHANGE.

10. CREATE A COMMUNITY.

# 1. Pursue the deep pleasure principle.

*There is pleasure*
*And there is bliss.*
*Forego the first to possess the second.*
— THE BUDDHA

"IT FEELS GOOD." Those three words state the prime motivation for human action. One could argue it is the ultimate urge of all mobile beings, from amoeba to zebra—all move toward that which feels good in some way, and away from that which does not.

Between feeling good while moving around in the womb and having a hand held as we die, we humans seek and find ways to feel good. Whether we grab instant gratification or aspire to longer-term emotional, intellectual or spiritual goals, we head toward pleasure; it provides the compass guidance of our choosing, which actually functions like a magnetic pull. This is true even for those whose psychological system has come to find pleasure in unhealthy actions like addictions, manias and even varieties of pain. It isn't just true; it is consequential: the pleasures we pursue determine the quality of our lives.

I like to think of healthy maturation as the slow expansion of pleasures to which an individual gains access through experience. It is like a palette of different colored pleasures to add to as we grow, enabling us to paint our lives in ever-richer ways. We all know people who have discovered arcane pleasures through experience—the violinist who experiences pleasure in the hours of practice alone in a room; the mystic who feels the positiveness of hours in meditative stillness; the seeker who finds pleasures in the challenges of the El Camino de Santiago pilgrimage.

Plato taught that there is one thing above all others that a society must accomplish in order to succeed. This essential key does not have to do with the economy, government or military, or any social institution. To succeed, he proposed, a culture must teach its young people to find pleasure in the right things. What are the right things? A sensitive question, isn't it? Throughout history, those in power have been only too willing to determine the right pleasures their populace should be trained for.

We ourselves, as individuals, decide which things we seek our pleasure through; it's a human right. I propose that there are some essentially human pleasures all people have the right to be introduced to when young, so they can mix a wide range of colors as they paint their lives. The list of ten commencements would be a pretty good set of primary palette colors.

Societies, cultures and families influence young people's pleasure choices in many ways. Young people pursue the pleasure principle, all right, but in the U.S. they are too often trained to seek pleasure in the least rewarding things—through their desires, which are shaped and manipulated ("colonized" as Sam Keen puts it) from our earliest years. Two days in a row, I listened to different groups of teenagers talking loudly on the New York subway. In both conversations, the kids spoke at length about fast food restaurants. They showed wit and sophistication about the burger joint world; clearly their pleasure explorations had been extensive. They not only had detailed opinions about the franchises overall, but even about whether McDonald's, Burger King or Wendy's french fries are better—and even which of the various McDonald's locations have the best fries. This seemed such a paltry target for their discriminating creative attention, such a literalization of their pleasure palette potential. They had poured so much time and skillful perception into such an unrewarding study, plying their skills of art in a medium that cannot provide fulfillment.

The deep pleasure principle has an odd relationship with gratification. In seeking deep pleasure, we incrementally learn to tolerate a delay in gratification (a necessary skill in the work of art, in any medium), yet the experience of delay does not feel like Spartan denial. We discover different kinds of pleasures throughout the process, *plus* the fulfillment in closure. The appeal of gratification is its speed; the trap is its binary and final nature—it has nowhere to go, and nothing more to offer than the moment itself. In the next moment, it demands another gratification. It does not "succeed" in us. (The etymology of the word *succeed* means *to have a follow-through*, as in the succession of queens and kings.) The work of art provides "success"; it finds pleasures in process, in stages and nuances along the way.

When we are less pulled by daily surface tensions like money, fears and desires—when we can partially detach from the imperatives of these demands and drives—something happens. We begin to attend to different things. We incline toward deeper pleasures, toward kindness and fairness, toward truth and beauty, toward deeper understandings of *the more*. As the Nobel Prize-winning writer Nadine Gordimer stated, "The truth isn't always beauty, but the hunger for it is."

Once released from the grip of survival necessity, Plato's rightest pleasures become those that fulfill our yearnings, not our desires. These are deeply personal pleasures, discovered, attained and rediscovered by the individual. Though they are sometimes sustained within a community—some write songs, some thrive in the chorus—the individual's experience is what counts. Whether these pleasures are pursued through works of art or spiritual play, they reliably produce the experiential results that count most with humans—and lead to the values that can sustain a society's success.

What does it mean to make the deep pleasure principle a guiding part of adult life? In simplest terms, it means that our yearning is actively invested in our everyday actions and that we habitually look under the surfaces of things. We develop a taste for, a feel for, the deeper pleasures. It appears in small scale as well as large: we direct our thoughts to the significance of a phrase we just heard, or the beauty of the light as we walk down the street, rather than (or in addition to) the logistical work of resolving transportation snafu. The deep pleasure principle is supported by habits like hobbies or amateur practices we love, by time dedicated to inner work, by idiosyncratic activities we love, by reading books that speak to this yearning part of ourselves. We have to give time to deep pleasures for them to thrive in our lives. In a personal religion, we maintain a regular practice of disengaging our attention to step back and witness the process.

The professional lives of artists and clergy are structured to encourage focus on deep pleasure. However, this hardly means that every artist and every cleric is a role model to follow; the pressures and distortions of their institutions, and the demands of the society they live in, can divert them as badly as anyone else. I know many amateur artists and non-affiliated religious seekers who embody the pursuit of the deep pleasure principle far better than many of their professional counterparts.

One simple guideline is always available—attend to what attracts. We are drawn to things: "what a great-looking coat," "what an interesting idea." Follow that attraction. Is the tickle of interest based in social conditioning, or does it derive from something deeper? Your attraction is a signal, and the inquiry engages the work of art. The deep pleasure principle is activated when you look under the surface for the source of that attraction. The alchemy of art begins to transform the experience; we can yearn our way toward sacred experience right there in Macy's coat department. Attraction leads to beauty. The experience of beauty announces the presence of the divine.

Beauty has always been central to religion, art, spirituality and creativity. By beauty, I mean the experience that we create inside. This experience is often sparked by encountering some beautiful object, but don't literalize its power by assuming the experience is happening just because something gorgeous is in your sites. How many homes are filled with beautiful objects d'art that are barely seen, much less related to? Conversely, we can create the experience of beauty in a smelting plant or in a paragraph of business prose. The experience is a spiritual act, a creative accomplishment. In the experience of beauty, we stop. For a time we don't want anything more; we suspend all other internal activities; we become aware. This transcendent moment of grace is a way the divine touches us through our senses.

In the experience of beauty, we participate in metaphor, recognizing some greater wholeness or order contained in a particular thing. We breathe a larger life into a lump of clay. Every lump of clay, be it a keyboard full of notes or a summation to the jury, holds the potential for beauty. We celebrate this truth by using the word "beautiful" to describe a job well done at shortstop, or at the symphony. (A friend once looked at the way I had refreshed my garden beds with manure and said I did a beautiful job.)

Beauty is love without goal or desire; its deep pleasure is an ego-free zone that quiets the restlessness of the spirit. The creation and discovery of beauty is a manifestation of our belief systems— look deeply enough, and we find our yearnings at work, and *the more* at the core.

Spiritual beings sense an ultimate kind of joy in connection with the divine, and a personal religious practice takes us toward the rightest pleasure. That is the experience of the complex truthful paradox—that beauty both means so much and doesn't mean anything, at the same time. If we can hold both, move past frustration and denial about the inherent contradiction, and find the pleasure of this bigger truth, we approach the "bliss," "nirvana," "state of grace" that so many wisdom traditions propose. *Nirvana* does not translate as *ecstasy* as is commonly thought; it actually means *cessation*. Slowing down to a stop in the experience of beauty, or in other occasions, is realization of the deep pleasure principle.

This intuition about the deep pleasure principle has drawn millions into spiritual practices of various kinds over millennia. As Roger Walsh, a scholar of spirituality, puts it: "Spiritual practices are so rewarding because they not only make us happier, but ultimately also open the door to bliss, a type of happiness that is infinitely more profound and satisfying than any of our usual pleasures." The yearning toward this achievable heaven grows stronger the more spiritual work one does. Spiritually successful people are having a great time.

## 2. Relax. Slow Down. And Sometimes Stop.

*Wisdom ... depends on the opportunity of leisure.*
*Only the one who has little business can be wise.*
    THE *TORAH*

WE HAVE TO RELAX. The attractions of deep pleasure may guide us, and skillful attention and intention may take us toward the divine, but tension keeps us away. Because a resting posture doesn't necessarily contain a relaxing spirit, there are inner relaxations, emotional, intellectual, spiritual easings up we must learn in order to expand our capacity to experience the divine. Meditation, of course, is the best known practice to accomplish this. There are many techniques of meditation, and cousins like yoga, mindfulness, prayer and contemplation, that provide similar inner relaxation.

The benefits of slowing are more than psychic—medical research offers a growing body of evidence confirming the health bonuses of spiritual practice. The "relaxation response" within a religious practice has been scientifically demonstrated to increase the sense of well being and peace, reduce anxiety, blood pressure, stress, cholesterol, insomnia, migraines and other chronic pain, and even add years of life. Other research suggests that spiritual practice enhances creativity and academic achievement, boosts self-control and sense of self-actualization, deepens empathy, increases marital satisfaction, and reduces drug and alcohol use and aggression. That's not a bad list of beneficial byproducts for committed practice of your personal religion.

Let us not suggest meditation is easy. Most people struggle to still the "monkey mind" and ingrained mental habits of thinking, planning, daydreaming and remembering. Gaining access to a quieter part of the self is not really a skill developed through effort; it is an adjustment in our attention, a letting go of our conditioned self. Gaining access to this unconditioned self makes all the difference in a personal religion. It *is* the little step back in awareness described throughout these pages. This experiential capacity expands the power and potential of all personal religious inquiries and practices. It is this not-socialized self, the authentic being without personae and identities, that takes personal religion beyond the head and heart and into the universal.

We do too much. Of course it is hard to slow and come to a stop. We live in tension, which is why stress is such a fact of life. When we "multitask" (as the current lingo describes it), we miss the experiences of each task entirely. Yet neuroscientists confirm there is no such thing as multitasking—merely finer and finer micro-tasking, switching focus faster and faster within our human limitation of being able to focus only on one thing at a time. The conscious full-attention experience of any single task can relax and fulfill us; when we combine them, slice our attention between them, we preclude satisfaction and discovery in favor of depleting efficiency. (Indeed, one recent night, I was mentally multitasking, while tooth brushing, at the john before bed; I flushed the toilet, got into the sheets, and realized I had forgotten to actually pee. So efficient and so removed, I had not only lost awareness of the act—I hadn't even performed the act. A spiritually bad moment.)

When we have too much to do, we experience stress in body and mind. Research shows that quickly switching the kind of mental work we do is a significant act in human experience; it puts a little stress on the individual. But when done at a gentle pace, the mind responds to the changed task with refreshed vigor—even on this minute level, people respond favorably to novelty. So, a little variety in our attention is good for us.

However, when this switching happens too frequently, or when it is happens because attention is yanked by outside demand, it can become a stressor. We all multitask, are interrupted often, and live almost every waking hour with dozens of redirections of our mental work, few of them self-generated. I have heard estimates that ten to fifteen mental redirections per hour is an optimum number before the shifting becomes stressful. But it differs for different individuals, in different settings; we can't just strap psychic redirection fitbits on our wrists. Most of us have dozens of mental redirections every hour, stress that dramatically influences the quality of our inner lives. Those who "want it all" pay a high price: they lose the inner relaxation that feeds spiritual experience.

> *The rush and pressure of modern life are a form, perhaps the most common form, of its innate violence. To allow oneself to be carried away by a multitude of conflicting concerns, to surrender to too many demands, to commit oneself to too many projects, to want to help everyone in everything, is to succumb to violence.*
> THOMAS MERTON

Thich Nhat Hanh, the Vietnamese Buddhist priest who has spent much time in America, recommends that we pause, breathe and relax before we answer the phone. It is a wise suggestion; such moments reduce the stress of the attention switch, preparing us to attend to the adventure that begins as we end the ringing alarm and enter another world. This commencement reminds us to graduate from the value system in which our minds jump to the demands of a dozen masters; and to slow down, even sometimes get to a stop, so that we can attend to our psychic work. Relaxation is not a pleasantry, not an enrichment; it's a lifeline. As the Zen slogan has it—don't just do something, sit there. This commencement sounds the most obvious, and is the most difficult to enact.

There are a thousand books, a thousand audio and videotapes, a thousand workshops, a thousand well-intentioned people who will tell us how to relax. Read, listen, watch; they can help. However, we already know everything we need to get started, and are merely unwilling to do it. We are unwilling for a very good reason—we can't manage to jam another anything into our already over-packed days. Relaxation, however, is not another important activity to schedule into each day; it is a way of thinking and living that informs our other daily activities. It is the white space of a different kind of calendar. In Turgenev's *Virgin Soil*, the despairing protagonist concludes, "I could not simplify myself."

Inner relaxation requires more than an extra yoga class; it means a change in lifestyle. It means shifting priorities and giving up things we like in order to invest in personal religious priorities. Quite simply, we have to sacrifice things in order to relax. Religions have always believed in sacrifice, sensing that we give up or give over something valued to gain something more valuable. In personal religion, sacrificing some of our activities to gain relaxation is a spiritual act. Etymologically, to *sacrifice* is to *make something sacred*.

Most people do not need more spiritual activities in the day as much as they need natural spiritual energy flowing into many ordinary activities throughout the day. The goal is to relax into discovery of the spiritual content of what surrounds us, more than to add new and different practices.

We can experience the divine when we stop, and cannot when we whir. Indeed, the divine runs on a different kind of time than our common linear, get-on-with-it pace. Divine experience, as every mystic has reported, feels timeless; and our glimpses of it open up a different sense of time. In the moment of experiencing beauty, of feeling grace, of being "in the zone," we experience that alternative sense of time.

We wish to change the experience of time so as to escape time's relentless inevitability. We try to overcome time's ravages by going faster and doing more. We try to extend lifetimes medically, literalizing the concern. But spiritual and artistic engagements change the experience of time more successfully. We enter a different reality that is not bound by the same schedules and content as daily life. Living in this other time is deeply rewarding, perhaps the greatest satisfaction we know. Many people rediscover this experience of time during death; art, religion and love are the best ways to get there in life.

Psychologists report that unresolved experiences cause tension. An incomplete connection, a serious question unanswered, an upset left unexplored—all increase our stress. The healthy response is to reflect on such experiences in order to gain clarity, to get a firmer handhold on something of personal significance as it whizzes by. However, we tend to move so fast that we deal only with the more superficial tensions in life, not attending to the big issues that go undigested in the spiritual gut. This makes us spiritually logy and undernourished. We become hasty in resolving tensions; we shortcut the reflective work that deep questions require. We become snap-judgmental and tight; we lose the natural relaxation and resilience that allows us to creatively invest ourselves in deep, interesting questions.

There is a distinction between tension and creative tension. The dancer is relaxed as he performs incredibly difficult feats. Absorption in a work of art brings focus, acuity, high energy, emotional and intellectual investment—within relaxation. The actor who is tense on stage or in shooting a film does not engage the audience. Learning to sustain creative tension within relaxation is one of the great accomplishments of artistry in any medium. Creative work requires a flexible, playful mind that is interested in dissonance and curious to explore it. A tense mind represses or rejects dissonance; it oversimplifies, snap-judges, rejects.

The work of art slows us down. Practices in spiritual traditions slow us down. Lifestyles of "voluntary simplicity" and even just "less doing" increase our access to the work of art and spirit. What will you sacrifice to gain greater experience of the divine? Give up some non-essentials to gain time in the art studio, the rehearsal hall, of the spirit. Among all the important things for us to do to make a difference to the world—improving the environment, striving for human rights and social equity, improving education, and countless more—there is no more critical task for each individual than this: slow down and sometimes get to a stop.

We must graduate from life in the fast lane, and commence the slowing down that gives us a chance to live in the divine. Less is *the more*.

### 3. Make things with personal meaning.

IN THE CHINESE MANDARIN ERA, young aristocrats spent many years studying astronomy, government, history and more; they learned a wide range of skills, absorbed many ways of thinking. And the culminating test for leadership was only about the arts, emphasizing creativity and imagination. Artistry was considered the ultimate demonstration of character.

In our time, students delve into many things during college and graduate studies. The management "guru" Peter Drucker was asked what single course, among all the possible subjects, every student preparing for a business career should be sure to take. He said that was an easy question: poetry, because it contained the essence of all the other courses and all the essential skills.

A little credo, on a tiny plaque, rests on my desk. Its two words keep my priorities in order; they remind me what to do when I am stuck. It says: make stuff.

We all need to make stuff all the time. We need to make stuff we care about and care about the stuff we make. We need to make worlds, of all kinds, and visit the worlds others have made and *make* connections to them. If we attend to this priority, protect and nurture it, life shifts into balance. World-making is the term I use for completing a whole "something" that holds personal meaning, no matter what it is made of. Those who attend to making worlds begin to attend more fully to worlds others have made, and to other parts of reality that are full of interesting bits. Those who create know divinity in an intimate way.

We value and remember what we make. We recall the creative projects from our schooling more than the content of the classes. We recall (and repeat) funny lines we came up with. We dwell upon creative projects we have given ourselves to, long after they are done. Tulane University researcher Daniel Mochon has named The IKEA Effect—we value furniture more if we have been involved in making it. In one experiment, he gave participants either a pre-assembled LEGO car, or LEGOS and instructions to build the car. Then he asked the volunteers how much they would pay to keep the car. They were willing to pay twice as much for the LEGO car if they just finished building it.

Why? Because creating is an act of spiritual consequence; it counts in us and in the world; it makes a mark on the map of a life journey.

Remember that the stuff we make need not be chipped from blocks of marble or typed into hundreds of pages of fiction. We can play with the actions of creating in the mundane media of conversation, in cooking, and in thoughts while driving or waiting in the checkout line.

Making stuff we love is not really about the stuff, even when the stuff is remarkable. The making makes the difference. We change inside when we make stuff we love. We spend time in flow; we develop critical skills; we live in deep pleasure; and we join the human species. As the saying goes, any jackass can kick down a barn, but only a human can build one.

Take whistling as a small but potent example of the impact of creating stuff. We can all whistle a tune, more or less. We have the ability to create in this medium; we all could make up a whistled tune if we tried—but we don't. Nonetheless, we have ready judgments about others—liking and disliking other people's performances based on unexamined criteria. So much changes if we actually try to create a tune for whistling. If we give ourselves to the task, we start paying attention to whistling and to melodies. We begin to notice things about our own whistling style and strengths; we discover difficulties and surprises about whistling. We want to get help to improve our skills—hello, YouTube. Suddenly whistling is everywhere—people doing little whistle-like things when "on hold" on the phone, friends doing unconscious little whistle fragments at odd times during the day, virtuosos performing at the shoeshine stand. The world of whistling begins to reveal itself, the various mixes of air and tone, the trills, the machines that whistle, etc. The world of whistling becomes engaging; the whistling of others holds ideas worth attending to, some not very rewarding, some quite amazing; the world becomes generous and surprising. All because we made something.

Remember that the making doesn't need to be *stuff* stuff. It can be a garden or a meal or a deepened relationship with a home-bound neighbor. The commencement lives in the verbs more than the nouns.

If you wish to make more stuff, start small. Make small things, work with few elements at a time, and work in small chunks of time, so you can build a habit of this modest practice before you demand too much change of your days. Working small enables you to accomplish enough to feel satisfied. Small satisfactions spark a burst of fresh energy to move toward greater challenges. If you decide to write poems, begin with a few minutes each day. Start with a subject you are burning about, but settle for a few notes or ideas rather than a finished stanza on any day. (If you were to decide out of the blue to spend ninety minutes a day writing poetry, the practice would disappear before it began. Start with ten.) Read poems that show how other poets dealt with your subject. Remember that thinking about doing it is not the same as doing it. It is the doing that counts. Begin small; but begin today. No other regular life practice has such a catalytic effect.

### 4. Balance process and product attention.

LET'S ASSUME WE HAVE a rewarding world-making practice underway. We are fascinated by the stuff we make and delighted by the satisfactions that accompany each completion. To enrich the spiritual potential of that practice, we must increase our attention to the processes involved to balance the natural passion for products. Artistry in every field brings a fascination with process—"how" becomes as interesting as "what," and the former holds more information about us as creators than the latter.

Our society is aggressively product-oriented. If we could reduce those inefficient, time-consuming creative processes, most of us would. We go for the gold. We admire hard work on the way to an achievement, but the quality and nature of that work is of little interest to most people in the face of the product. Students are occasionally taught to focus on the process of a math solution, but are drilled into product addiction most of the time and graded on the answer. Poetry is all about process—and look at its position on the periphery of American life. We live in gross imbalance.

Fortunately, most people readily regain an interest in process. For example, I ask workshop participants to compose a particular kind of sentence. Before we indulge in the natural fruition of reading the sentences aloud and receiving feedback on our small creations, I ask the group to jot down everything they can remember about what they did during the two minutes of the process. They are stunned to realize how much is going on, frequently finding over ten different cognitive, creative and aesthetic tasks. I might ask them to make a map of their sentence creation process. They trace roots for some of the actions—the search for the perfect adjective might remind someone of a poem written in eighth-grade English class. When they share their process journeys, they delight in the idiosyncratic play of each individual's creative improvisation. And *then* we read the sentences we created. The group responds to those sentences very differently than the groups that skip careful attention to the process. The non-process-attending groups enjoy each sentence as it is read, but tend to judge, get bored quickly and want to move on. When we have attended to process, the group moves more slowly. The listeners want to take time with each sentence to consider how the choices evident in the final sentence have emerged from the process just described. The amusing sentences get deep laughs. We ask to hear some sentences two or three times. The ambitious sentences are appreciated, even if the writer couldn't quite pull off the attempt. It is a richer dialogue. It binds the group, and sets a tone for much deeper work. It is much more fun. They learn more about writing, about art and about themselves.

We cannot merely try to remember to focus on the process, or we forget. We need to develop a habit of process-focus that builds over time. In a class where the teacher repeatedly attends to process, students begin to internalize that practice. Apprenticeship is a glorious way to learn attention to process; most mentors share their own process-focus as a part of the teaching, and the apprentice inculcates it for life. Many artists develop exemplary habits of process-attention, integrating it with product-attention.

If we document our process in some way as it unfolds, we know and remember it better. Without this, details are lost, insights are forgotten; the choices and accomplishments along the way disappear unacknowledged. At a minimum, it is helpful to document the process at the end, in hindsight—particularly in short-term projects. But for longer-term projects, we need to document as we go. Especially our personal religion inquiries. Spiritual inquiries produce fewer documents in the natural way that artistic media provide, so we must make an effort to document our spiritual explorations as we go. Use that journal, tape recorder, note cards, whatever, even though you need to go a little out of your way to produce the documents. That habit will advance the results manyfold.

Whatever documents we gather, we must reflect on them periodically to rediscover what they hold. With this process we shift our attention, balancing our interest in process and product. We perceive the product *and* the richness of the way it came to be— which requires a little step back in awareness to take in a broader and more complex story. This is necessary to offset the damages from critics and even feedback from friends—even their positive responses can impair our "success" if we are not well grounded in process-passion. Process-awareness illuminates the life of the spirit; it gives the work of spirit a chance to breathe, to inspire, our lives. It is said that the great masters of Chinese painting did not paint the subject they looked at, they painted the forces that led to it. So may we.

## 5. Develop a creative prayer practice.

PRAYER IS RELIGION'S most universally shared feature. We all pray—in different ways, at different times, for different reasons. The capacity to pray, the internal actions of prayer, lies at the heart of all religion, organized or disorganized. To get good at it, as with any complex skill, we must practice.

As universal as prayer is, though, few religions really delve into its essential skills and train practitioners to become more adept over time. I am convinced that one reason Buddhism is growing so quickly in America is that it provides such good training—followers feel results; they experience a difference. Evangelical churches provide experientially vivid forms of prayer, and their numbers are growing. Mainline Protestant churches that are losing membership would do well to develop a similar training that makes an experiential difference. They would also do well to shift attention more toward the experience during prayer than toward its hoped-for results.

The bestselling author Karen Armstrong, a Catholic nun for seven years, describes her mighty efforts to learn how to pray well. All her peers told her that she should hear God's voice, and try as she might, she couldn't. This frustration precipitated her departure from the church to become a freelance monotheist. Yet in describing her experiences while studying and writing about religion, she describes prayer precisely as we use the term here. She has remarkable natural skills of prayer, but because her order was narrow in its definition of prayer, because they left the skills of prayer to the figure-it-out-yourself system, she had to find her way into a personal religion, which she practices masterfully.

What adjustments do we make to everyday thinking when we slip into prayer? We stop doing everything else for a time—which, if for no other reason, gives prayer significance. We sacrifice some other kind of activity to sacralize the occasion. We get still and focused. We empty ourselves of certain burdens we carry through the rest of our day. We open the heart and mind to reach beyond our quotidian concerns. We stop talking to ourselves and our colleagues in life; we stop planning and recalling, and yearn toward something larger than us. We pray with the voice of the heart, with the direct, truthful expression of who we are and what we need to say.

In good praying, we attend carefully, exquisitely, listening to whatever arises in the improvisation. This is the work of art, and it enables us to do extraordinary things like make contact with the divine and get answers to complex questions.

The capacity to pray awakes the voice of the divine in us. The capacity to pray is the answer to prayer. To give ourselves over to prayer is to begin receiving the satisfactions of prayer; to fully address the divine is to begin to be answered by the divine.

Thomas Merton writes, "Prayer and love are learned in the hour when prayer becomes impossible and your heart has turned to stone." We grow and change; circumstances wear on us; the patterns that once provided spiritual sustenance fail. This can lead to shutting down, or to an inquiry. Prayer can become an act of imagination. We focus and offer our communication as if there were a something that receives it. Because we "believe," we give ourselves to this possibility so fully that we function as if it were so. (Faith is the willingness to believe that connections are made through prayer, even when we don't feel anything coming back, even when we have reason to doubt there is anything "out there.")

Why do we tend to close our eyes in prayer? The instinct is artistic. We know, unconsciously, that we do a different kind of attentive work when we close our eyes in prayer—in thought, in recollection, in listening to music. Those eyes-closed images are mysterious; they are embellishments, distillations, imaginative re-configurations of eyes-open seeing. The reduced visual input enhances certain kinds of concentration and helps us follow the intuitive image-streams of the artist in us. We paint on a wider and wilder canvas when we close our eyes.

Some complain that their prayers are not answered. It is a common reason for giving up on prayer. Of course, this usually means that what was sought was not given. But remember, a spiritual request line is not the kind of prayer we address here. In creative prayer and meditation, we get what we make, and the more we give ourselves over to the action of prayer, the more we get.

Here are a few more thoughts about prayer:

⮞ The quality of prayer is determined more by the attitude toward praying than the particular method used.

⮞ The tiniest elements of a prayer are the most important: how we reach out with the heart and mind, and how we listen to hear a response.

⮞ Praying doesn't always look like praying; sometimes we enter prayer through unplanned means, like making something, discovering beauty, feeling wonder. Sometimes it just hits us, like a burst of love or a wave of gratitude, as reverence when we enter a sacred space like the 9/11 Memorial. As we stay within those moments, we pray.

⮞ Formulaic prayer, in which we repeat certain words, can provide a useful approach, but it demands a special attention to stay aware and exploratory.

⮞ An angry person struggles in prayer, whether the anger is aimed at God or something else. Anger can sharpen the authentic voice, but closes off creative listening. Anger (in its various guises) and hopelessness are the main reasons that people stop praying.

🖎 Many adults have not developed their skills of prayer. They pray as if they were children, using the tone and perspective of a 10-year-old. You may recall I outgrew and shed the personal prayer of my youth that I described in Chapter 6; my praying has slowly evolved in subsequent decades, until now it is often hard to separate it from action.

🖎 The more adept we are in prayer, the more our prayer experience transforms our outer experience. Prayer does not take place in isolation from the rest of our interests—prayer is serious play with yearnings that express themselves throughout our day.

🖎 The act of emptying oneself is an often overlooked, but essential, aspect of prayer. Out with the secular air, in with the fresh air. We must let go of our mental, emotional and practical attachments—the connecting wires that draw energy away from the creative prayer occasion. The divine struggles to enter a busy awareness.

What about the other kinds of prayer? Can they too become filled with creative content? Desire prayer is literal; we want something. But if we can look under the surface of that desire, we can awaken the work of art. For example, say we want, and pray for, a new couch. If we add a jot of awareness, we begin to transform that prayer. The little step back changes "I want [or need] a new couch" into "I seem to be driven by the desire for a couch, and I am not sure what is going on in my heart"; the request line becomes an inquiry that requires the work of art to pursue. The literalized desire for a couch may clarify as a yearning for the relaxation experiences associated with a couch, or the kinds of great conversations associated with a couch, or a feeling of "home" buried in childhood memories. Delving into the bigger truth under the desire doesn't mean that you don't get the couch—it means you sacralize the acquisition process to enrich your life even more.

The same pattern applies to comfort prayer. We are over-whelmed and turn to prayer to find some kind of respite, some haven. The moment we relax the demand to feel better and open to the yearning underneath that desire—feeling what we actually feel rather than seeking to escape it—we begin to create answers to that yearning. We begin to find our way toward divine experience.

If we disallow the split between the words of a prayer and our full attention, and put our attention into the prayer itself, we begin to slip into the work of art. Try saying the 23rd Psalm, "The Lord is my shepherd...", and pay attention to every image. Pause to notice how each image strikes you today; play with the poetic implications of having a shepherd today. In what way do you lie down by still waters today?

As you can see, you attend to the images as if they were from a work of art, which, of course, they are. In exploring them as worlds, rather than reiterating them as verbal things, you awaken their power to transform, to deliver comfort and satisfaction. You invoke the divine by actually praying rather than just saying prayers. We pray more successfully by attending to one short poem by Emily Dickinson or Rumi than by repeating twelve "Hail Marys" while worrying about taxes.

Buddhism invites the koan question, "Who is praying?" In Buddhist practice, the question is, "Who is meditating when you meditate?" The answer is not so simple, and the answering process provides necessary learning—the purpose of koans. Meditation facilitates access to no-self awareness, a still place apart from the concerns that appear in prayer. Creative prayer is rich with aware-ness, often has stillness, but tends to stay engaged with realities of the world. Similar and yet different.

### 6. Look at things in different ways.

WE TRUST WHAT WE SEE. Natural as this is, it is a limitation to our spiritual growth, because we observe through our existing prejudices and use a small palette of ways to make sense of things. We usually arrive at conclusions that conform to our expectations (called "confirmation bias" in psychology)—if we always do what we have always done, we will always get what we have always gotten. The solution is not to distrust the way we take things in (a paranoid view), but rather to sometimes use our attention in more skillful, playful, non-automatic ways.

TRY THIS.

*Recall a recent experience in which you learned something—it can be something small. Tell that little story in twenty seconds. Now shift your perspective of that story to tell it again (making whatever changes are necessary) as if you were telling it three years from now. Now, tell the story again (again making whatever changes you wish to fit the setting), and this time, make it your "Rosebud" story, the final story you tell on your deathbed. And finally, it is now a thousand years later, and people still tell this story for some reason; retell it (making whatever changes are necessary) to fit this setting. There are an infinite number of other ways you could tell it. For example: retell the original story, giving it a slant to make it the story that a highly political person would tell. Make it a story a 14-year-old boy might tell. Finally, tell it again from the perspective of one small object in the story. As we adopt other perspectives, the content, purpose and style of the story change as a result.*

I call these different perspectives "lenses of perceiving," through which we see (and usually interpret to create meaning) what is going on. In workshops, I introduce the game of "lenses of perceiving" by having us look at a work of art several times. Let's say we are looking at a student dance piece. On the first viewing, we just look at it, shifting instinctively between the various kinds of attention people naturally use when grappling with a complex piece of information: looking for a story, looking for repeated movements, following how the music and dance interrelate, following a particular dancer, etc. After seeing it, we share observations about the dance—I emphasize observations, and discourage spoken interpretations or judgments about it for the time being. Then we watch it again, adopting a particular lens that seems interesting—say, "see what we can glean about the choreographic process." Using that perspective, we discover different things in the dance. Sometimes, we view it again, this time looking for "what might come next in the continuing development of this piece," or "what it feels like to dance in this piece," or "what is the choreographer working on as an artist?" I have used as many as seven different lenses on the same work, and each time we discover something important we hadn't noticed before. After our first viewing, we thought we knew "the truth" about the dance; after our fourth viewing, we can still see that earlier truth, but our interpretations find much richer truths. After seven viewings, I am happiest if we feel paradoxically that we know the piece well and that we really know very little about the truths of that piece. That's an ideal moment to meet or learn about the creator of the piece.

We tend to forget that we experience life through lenses, usually in single glances, and assume we see the singular truth. The more we stick with our subjective lenses, assuming snap judgments are absolute truth, the further we have to go to find the divine. The divine lives in the lens-less perspective, in capital-T Truth, as so many spiritual traditions tell us. We can only come to know the Truth by knowing about our lenses, recognizing their influence, and learning to set them aside.

One good way to become more aware of our lenses is by intentionally switching them and then attending to the results. This practice creates a little distance between the observer and the observation, a little step back from identification with what we see. That playful little bit of distance makes all the difference in loosening the grip of our subjective lenses, allowing some space for the divine to come in. Those happy few who have learned how to see without lenses see the divine everywhere.

Divine perception is not seeing new things, but seeing the same things in a new way. It enables us to see into things, under the surfaces of things—as Buddhists say, "to see things as they are." The work of art develops this capacity for seeing in various ways, preparing us to see things in the multiple ways they live and speak.

As Wallace Stevens wrote in "The Man With a Blue Guitar":

They said, "You have a blue guitar,
You do not play things as they are."
The man replied, "Things as they are
Are changed upon the blue guitar."
And they said then, "But play, you must,
A tune beyond us, yet ourselves,
A tune beyond the blue guitar
Of things exactly as they are."[36]

The rules of playing with lenses of perceiving are simple: try on a different lens and notice what you see. The goal is to develop flexibility and intentionality in the way we look at things—not to see the divine, which may or may not happen. The divine reveals itself as a gift, an act of grace, not as a payoff for enough practice. So play with lenses the ways children play with toys, merely for the pleasure of the play. Divine light will have a much easier time getting in.

≤ STAY ON THE LOOKOUT FOR THE NEW. Wear a lens that attends to novelty everywhere. Look for the surprising bits you didn't expect, the aspects you overlooked before, the changes, the new within the known, the novel experiences within you.

≤ BE ON A SCAVENGER HUNT FOR BEAUTY. Look especially in unlikely places—find beauty at the office, in the cabinet under the sink, in the phraseology of the delivery man. Remembering that we *make* beauty, use an intentional lens to practice creating it everywhere.

∽ LOOK FOR PATTERNS. Patterns in the day. Patterns in the words or metaphors that arise in a day, visual and sound patterns as you walk down the street. Patterns in what you notice in store windows. Patterns in the kinds of feelings and thoughts you have. Patterns in seemingly unconnected phenomena like items in the news and aspects of the self. To identify patterns, you have to step back in the psyche and observe in a less automatic way.

∽ ATTEND TO TOOLS. We usually overlook the humble tools we use: the computer, the pen, the dish sponge, the hair brush. Notice their nature the way a violinist notices the nuances of differ-ence between various bows. Flip the occasion—attend to an action from the perspective of the tool itself: what is it like for that sponge to be used by you in cleaning that cup?

∽ LOOK OUT FOR METAPHORS. See the metaphors in the language you use and that others use to communicate with you. Look for them in your home: what artworks are given prominence, what does the arrangement of the furniture say? Attend to the accidental poetry that surrounds us: the broken limb across the front yard walkway; the snippet of song that stays in the mind— what do they suggest? The panhandler in front of the bank, the security guard sleeping in the mall office—if you saw these things in a movie or play, you would know they meant something. View them "as if" they held some meaning.

The metaphoric mind connects two different kinds of truth, scientific (or literal) and aesthetic (or symbolic). Regular practice with the metaphoric mind loosens up our attachment to certainty, both scientific and aesthetic, in such a way a third kind of truth can begin to appear: spiritual truth. Spiritual truth recognizes the greater truth that contains both scientific and aesthetic truth. Spiritual inquiry steps back from the truths of the other two, holds them both with affection and respect, and offers access to a truth in which metaphors are artifacts, often elegant but incomplete. Spiritual perspective begins to see the whole.

≤ CATCH THE COMEDY. Many people naturally do this; they wear a lens that enables them to see what is funny, weird or incongruous in what they encounter. The bird dropping on the nose of the park statue, the sign above a shop that reads "Taxidermy Trampolines Cheese."

≤ LOOK SMALL. Pay close attention to little places: the inside of a tomato, the actions of unlocking a door, the way we tell the story of our day, the inside-the-mouth experience of tooth-brushing. Look for the little sequences and watch the subtle dramas unfold, like that of figuring out the new remote control. Humble attention to the small and ordinary provides the simple stones with which we build our inner sanctuaries.

≤ LOOK FOR A GLINT OF CONSCIOUSNESS in other people. You may sense a glimmer of light in the eye, a turn of mind, an intuitive warmth, a signal of a shared value. This lens keeps us poised to find deeper contact with all people, attuned to the breadth of divine presence that surrounds us. The intent to find this glimmer in people tends to draw it out in them. It is my practice to try to make a connection-with-glint with a person from another race every time I get into a New York City subway car. I succeed on about 75 percent of my rides.

Just as there are lenses of perceiving the world, we wear mental lenses through which we identify who we are. "I am the kind of person who..." We rarely change these lenses of identity—we "are" female, or gay, or Hispanic, or ... a lawyer, an American, an "artistic person," a reliable friend, bad at math, shy, a good cook. We fuse these identities in front like masks worn in Greek tragedies—the etymology of the word *persona* is *mask*. Sure, we probably *are* these various things that form our constructed identity, our persona. And we are also more. Practice the more.

I am an aging white male, but I have a number of feminine attributes. I used to be listed as "general ethnic" as an actor because I don't look like an all-American guy. I am young in many ways. So,

I am partly the handy identifiers, and partly their opposite. How much smaller I and my experiments in life become if my persona mask represents only half of who I am.

In a spiritual realm, we are often the opposite of our identified persona. And more—there is no such thing as men and women, or Caucasian or black or Hispanic in spiritual truth; these are irrelevant and limiting distinctions. From the perspective of eternity, even being "young" or "old" is meaningless irrelevance. Yet we cling to the lesser lens of ourselves, rather than yearn toward our divine aspects.

The spiritual benefit lies in holding our identities more loosely, so that the mask of persona is not glued to our face. We can open up a little space that allows another sense of self to enter into in, the not-self that is not separate from other people and the world around us.

Just as we can practice changing the lenses of perceiving throughout the day, we can experiment with spiritual exercises that loosen our death-grip hold on our identities. Try on different lenses. Try: "I am the kind of person who is able to find the good in everyone" for a day, even an hour. It doesn't mean you run around like Pollyanna, merely that you look for the goodness in every encounter and pay attention to the experience that ensues. Different lenses provide different qualities of discovery. Normally, we view our own actions as prompted by external causes, and we attribute the actions of others to internal causes—flip those lenses, and see what you get.

Here is a lens that serves us well: "Where is the universal element in this person, this situation, this moment?" Many religious and spiritual traditions use the metaphor of an inner eye that provides the vision of the soul. Third eyes, and other metaphors of a different kind of sight, see the sacred. They see without lenses; they see beneath the surface games to the larger truths underneath.

I was standing on a street corner in Memphis waiting for my ride to pick me up. Two young men approached me on the sidewalk. They were about twenty, tipsy if not outright drunk.

They were loud and obnoxious. I disliked them at fifty yards. They made comments to people they passed, not exactly rude, but blunt and sloppy. They found themselves very amusing. I was seething with disapproval, working quickly to prepare withering rejoinders for the insult they would doubtless toss at me. Then I noticed the tense drama I was creating with my instinctive lens, and I decided to change it. I chose to look at them with love and see what I saw. Immediately I saw two young men who loved each other with a depth that would be with them for the rest of their lives. I noticed they were of different races; how wonderful, a young black man and young white man with no racial impediment to their fusion. I noticed that as clumsy as they were in their remarks to people or to one another, they were basically well-intentioned. In their inept way, they were giving what they had. Then they reached me. I held on to the positive lens, and as they passed, one said, "You look like a nice guy, I hope you have a great evening."

THERE IS A SUFI TALE of a wise old man who lives in a little shack on the outskirts of town. A traveler arrives and asks the old man about the people who inhabit the town.

The old man requests of the newcomer: "Tell me about the people in your hometown."

"They were terrible people. Crooks, cheats, busybodies, idiots; it was impossible to live with them. That's why I left."

"I am afraid you will discover the people in this town are just the same," responds the old man.

A little while afterwards, the old man encounters another traveler who asks him about the people in his town.

"What were the people like in your hometown?" asks the old man.

"They were wonderful! They were honest, hard-working, kind and thoughtful; I was sad to have to leave."

"Lucky you; the people in this town are just the same."

### 7. **Play with the way you know.**

WE ARE OVERLY RELIANT on logical thinking; we dismiss every other kind of knowing as fluff by comparison. We are addicted to certain ways of explaining things and we contort our experience to accommodate that preference, overlooking the richness in life that responds poorly to logical thought.

The previous commencement reminds us to intentionally play with multiple lenses of perceiving; this one goes a step further, reminding us to play with the ways we know things. We each have a small set of old reliable ways we know things that get us through life, but we can go deeper.

Psychologist Howard Gardner proposed the theory of multiple intelligences in 1983, positing that we have seven (later, eight) distinct kinds of smarts. The theory has been widely adopted (and adapted, usually without Gardner's enthusiasm), and it has had significant impact on the way we think about learners, even as most schooling has been slow to reform based on new understandings. These intelligences include the SAT standards of verbal-linguistic and logical-mathematical intelligence, but also musical, interpersonal, intrapersonal, visual-spatial (think architect and interior designer), bodily kinesthetic (dancer, athlete) and naturalist (knowing in nature). Gardner's legacy is the wide recognition that learning and knowing involves a complex mix of natural capacities and developed skills.

It's time to play with ways of knowing. Here are some suggested ways:

꒰ TO BEGIN, WE MUST GET BETTER AT NOT-KNOWING. We must be able to relax within uncertainty, to continue internal and external inquiries even when our discomfort prompts us to conclude. I recall a chemist I met at a conference of the Association of Managers of Innovation, where I was speaking. He admitted he was extremely logical-dominant in his thinking. He said it was good for him to hang out with "the creative types" at the conference because it shook up his mental norms. He confessed he didn't like it at the time; the challenge to his thinking made him uncomfortable, and the activities were awkward for him. However, he noticed that a week or two later, his thinking was broader, his imagination provided more ideas, and he was producing better work.

Can you let go of certainty sometimes? Especially in instances when you really don't know, but are in the habit of convincing yourself and others that you do? Can you recognize that you really don't know how someone else may react to a moment, or why other people love you? Can you catch the moment before you snap to certainty, to pause and question whether you do indeed "know"? Can you do it ten times a day? Can you relax when you admit that you do not know—relax, and see what happens?

≈ WE MUST DEVELOP A TASTE for paradox and ambiguity. It is not enough to merely tolerate them; we must actually find a pleasure in the experiential sparks they provoke. They offer us a chance to go deeper. Psychologists tell us that interest in the things that don't fit, in baffling contradictions or anomalies, appears consistently in highly creative people. The poet Rainer Maria Rilke famously advised a young friend: "Have patience with everything that remains unsolved in your heart . . . live in the question."

There is a reason that koans have been a basis in Zen teaching for so long: they freeze the logical thinking gears that grind relentlessly, thus enabling other kinds of wisdom to appear and engage. Where there is no right answer, other kinds of answering processes begin. Here are two famous koans: what is your original face before you were born? When you can do nothing, what can you do? Do you find yourself brushing the invitation of these koans aside, or playfully engaging with them? If the latter, can you sense what it would be like to inquire further, what you would have to do inside to continue engaging with it? It is a different quality of experience from question-answering, isn't it?

Underneath the inherent frustrations of ambiguity and paradox lies a quiet delight, almost wonder, that the world can truthfully be like that too. Speaking for myself, I am both an expert and a beginner at the same time; that contradiction astonishes me, and when I accept its truth, it liberates me. Remember the guideline I use throughout my life and work, from the twentieth-century physicist David Bohm: "Any time you see seeming opposites, look for the greater truth that contains them both."

⮑ We must be on the lookout for the invisible. For example, I just asked myself "What is moving invisibly?" as I write this paragraph. I found several things: the pea shoots in the garden outside my window are beginning to break ground today; my heart aches as my partner rises to take her first painful steps on her injured ankle; there is a surge of national anxiety as the Nasdaq stocks suffer a drop in value. Each is invisible; each is an active event in me today.

⮑ We must engage the metaphoric mind, the poetic imagination, to grasp things in a deeper way. To do this, we attend to the metaphors we and others use. Metaphors surround us; we must notice them. We also must generate metaphors, discover the truth of one experience in terms of another. Take care to create good metaphors that go beyond the generic, and enjoy the opportunity for mini-creations throughout the day—go past the warhorse "It's pea soup fog out there" to try out "The fog is my memory of mitochondria."

⮑ We need access to the poles. Polarities are often named in discussing ways of knowing—right and left brain, hard and soft, slow and fast thinking, logos and mythos, lateral and penetrative thought, yin and yang, logic and analogic, male and female, and so on. There are nuances of difference between these metaphors, but they all tap variables recognizable in ourselves. The names are not important, but ready access to both experiences is. The goal is not balance as much as the flexibility to work back and forth between the extremes, to recognize where we find ourselves on a continuum. You probably rely on one kind of thinking more than the other—provoke yourself to try out the other. Like the chemist I met, practice the kind of thinking that is unfamiliar to you; we expand our creative potential when we shuttle back and forth between ways of knowing.

⤳ We must *notice* the action of the mind and spirit, rather than treat this work as an autonomic system like digestive peristalsis. In our spiritual ecology, we must not treat these inner resources as stuff to be used and discarded. The industrial mindset believes the planet's resources are there to be used until depleted; this mindset that causes so much planetary trouble applies internally as well. We need to recognize that the sensitive acts of creating images and carefully perceiving them, as well as the constructive acts of thinking and making informed judgments, are all significant acts that form who we are and where we are going. We begin to create a sustainable world by the way we respect and attend to internal environmental resources, not just external ones.

⤳ We know in mysterious ways we cannot name. There is an abundant underworld of knowing that goes by the name of intuition, or immediate knowing. The action in this sub-liminal system is not justifiable in the court of logic. When you "just know," you can't articulate the knowing, but you know you know. Although this sense is widely dismissed, that does not make it less valid or less consequential to the individual. Such knowing can ground lifetimes of altruistic service.

INNER CERTAINTY IS A SIGNIFICANT occasion. Immediate whole knowing has been described by philosophers for millennia, and is as significant today as ever, even though it is not celebrated by our overly literal culture. Inner certainty taps a deeper truth; we "just know" a lot more than we admit to ourselves, like when someone is lying or when we shouldn't be doing something. We often know when we hear an uncomfortable truth, although we frequently distrust it. Our inner ethical selves sometimes just know when a choice is right and when it isn't. In such knowing, we tap deeper understandings and intelligences. Those deeper certainties provide a different kind of authority than logical conclusion—perhaps not the authority you want to invoke in a formal debate, but the authority you want to find in making a major life decision like whom to marry or which job to take.

Artists apply "just knowing" to many of the choices they make in their creative processes. The poet just knows that certain phrases work, or that certain turns in the flow of a poem are right. This artistic skill is developed partly from study of the medium, partly from experience in the medium; and partly, it emerges from that individual creator's heart or aesthetic soul. We all develop intimate knowing from the media we invest ourselves in over time. In the medium of life, this is the wisdom we used to revere in elders.

Big decision to make? Sleep on it. There is wisdom in giving ourselves some time away from active focus on a question, to allow the dust to settle and to allow our mysterious skills to play with it. We intentionally use sleep, the obvious tool of not-thinking, as a workshop to complete a decision. We allow our inner knowing to emerge, and it usually does. I believe we can assign much more work to that inner knowing. We must graduate from monochromatic knowing and graduate into the full palette with which we were born to paint.

### 8. Delve into existing traditions.

NOVICE MOUNTAINEERS do not attempt Mt. Everest, even in the crowded modern climbing era. One has to develop skills to succeed in such an endeavor. Everest climbers have made many simpler climbs, called Class 1 and 2 climbs, which are walking and steep walking; these develop essential physical and mental skills. They undertake many Class 3 and 4 challenges to prepare for this ultimate Class 5 climb in brutal conditions. Aside from the physical and mental skills such practice builds, there is another, subtler reason for making repeated climbs prior to the big challenge: to embed procedures. Repetition of procedures builds habits of mind and body. This is necessary for success on a Class 5 climb, because the stress of the situation becomes so great: altitude makes effective decision making unreliable; deprivations of oxygen, food, warmth and sleep scream their demands; fear of death is actively present. Under such stress, procedure holds up better than anything else. The ingrained habits that derive from endless practice with equipment, with protocol, with repeating the basics, become the single most reliable tool to survive and to achieve the summit.

Religions know this. Since all paths lead to the same summit, they emphasize procedures—going to mass, kneeling in prayer five times a day, meditating every day for decades—to support our spiritual climb. They keep us going when the spiritual going gets rough: when we are surrounded by great mysteries and suffering; when we are hurt and frightened; when we experience loss, illness and inexplicably bad realities; when we get depressed; when we are constantly distracted from our greatest aspirations. The procedures we learn through religious traditions support us when we encounter stress. The arts know this too. Artists learn techniques, and practice them continuously, so they can function optimally in the challenging moments of creation.

While a personal religion requires the ongoing development of practices that work for the individual, we need not invent every practice. Our ancestors in many cultures have done superb work for us, creating effective practices that advance spiritual experience. Why not receive the gifts they have crafted for us? Indeed, the spiritual practices of different traditions represent the best creative work of generations of brilliant, dedicated individuals. It is arrogant to turn casually away from such accomplishment.

From Dorotheus of Gaza and Marcus Aurelius of Rome to Ignatius of Loyola and Nikos Kazantzakis of Greece, bookstores (physical and online) across the world are lined with religious and spiritual texts that present a range of practices such as humans have never seen before. If we dedicate ourselves to the rigors of any great tradition, we head toward the summit.

One hallmark of our spiritual times is that people *are* exploring other traditions as never before. Buddhism, for example, is the fastest growing religion in the West. Many people are delving into intensified spiritual experiments, rediscovering traditional practices, exploring wisdom traditions. They give themselves over to a tradition and invest themselves in the style of inquiry it offers, as young artists explore the styles of historical greats.

Experimenting can be dabbling. Dabbling looks for the quick fix, the immediate sensation, access to an unusual state of experience without respect for the depth the tradition offers. This kind of visit to the spiritual amusement park is not the same as learning from a wisdom tradition.

Before committing to a spiritual practice, we go through an initial phase of learning its techniques. This phase challenges our beliefs and biases, often causing volatile reactions and overt changes in the way we function. Many bail out. Then, at some point, some make a commitment to long-term practice. This works in deeper ways: we internalize the practice so that we can respond to new situations with the wisdom from that practice; we tolerate its difficulties and work out conflicts with the way we live our lives; we absorb the internal logic of the practice; we create new beliefs; we develop a consistent perspective for making choices. We learn how to improvise in that style, and use it to rewrite our personal narratives.

The training process in any tradition is hard, often discouraging work, because it addresses subtle habits of mind and heart. All dedicated religious training requires significant sacrifice, patient practice and many internal changes. I wish I knew a shortcut—I would have taken it myself. If one existed, some American would be getting rich off of it right now. Indeed, there *are* shortcuts for sale that promise helicopter rides to the summit. I am pretty skeptical myself but have been suckered a few times—I remember purchasing a set of eyeglasses with various colored lenses said to activate underused aspects of my spiritual panoply. You can guess how effective they were.

A traditional practice can balance the more individualized aspects of our personal religion. The balance is paradoxical—full dedication to the path, and at the same time, a full dedication to our own personal religious development. The tradition is more than a resource, or a vendor of experiences from which we pick and choose. It is, hopefully, a good parent. An ideal parent freely gives—and we fully receive—love. This wholehearted (idealized) exchange happens even though we know we are different than our parents and that we will leave them when the time is right. The good parent loves the child unconditionally, gives bountifully within clear boundaries, and supports the unpredictable development of the child as an individual. The wise child loves her parents unconditionally, gives bountifully in learning the parents' ways, and keeps a more important focus on her own personal development. The great religious traditions want us to merge and move in for life; honorably so, they feel they have much to give a lifelong journey within a faithful community. With response-ability, we must follow our individual path as it joins a separate, time-honored path. This may only be for a while, before the direction turns to a path less traveled. But we cannot play around with a tradition for some quick hits of experience, take what we want, and dump it. Rather, we wholeheartedly commit, even if not "whole-lifedly."

## 9. Practice change.

OF ALL THE BIG THEMES the divine playwright wove through the unfolding plotline of the universe, perhaps the greatest is the tension between the status quo and change. The conflict is omnipresent. Our cells enact the drama, as do the molecules that comprise those cells; mountains improvise their scenery slowly; the Hubble telescope snaps vivid moments in a distant tableau that happened seventy-two million years ago.

The human psyche presents an endless sequence of improvised confrontations between the old and the new. The forces behind each side are strong and deep. The status quo represents safety, relaxation and comfort, even when its norms are unsafe, anxious and uncomfortable. The status quo is like family, a word that shares its etymology with *familiar*. People fear and resist change—research shows how doggedly we cling to a known situation, even if it is meager or bad and something "better" is offered. Species resist change, even though adaptive flexibility is the key determinant of a species' survival. Relationships, organizations, even ecosystems prefer not to transform themselves. The pull of the status quo strengthens with time; as a female friend says, it's easier to train a 22-year-old bachelor than a 52-year-old one.

We especially resist change when it is thrust on us. I know of no better way to entrench bad teaching than telling teachers they have to change. And contemporary humans have been coping with a pace of imposed change that is insane by species standards. On the most basic level, we are dealing with a radical expansion of human life span. Firmly carved in our species memory is the hope we might live forty-five years, if we are lucky—yet in recent generations that expectation has practically doubled. It's as if we have suddenly moved from a two-room apartment to a four-room house with the same psychic furniture.

We wear confirmation lenses as we encounter the world. We say we are willing to change, but the change we usually want is for the rest of the world to conform to our individual wishes and beliefs. We do not deal easily with transformation, with metaphor or uncertainty—no wonder the arts love all three. No wonder the arts can be an awkward option in a comfort-and-gratification culture.

We like newness when it distracts, not when it dislodges. It confirms what we already think and feel. We may laugh, or cry, or get excited, but underneath the offering says what we love to hear—that the world is indeed the way we think it is and has some interesting new bits for us. Conversely, art happens outside of what we already know; artistic experience changes us in some way. Inherent in the artistic experience is making connections outside of what we know, expanding our sense of the way the world is or might be, expanding our sense of the possible. The creative act of *making* those new connections *is* the artistic experience. Sometimes we even have that artistic experience while engaged with "entertainment," like a pop concert, a conversation, a sunset—things the culture doesn't label as "works of art" but that we experience as art.

In general, things we experience as entertainment use variety and novelty to confirm what we know; things we experience as art invite us to expand how we see or understand the world. Indeed, artistic experience *is* that expansion of the status quo. It makes sense that Americans, who are conflicted about art, lead the world in creating and selling items for entertainment.

Our control instincts settle us down to routines and simpler ways. But like golf balls hit by life's three-iron of change, we are sometimes whacked out of the status quo; we fly free for a while, land in a new location, slow down until we stop. We settle into new habituated patterns or return to the old. How readily people who live through major life disruptions like divorce and illness re-establish new or old habits and settle in.

All change is exchange (*exchange* is the etymological meaning of *change*); we have to give up something to get something new. Some accept a miserable status quo rather than change—addictions and abusive relationships are examples.

NOT ALL PEOPLE ARE SO CHANGE-AVERSE. Psychographic research posits that some 15 to 20 percent of the U.S. population may be change-eager. Yet even among those who seemingly welcome change, there are many less obvious resistances. We attach to our opinions, our ways of presenting ourselves, our looks, our ways of thinking, our self-identifications like gender, height and profession. We meet open-minded people who inflexibly insist others be equally open-minded.

Yet change can spark vitality and excitement. Change within sufficiently safe circumstances is pleasurable and inspiring, and disruption of the old is necessary for a discovery of the new. Research shows that many significant scientific breakthroughs come from scientists who have just made changes in their focus; I have heard that *most* Nobel prizes in the sciences recognize work done in the first five years after a scientist changes fields. Change is essential to growth, in individuals, corporations, and relationships. Change is the only constant in the universe, as we have often heard. For species to survive, they must be good at staying very much the same *and* at making small essential changes.

We need an attitude of willingness toward change. This does not mean we become un-rooted tumbleweed, blown every direction by whatever comes along. Willingness to change means we encounter and explore new experiences actively, openly and fully to discover the truth and value they contain. We inquire, willing to change what we think and do as a result of what we discover. Arts experience provide an excellent gym for us to keep that openness in good shape.

## Habits

HUMANS LOVE HABITS. We depend on them. They help us cope with the complex input of daily life. Children find comfort and stability in routines; those routines allow them to focus their learning on particular areas of necessary growth, like figuring out how everything works. The pattern does not change much for adults. We create habits and routines that are psychically and physically energy-efficient, so we can direct our conscious attention toward matters of greater interest and import. Habits hate change.

Etymologically, a *habit* originally meant *what one has* and later *what one is*, and it is that latter sense that fascinates me. Use that little step back in awareness that supports a personal religion to perceive habits as artistic creations. Think of them as little dramas, little dances, we intentionally create. Investigate a habit as a small work of art that describes who we are and see what it suggests, what values it is based upon and what it aspires toward.

For example, I warm up my car before I drive it for the first time on cold days. I know it is not actually necessary, and pollutes the air just a little—but I do it anyway, or feel guilty if I don't. If I look at this habit as a creation, I see that I have developed a magical practice that makes me think I am pleasing the car, and that it will stay healthy longer. Using my own body experience of morning-stiff joints, I anthropomorphically assume the car needs the same bit of time to get loose. I make the small sacrifice of time to the incomprehensible deity of modern cars in hopes it will reward me over the years with fewer repair bills. I make my puny offering out of projected empathy, fear of the incomprehensible and hope for a better future. I am confirmed in the efficacy of this paganism because my last three cars have needed no repairs. (And now I will have to warm it up longer tomorrow to allay the auto deity's potential retribution for my hubris.)

If we can playfully see a habit as a personal creation in the medium of daily living, with a story to tell, we accomplish a spiritual act. If we bring awareness into the habit, and a little distance from its automaticity, we increase the spiritual content of daily life and open up our willingness to play with change. Indeed, after writing the previous paragraph I did a little research to learn whether warming up a car does help it last longer, and found out it doesn't really make any difference. I changed my habit. Score one for logic over superstition.

## Comfort and Boredom

THERE IS COMFORT IN THE STATUS QUO, and Americans hate discomfort. Comfort is a guiding principle, an inalienable right, a quasi-religious value in this country. Fear of physical discomfort, caution to avoid situations where we might experience discomfort of some kind, dictates much of what we do. Our living conditions are more comfortable than those of any populace in human history, and we want more.

This cultural priority has ramifications. We avoid mental and emotional encounters that are likely to cause disruption. Comfort-mania lulls us away from opportunities for learning and change; focus on comfort diminishes awareness and yearning. All high-commitment spiritual traditions bypass issues of comfort, requiring us to do things (like sit in the same position for a long time, or eat less, or not talk) that pass us through discomfort. Religions are generally more attentive to issues of comfort during attendance—I remember being fascinated with the drive-in church my grandmother lived near in Florida, where the faithful didn't have to get out of their cars, but pulled up to a post holding a speaker to hitch onto their car window. Parishioners watched the service performed in a glass sanctuary where a movie screen might have hung.

DISCOMFORT IS NOT A GOAL. Ideally, we treat comfort as what it is: a shallow, temporary sensation that is less important than it seems. Comfort is a habit that, once broken, allows for new experiences. We might be troubled by a wooden chair at a movie theater when we expect a cushy sink-in seat; but if the movie is good, we forget the comfort-disappointment quickly and become grateful to be there. If we are not actively engaged in the movie, the seat issue gains significance. The issue is the engagement, not the seat.

Every important act includes a little discomfort. Look at the scrunched face of a child learning to write what he thinks. To live a life avoiding discomfort is to live small. The comfort compass guides many through life, but it does not lead us to fulfillment; it guides us simply toward comfort and a plush, padded coffin.

I see the comfort issue in the work of art—the encounter with the new, the reaching out of known thinking is a little uncomfortable. People pass by challenging paintings on the museum walls and skip the "modern music" in the symphony hall. Yet as an educator, I know that those minutes when we tolerate discomfort to experience something that challenges our status quo are golden minutes for the spirit.

Another symptom of American comfort-mania is our horror of boredom. We fear it; we run from it; we go to great lengths and expense to avoid this enemy; and we react quickly and decisively when its early indications appear. Our weapons are the remote control, the phone app, the next text—not to mention the entertainment industry and mass consumer culture. We will change jobs, change spouses or take experience-altering substances to escape boredom. We "pay" attention and expect the activity to give us what we want. If it does not, or does not sustain in doing so, we get bored. Boredom and blame. If we are bored, something is wrong—wrong with "it" or "them" or "something" other than ourselves.

As one who spends wilderness weeks without any toys for distraction (a circumstance that may qualify as the most boring setup in the world), I have learned a few things. I've learned that the habits of distraction can be set aside—externally first, leading to an internal override of the addiction. I've learned that the habit of distraction places the onus of personal engagement on others; it is quick to blame and bolt, avoiding our own responsibility for the quality of attention and interest we bring to life. Habits of distraction make us demanding consumers, and they make us spiritually lazy. I have also learned that just on the other side of boredom lies a world of interesting invitations to attend and discover things that matter much more than the distractions that block them.

Do not seek boredom, and do not flee it. In a situation that is boring, *do* something with your mind and attention to change the status quo. This is spiritually creative work. Say you are stuck in a boring meeting. The impulse to daydream is natural, but do something more intentional. Wake up your attention. Provoke it with good questions. Count the beliefs present in the room that allow this group to function together. Find metaphors that capture the deeper truth going on. Where is love present in the room? This mental practice builds strength of spirit. It builds habits of looking under the surfaces of daily life. It says yes to what is, and practices creative attending.

We do not play with change just for the sake of change Find and follow curiosities. We expand our comfort zone of experimentation and follow our inquiries even when they prompt change. The saxophone player practices the melody a dozen different ways so that in the performance moment he can freely create and change everything. We stay changeable so that we can flexibly shape what we do to explore our beliefs. Otherwise we only dabble in spiritual experiences as esoteric entertainments.

Play with change. Say, for example, you watch two hours of TV most nights. Stop for a month and experiment with the ways you can spend that time. I know a family that did this—a year later, they can't imagine giving up what they have gained. Make a reasonable deal with yourself to make changes large and especially small. Break some habits and experiment with alternatives. Try this every day: if you are about to do something automatically, do something else. Righties, open the door with your left hand, and vice versa. Walk down the corridor in your home with your eyes closed (carefully); and notice the experience. Creative choice and attention to consequence—do it every day. Do it partly for its own sake, to enjoy the little experiments, partly to reduce the change-barrier of discomfort, but more to train the mind to play with alternatives and attend to the potential of new experiences.

These experience experiments shake up our routines, setting us up to better align our actions and beliefs. Adjust what has fallen out of whack but is held in place by habit. Be willing to sacrifice, to give up something to gain something more. We sacrifice the comfort of a lazy weekend and some money to attend a weekend workshop. We sacrifice the certainty of our opinions to gain a wider view. Sacrifice itself—paying for a workshop, loosening a certainty—does not necessarily produce new fulfillment, but it does offer the potential to create positive change. The yearly Catholic observance of Lent can be a meaningless deprivation, or it can be an opportunity.

Spiritual exercises are more than the activities we do to spark spiritual experiences (although they can). Spiritual exercises are the things we do to bring about a changed life. The Buddha did not sit under the lotus tree to have some fascinating experiences; Jesus did not spend time in the wilderness because he liked desert camping. Spiritually creative people seek to change their lives so they can live in greater spiritual alignment. We give up aspects of the status quo to gain *the more*.

## 10. Create a community.

*We are here to awake from the illusion of our separateness.*
— THICH NHAT HANH

AMONG THE GREAT ELEMENTAL THEMES in this divine comedy (or tragedy, depending on how you think things will shake out in the universal play), the Western cultural tradition, especially in America, loves one conflict plot line in particular: the individual's essential aloneness versus the need to be part of a group.

We *are* alone, and celebrate that in our reverence for lone cowboy individualism and in our bedrock beliefs in personal responsibility and opportunity. Conversely, as de Tocqueville and others have noted, Americans have always been great joiners, attracted to endeavors and accomplishments that cannot be achieved alone. Individualism *and* community. Our Puritan heritage was split between the Calvinists' absolute individual responsibility in relation to God, and the settlers' absolute dependence on one another for survival. It takes personal grit *and* a village.

Both have deep roots. Individualism is supported by the fact that we experience things individually, and live idiosyncratic lives of solo learning and experience. Community goes back to our ancient roots. Stone Age hunting parties had a core of about ten people; this is reported as the average size of a business working group. Anthropologists surmise that the most efficient size for a tribe was probably about 100–150—and 150 was once the average number of names in an American address book, until the electronic variety came along. These were the basic social units, and this community organization of the hunter-gatherer tribe was a successful template for humans for about 2,990,000 years of our 3,000,000-year history.

The dynamic tension between individualism and community is clearly evident in the arts. In contemporary Western culture, art-making is the kingdom of individualism—a creator makes a unique world out of her understandings. At the same time, the audience is rarely far from the artist's awareness; she even role-plays the audience regularly in her mind, assuming their perspective to assess how the work is developing. We share our experiences of works of art, either attending them together or talking about their impact on us. When I ask any group to list the benefits of having artistic experiences, they always say that artistic experience makes them part of some kind of community of experiencers who meet beyond the mundane.

In Part One, I described my ragtag sense of a disorganized but helpful personal religious community. It includes friends and family with whom we inquire into spiritual questions, those with whom we naturally fall into dialogue that lingers and resonates after we part, those who tap our creativity, those who draw us into playful invention, those who challenge what we know.

Friendship has become strained in our time. In ancient Greece, Aristotle and other wise men took friendship seriously. They cited three components to friendship: friends enjoyed one another's company; friends were useful to one another; and friends shared a common commitment to the good.

In modern America, our sense of friendship is more limited. We rely on the first aspect almost entirely, although we do include some of the second. We overlook that critical third aspect. For the ancient Greeks, the third element made friendship a fundamental tool of creating a good society; it brough morality and ongoing improvement into daily life. Friends did not just hang out together but actively made one another better people. The primary institution that attended to the link between standards and behavior was friendship—not the law, as it is today. We were accountable to our friends for the quality of our actions. Friends loved the good in one another and were dedicated to developing it. The opposite of a friend was not an enemy, but a flatterer.

These are the friendships I envision comprising a personal religious community. Fellow yearners, fellow inquirers. People who take care to understand what we are inquiring into, and support that growth above all. These friends will take the time to help clarify our yearnings and priorities, and (compassionately) point out choices we make that conflict with our intent. The Buddha said, "Do not live with people who do not care and find friends who love the truth."

## Service

AMERICAN RELIGIONS ADVOCATE SERVICE, and celebrate many generous gifts of service from their faithful. However, service is more commonly seen as a generous act of voluntary charity rather than a necessary practice of faith. In many spiritual traditions, service is seen as a means to wisdom, as a part of spiritual development—witness Mother Teresa. Service changes the ego, balancing the dominance of individualism with the humble power of community. Service develops compassion amid the egocentric pressures of our culture.

We must serve as an ongoing part of what we do. Service can take many forms. Certainly, volunteer work at a hospital or literacy program can be service work. However, much of what we do already is close to being service—we just do not view it that way. I am a teacher, so helping students learn is a part of my job. But I go an extra step to work with students in the evening, via calls or emails on the weekend if they need it; I spend some ten hours a week supporting the growth of my friends and former students. Placing what I know at their service, giving them the precious commodity of time is one way I serve, and the experience serves me too. When we help a younger colleague at work, we are teachers; if we take care with the colleague, attend to the deeper issues of concern, advise and guide with full attention and caring follow-through, we have served that individual.

We are all teachers all the time, mostly by example. Are we teaching well? To be attentive to this responsibility at work, at home, in a store, is to serve. Our days are filled with opportunities to serve others by example—to teach through the way we look at things, the quality of our questions, our interest in looking under the surface, our willingness to change. If we embody our beliefs and actively pursue our inquiries in daily interactions, we serve those we live with. Through habit-adjustments, I have now reduced my trash reduced to two (admittedly large) garbage bags a year. Few people know this about me, but it feels like serving a greater good to make new habits that lead to that result. It *feels* like service, and it feels good, even though few know about it.

The key to service is that it is an inner act as much as an outer one. The etymology of the word *service* means *the condition or work of a slave*. Indeed, in service we willingly subjugate our individual power, our egocentric worldview and our self-importance by becoming servants to something larger and more important than ourselves. In service, we serve our beliefs rather than our preferences.

If you do not already have an active kind of service, start small. Help people on the street, at work; help neighbors. Attend to the inner act. As you help carry someone's grocery bags, connect the action with the belief and do it with your whole heart. A simple way to do this is to dedicate an act. As you perform any act of service, make a formal little dedication, a conscious prayer. As you carry the older person's groceries, speaking pleasantries, say to yourself, "I dedicate this act to the care of older people, who have much wisdom even if I find them annoying." Or, "I dedicate this act to the welcome surprise of a helping hand when we're in need." Centuries of wise people have said it is a privilege to serve others, not social dues we pay to get into the fraternity called heaven.

# PART IV
## PAST, PRESENT, AND FUTURE

## ◆ CHAPTER 16 ◆

# THE PAST AS PROLOGUE

AROUND THE MIDDLE OF my wilderness week, senses sharpen and rhythms slow. I decide to tour my circular realm—104-foot diameter means how big a circumference? Hard to answer out there without paper. There is no hurry, so I walk as slowly as I can while still moving. It takes me an hour to walk the circuit: I add fifteen minutes for a detour to get a gulp of water. I then journey inland, inside the perimeter, to visit interesting destinations. I look for the history of the place—evidence of weather, animal visitations, human presence. It shyly reveals its past. On retreats in Colorado, New Mexico, and twice in the Adirondacks, I have been stunned to discover that my area contained a stone circle that had to have been placed by humans. It is a shock every time, because I had been oblivious to it for days. Repeatedly, unwittingly, I have found my way to sites of ancient sacred practice. Too implausible for coincidence, too invisible for intention, too wonderful for words.

We live within ancient circles, visible or not. Even without knowing it, we find our way to sacred sites our ancestors blessed. We perceive them when we slow down enough to see. When we see, there are implications. When we carry those implications out of dedicated spiritual times and places, we make different choices about the way to live.

We take a slight detour in this chapter to honor the lineage of personal religion, noting its origins in human survival and evolution and its relationship to organized religions.

Anthropological discoveries tell us that personal religion is our ancient legacy, and an enduring art of the spirit. Twenty times longer than there has been anything like "a religion," human spiritual needs and yearnings found expression through the work of art. These same practices will be active, if still overlooked, long after today's religions have evolved into something we cannot imagine today.

We live today because our ancestors adapted well to the crises of their times. Our primate progenitors encountered a thinning of the forest canopy five million years ago. Bad news for apes. Some pioneers came down to the forest floor and went to work on a new ankle design that allowed for walking. They exchanged brain space dedicated to olfactory work for increased visual acuity. Before our "human history," our proto-human ancestors lived successfully in hunter-gatherer bands for about three million years. Along the way, in a mere million years, our ancestors evolved from terrestrial vegetarians who served as dinner for local carnivores, to clever scavengers, and then to skilled carnivorous hunters, the only animal that can kill from a distance. This took brain power, and indeed the brain and its cranium grew rapidly. So rapidly that childbirth became dangerous. Because of female pelvic anatomy, newborn heads could be only so big, and when we hit the max, we developed a brilliant solution called culture— the brain's continued development after its passage through the unforgiving gate of the pubic bone. Lifelong learning became our species' greatest invention. We celebrated this breakthrough by adding a full pound of neocortex to our mature brains over the next million years.

BY ONE HUNDRED THOUSAND YEARS AGO, most of evolution's obvious business had been completed: we walked well, fingers were in good position, posture needed some work but was definitely upright. It was time to focus on evolution inside the skull. We differentiated the functions of the two brain hemispheres and areas therein, teaming them to work together. Language skills rapidly increased in complexity, and our artistic skills were born. Pattern recognition had always been a strength for humans ("hmm, it is always warm around that jumpy yellow light that leaps from the trees when lightning hits"), and at this time, we expanded this capacity rapidly. The anthropological record makes me believe art was born from our participating in patterns.

Not coincidentally, our forebears made two additional discoveries at roughly this same time. They discovered that if they stuck seeds in the earth, the food they had been wearing out their feet to gather grew right where they placed that seed. They realized that some animals could be kept in captivity, so the hunt could stay in the backyard. Agriculture and the domestication of animals enabled humans to stay put. It gave us a little control over our environment, and launched the long history of taming nature to serve our wishes.

We are inherently a homey species (or perhaps a lazy one); over the next dozens of millennia, wherever hunter-gatherer tribes encountered farmer-herder ones, the former eventually converted to the ways of the latter. Even barbaric tribes grew tired of sacking and pillaging on the road and settled down to farming and herding. With a planted field and a corral of steaks, our ambitious ancient relatives were free to turn their innate inventiveness to complex communication.

Language and art grew from the need to communicate essentials. Verbal languages proved useful in solving many problems, and the other languages like dance, music, visual images and theater were effective in solving other essential problems, like weather, childbirth, aiding the hunt, keeping the clan united, educating the young and making big decisions.

There was no bearded sage with a starter pistol marking the beginning of human history, not even a poll selecting the five greatest events of prehistory. It is said that the dividing line between history and prehistory is "the sense of history," when humans began telling stories of the past, passing on remembrances to future generations. How appropriate that storytelling, a work of art, designates our official start, perhaps forty thousand years ago.

We have shards of evidence from that time indicating that the artistic and spiritual impulses were working together to address the mysterious aspects of life. Our ancestors were making music forty thousand years ago, and there has been no human culture without music since then. Early drumming and piping was not Friday night club music, but is surprisingly similar in the way it speaks to and with divine forces in the dancers. The relatively modern art of cave wall–painting in Borneo, the Ural Mountains, France and Spain left complete but ambiguous documents of our artistic-spiritual inquiry thirty-four to twenty thousand years ago. Art and religion were the same activity to the Chauvet cave painters. The elegant animal images were not made to improve cave resale value, but to connect to, to please, to get lucky with some greater power that provided essential sustenance.

There was a widespread period of goddess worship about five to ten thousand years ago, with female-figure sculptures found in many locations that had no contact with one another. With child mortality so high (75 percent in some periods), the worship of goddesses through artistic expression was no Sunday morning social event, but a survival necessity. The "Venuses," always with huge thighs and breasts and tiny heads, were not an artistic fad; they were an impulse from a species' soul and loins, not its the head. The artistic impulse is still a survival necessity, a form of worship, and those who communicate with the divine still sculpt with any media at hand.

IF HUMAN HISTORY STARTED forty thousand years ago, that means it has stretched only two thousand generations, allowing twenty years as a generation. Two thousand rounds of fireside tellings, and later media inventions, for the various arts to document the unfolding story of our spirit. The old folks still painted on cave walls 850 generations ago. Our progenitors realized grander artistic-religious ambitions by dragging stones up the sides of pyramids in Egypt and into circles in England, about 180 grandpas ago. A mere 167 generations back, Moses was busy carrying heavy documents downhill, advocating the first monotheism and rejecting golden sculptures of forbidden religious expression.

The religions we commonly think of as religions appeared with Judaism about two hundred generations ago, although Zarathustra launched Zoroastrianism, the longest continuously practiced religion, twenty-five generations earlier. The Hindu Vedas appeared 175 generations ago. The Buddha, Lao Tzu and Confucius were working the East at the same time, the Axial Age, 130 generations ago—while Pythagoras, Orpheus, Dionysus and the mystery cults were at work in the West during the same few amazing generations. Christ offered new ideas one hundred generations ago. Mohammed rethought the Hebrew Bible thirty generations later. Martin Luther hammered a paper onto a church door just twenty-four generations ago. It was only about eight grannies ago that the last American state (Massachusetts) stopped using public taxes to support a state church. We began to hear the Catholic Mass in a language we could understand fewer than three generations ago.

Before formal religions appeared, the lives of believers had always been filled with a mix of spiritual and artistic practices. Indeed, there was no word for religion in the Egyptian, Mesopotamian, Sanskrit or Hebrew languages because the spiritual impulse was integrated as a part of life, not separated as a special practice. The subsequent formal religions that grew from prehistoric practices always included artistic expression as a fundamental part of religious practice.

In the long human line of passing what we know from generation to generation, our last few generations (our time) are the first to feel that art and religion are two separate things. Many vestiges of artistic expression remain in the traditional practices of religion; we sing and move in choreographed ways. Religious settings are beautiful and filled with symbolic things, but they are less full, less dynamic, less engaging than before, because artistic participation has split off and specialized away from the average person's life concerns. However, we have not entirely shed the ancient history of our species that successfully linked art, spiritual yearning and daily life for 1,997 of our 2,000-generation history.

## Personal Religion Within Organized Religions

NO MATTER HOW ORGANIZED any religion becomes, idiosyncratic personal religions must thrive inside and outside officialdom to keep it vital. For a formal religion to stay alive, personal religion must be alive alongside it. The devout parishioner who makes up her own prayer and the cave dweller who fashioned her own clay figure both count as practitioners of their own religion.

Here is the originating plotline of our major "religions." Each grew from a success story of personal religion. A charismatic (etymologically *spiritually gifted*) artist of the spirit, steeped in the traditions of the time, devised original ways to satisfy essential needs. This seeker/yearner creatively delved into spiritual inquiries to realize divergent ideas, often spending time in solitude to do so. This artist-of-spirit then taught, sharing the accomplishments of the creative work, further developing the new ideas and improvising ways of expressing them. The teacher's innovations provided rewarding experiences to others, so the teaching attracted followers. The originator's spiritual inspirations led to the development of sects, some of which became religions, which muddled the originator's impulse, as William James describes:

> As a rule, religious geniuses attract disciples, and produce groups of sympathizers. When these groups get strong enough to "organize" themselves, they become ecclesiastical institutions with corporate ambitions of their own. The spirit of politics and the lust of dogmatic rule are then apt to enter and to contaminate the originally innocent thing ... to some persons the word "church" suggests so much hypocrisy and tyranny and meanness and tenacity of superstition that in a wholesale undiscerning way they glory in saying that they are "down" on religion altogether. Even we who belong to churches do not exempt other churches than our own from the general condemnation.[37]

Religions grow secular. The members of the sect are driven by their enthusiasm for the spiritual content of the "new way," but also by practical, personal and political considerations. Generation after generation of followers deal with "corporate" problems, and the successful sect inexorably becomes a religion with dogma, clergy, a distinctive style of practice, and the games of power and politics. The "contamination" (James' term) we may blame on organized religion is really just the same impulse of corporate dominion we see in all powerful institutions. Religious institutions are no baser than those in other fields; however, because religions purport to be different, their power politics show in stronger relief. Religions can drift far from the creator's original intent. More than a few have commented that, if living today, Jesus would probably not be a Christian.

Remember the game of telephone you played as a child, when a whisper was passed down a line, and the initial statement was compared with the garbled one at the end? Spiritual innovators would be stunned at the distortions wrought by generations of institutional whispering among the faithful. The gentle, loving Mohammed would not delight in female genital mutilation practiced in his name; Jesus would weep at the mountains of bones of those killed in his name; Abraham would recoil at a follower spraying bullets in his name in a Jerusalem mosque; the Buddha would be confounded by the power politics within and between different Buddhist groups, and by the brutal oppression of the Muslim Rohingya people by the Buddhist government of Myanmar.

Over time, the new becomes the old. Then, invariably, spiritually inspired individuals dissent from the secularized old religion, offer new ideas, gather a sect, and repeat the cycle. Every successful heresy becomes an orthodoxy. The pattern—individual to sect to religion to dissenting new sect—applies to art history as well. Indeed, this human pattern applies to most major institutions.

Personal religion returns to the fundamental impulse under all religions—we each adapt the traditions we grew up in to create new answers to essential questions. We may need some solitude along the way. We teach, especially through example, and share our discoveries with those in our "community." We find fulfilling experiences, and we make a difference in the world. We are the spiritual innovators the world cries out to find.

## Jesus, Christianity and Personal Religion

CHRISTIANITY, THE WORLD'S LARGEST religion, was born in personal religion. Jesus was a Jewish spiritual innovator who adapted aspects of his contemporary theology. He was the first major Western figure to argue nonviolence as a response to aggression. His emphasis on love was a radical departure from tradition, especially the idea of unconditional love for all other humans. He prioritized personal experience and responsibility. A strong stand against hypocrisy was a recurrent theme in his teaching; he emphasized the importance of filling ritual and religious action with personal spiritual experience, attacking the Pharisees for empty ritual performance. Jesus did not focus on the notion of a chosen people; rather, he focused on the personal choice of the individual—each could choose to believe and act in accordance with the divine. Some scholars propose that Jesus' teaching was shaped by, and is deeply consistent with, "the wisdom traditions." These comprise a kind of perennial "enlightenment" philosophy distilled from mystics prior to and within Hinduism, Confucianism, Taoism, Sufism and Christianity.

In style, Jesus was an artist. He disdained legalistic, literal, prescriptive thinking, preferring analogical, metaphoric communication. He spoke in parables, in memorable stories, cryptic aphorisms and images that lingered (for a couple thousand years) in the minds and hearts of followers.

His teachings required full attention and artistic interpretation from his audience; we have spent two millennia arguing over those interpretations. Jesus himself seems to be consistently annoyed at the quality of attention and understanding his disciples brought to his teaching, which makes for poetically evocative reading even for non-believers. He made contemplation and reflection essential aspects of spiritual practice. He was a performance artist; he avoided having his teachings written down, knowing the live moment was the potent one, and that transcriptions are subject to misinterpretation and mischief. He was a master of "the teachable moment," a modern education term for recognizing a serendipitous occasion when learners are ripe for a particular kind of learning. He performed when the spirit moved him, not at scheduled places and times—his ministry was an ongoing improvisation. Following Jesus must have been a fascinating, unsettling, edgy learning experience. Sadly, most Christians do not feel the same improvisatory, creative excitement in following Jesus today.

The Gnostics adapted Jesus' message in a direction that adhered to its artistic nature. They believed in Jesus' story as a kind of metaphor; they received his messages as complex works of art to be explored on multiple levels of meaning; and they revered the crucifixion and resurrection as symbolic events. They were amazed that the Orthodox Christians took such a literal view. Both approaches, the literal and the artistic interpretations of Jesus' life and teachings, were thriving until the Emperor Constantine's ironically titled "decree of tolerance" of Christianity (marked by the Edict of Milan in 313). This designated the Orthodox leadership to administer the new state religion over the various Gnostic sects. The Gnostics were wiped out so systematically and thoroughly that their existence was almost erased from history.

With the Orthodox in leadership, the long sequence of interpreting Jesus' life and work began; this trail has given us modern Christian religions that are strangely dissimilar to the message and style of the man. Christians are invited to follow Jesus' model, but an interpreted version of it; his actual model is an exemplary integration of art and religion. The actual model means making up parables to describe what you know. It means paying attention to everyday events, to bring about small miracles in them. It means teaching what you know and aspiring toward unconditional love. We inherited the orthodox view of Jesus' life and teaching over the Gnostic view. The etymology of the word *orthodox* means *having the right opinion*; the etymology of the word *gnostic* is *perceiving, coming to know*—basically, *learning*.

All religions deal with a mix of sacred and secular concerns. The early centuries of Christian practice allowed for a variety personal religious expression within organized practice: individuals could worship in nature, could hold pagan passions and even practices, as long as they adhered to certain religious guidelines. Christian holidays absorbed pagan celebrations. This flexibility supported Christianity's success. Sacred experience was allowable in a variety of ways. Over time, the Christian church increasingly reduced that flexibility in how sacred experience was to be approached.

Martin Luther nailed his ninety-five refutations of Papal Orthodoxy onto a church door at Wittenberg in 1517, believing that "every man is his own priest." The Reformists believed that personal encounter with Jesus' words—aphorisms, parables, the Sermon on the Mount—must serve as the basis for Christian life, not the inventions of orthodox theologians, such as papal infallibility, that Jesus did not teach. An irrepressible personal religious impulse simmered underneath the Reformation's many arguments against the Papacy's excesses and secular preoccupations. However, the Protestants' outburst was hardly a ringing endorsement of the priorities found in this book. They did emphasize the personal relationship to God and individual responsibility, but their harsh suppression of Jesus' message of love, compassion, joy and artistry squelched the personal religious impulse as successfully as the baroque ornaments of Catholicism had done. Protestantism was just a change in style.

# · CHAPTER 17 ·

# PERSONAL RELIGION, AMERICAN STYLE

A SEED FROM THE PROTESTANT EXPLOSION eventually crossed the ocean to grow on American soil, in the form of the Puritan settlers. It is hard to overestimate the formative influence the Puritan ethic has had, and continues to have, on America. That ethic emphasized hard work, self-reliance, personal responsibility and moral rectitude; it discouraged imagination, playfulness, compassion, mysticism, tolerance of dissent, love of nature and nonviolence—all messages of Jesus. The writer Christopher Marley quipped that our history would have been a lot more pleasant if Plymouth Rock had landed on the Puritans, rather than the other way around. During President Clinton's impeachment, an Australian journalist wrote, "Thank God we got the criminals, while America got the Puritans."

Early Puritan influence was widespread; the day the Declaration of Independence was signed, over two centuries after the Plymouth community started, four-fifths of the European-American population belonged to Puritan or Puritan-like churches. This makes early Americans the most Protestant people in history.

As uptight as they may have been, our Puritan ancestors set foundations that partially predispose us toward reliance on a personal religion. Puritanism urged individual responsibility for creating a relationship with God, an infusion of sacred awareness throughout daily life, a personal and social order based on simplicity, and a belief that we live to fulfill divine purposes that are known only by individuals. Puritanism also emphasized the primacy of personal experience over theory, launching an anti-intellectualism that still colors our public dialogue today.

Our Founding Fathers were even more attuned to personal religion than were the Puritans. Steeped in Puritan-derived theology, they were seriously religious even though few were serious church activists. Morality, divine order, personal responsibility, the sense of being an instrument of divine purpose—these were in their hearts and minds. Separating church and state did not suppress our religiosity, which has steadily grown. Thomas Jefferson said simply: "I am a sect myself." He cut and glued together his own forty five-page Bible of only direct quotations from Jesus, so he could consider the teaching without mediation from other people. He argued for freedom in religious search, insisting that: 1) the human spirit is naturally inclined to think freely, be curious and explore alternatives, and 2) convictions reached without such explorations are less genuine. He said that unexplored beliefs tended "only to beget habits of hypocrisy and meanness." The Founders believed our highest good was an individually discovered faith in God and the fulfillment of America's divine purpose.

In the subsequent two hundred–plus years of our national im-provisation, overt religiousness has increased—to the point that we are the most overtly religious nation on Earth. G.K. Chesterton called America a nation with the soul of a church. Dwight Eisenhower said America had to be a religious nation, and he didn't care what reli-gion it had as long as it had one. Today we still believe in religion apart from Religion: "Nine out of ten [American adults in a survey] feel one can be a good Christian or Jew without going to religious services; and seven out of ten say all religions are equally good ways of finding ultimate truth."

With this tradition of organized and disorganized religion, why do Americans struggle for spiritual fulfillment? Our history also contains a consistent thread of a very different color—secularism. The Puritans were diligent workers; indeed, it was a badge of honor among them to work on religious holidays, demonstrating that they were not bound by hollow rituals as the Papists were. Soon secular reasons motivated people to try their luck in the colonies, and in

America's century and a half between settling on the East Coast and settling on a Constitution, secular concerns came to predominate. That tension between religious and secular impulses has been a recurrent conflict at the heart of America, giving our religions a pragmatic bent. America has been, and still is, the most religious *and* the most secular nation on Earth, simultaneously. Religions have not resolved this dilemma for their faithful: Americans struggle to find spiritual expression in the world's most aggressively commercial culture.

## The American Religion

AMERICAN HISTORY HAS DEVELOPED certain socio-religious values that supersede the boundaries of religious institutions. These themes and feelings comprise what is sometimes called "the American Religion"—the general amalgam of values that we stamp on our money and demand of our politicians. Distilled from our initial Protestantism, it is a core set of beliefs, ethics and values that "Americans" are expected to embrace. Many fine writers have taken up this subject; the notion of some kind of a national belief system is easy to challenge, because it contains so many exceptions and contradictions. Nonetheless, these values inform the norms of our national public life and our sense of who we are as a country, so they matter. Several tenets of this secular "religion" align remarkably with the priorities of a personal religion.

Americans believe religion is a matter for individuals to resolve. Each individual forms her own understandings, and should base her actions on them. This self-reliance means that we are expected not only to leave home to find our way in the world, but to leave the church too and find the religious expression that is right for us.

American Religion celebrates the freedom of the individual. (Ironically, individualism is celebrated in just about every part of American culture *except* organized religion.) Anything that violates the God-given American right to think, feel, judge, decide and live as we choose is deemed not just immoral but sacrilegious.

We believe in our laws and the limitations they impose, but we culturally revere individual potential within those laws. The goal of the American Religion is to create oneself—our heroes are people who have done that. We confer special authority on those who have made themselves great from humble beginnings.

Our religiosity may be overt and outspoken, but American Religion believes our spiritual responsibility comes one-on-one, in the quiet. To recall James, "Religion...shall mean for us the feelings, acts, and experiences of individual men in their solitude, so far as they apprehend themselves to stand in relationship whatever they may consider the divine."

American Religion is fundamentally experiential. We feel we must *know* our religion, be able to feel it and act upon it, rather than just discuss it or accede to beliefs. It is not far-reaching; we prefer to stay within a narrow, comfortable arena of recognizable feelings, avoiding mystical experience and spiritual challenges to the status quo. American Religion is cautious about religious information: we want to know more (religious books and other media sell well) but prefer to study within a narrow, familiar range of inquiry.

American Religion believes in "soul competency," a term used by Southern Baptists such as E.Y. Mullins: "What we know most indubitably are the facts of inner experience. We believe every individual is competent to make religious choices, and to live according to religious precepts—and we hold people to such competency." (This belief is akin to aesthetic education's belief that we are all artistically competent, able to do worthwhile creative work in any artistic discipline if given an appropriate challenge.) American Religion requires us to do something with our soul competency: over 80 percent of Americans say that we should arrive at our own religious beliefs independently of any church or synagogue. Americans believe one should pray directly to God, and use our soul competency to form a personal relationship with God—indeed, in various polls, over 90 percent of Americans say they have done that.

American Religion believes that we are personally loved by God, and that God communicates with us individually. Ralph Waldo Emerson wrote, "It is by yourself without ambassador that God speaks to you." Consequently, American Religion believes that our actions should be appropriate to someone in touch with God. We believe America is a leading nation not because God ordained it, but because we have worked to fulfill our higher purpose and have inclined God in our favor as a result of our efforts. Our bargain with God has been that we will work hard, and be good, to merit the divine blessing—we feel we have earned our good fortune. American Religion feels a moral responsibility to be a divine instrument for good in the world. (At least until current times, when fundamental disagreements about America's global role has confused our sense of who we should be toward the rest of the world.)

Religious fundamentalism enjoys repeated resurgences in American history, but it is more an issue of style and emphasis than a distinctive aspect of American Religion. It reappears predominantly as a reaction against change, and against modernism in particular. Its style stresses literal understandings and reassuring simplifications. (As Harold Bloom writes, "Fundamentalists cannot sustain a metaphor.") It provides a safe place in a turbulent world. It is the American Religion with a narrower range and a stronger emotive element. Fundamentalism has been growing in recent decades, but there has always been an ebb and flow to the American fundamentalist phenomenon. It will probably grow as we grapple with an ever-more complex world; and it will wane as people increasingly piece together their own spiritual answers—to say nothing of public outrage over revelations of the excesses (usually sexual) of fundamentalist leaders, as has cyclically happened throughout American history.

With such assurance of a special connection to God, it seems that the American Religion should make us self-assured and maturely self-confident. In actuality, Americans are cautious in their religious sensibilities, insecure about spirituality, and unhappy when challenged to experience religion differently. This may be because American Religion is based in temperament more than theology, or because America is an insecure nation overall. De Tocqueville noted this 180 years ago, citing our "restlessness in the midst of prosperity" with "minds that are anxious and on edge." Almost 120 years ago, the psychologist George M. Beard noted a spiritual malaise in large numbers of educated, refined, civilized Americans, calling us "the most nervous people in all history."

## Today

THE IDEALIZED IMAGE of the American Religion reached its apex in the 1950s, as we became a world-leading nation. Not co-incidentally, organized religions reached their apex then as well; 80 percent of Americans belonged to an organized religion (pre-dominantly Protestant and Catholic), compared with 45 percent a hundred years prior. This was the high point in American church membership, and it will never be achieved again. About 80 per-cent of American children went to Sunday school at least some of the time; 60 percent of those '50s youngsters now say religion was a very important part of their upbringing. Over two-thirds of families said grace every day; today, fewer than 30 percent do. It was during the '50s that "In God We Trust" was added to paper currency and "under God" was added to the Pledge of Allegiance.

The religiousness of the '50s demanded little, and affirmed the nation's basic values and institutions. As the '60s began, the prospect of nuclear annihilation was becoming real to us, seeping into us. The question "Is God Dead?" appeared on the cover of *Time* magazine, marking a spiritual turning point we did not grasp at the time. The tension between the individual yearning for answers and the Sunday morning experience, with its predictable words from the experts, began tearing the comfortable fabric of America's self-image.

In the '60s and early '70s, the American tradition of individual creative idealism reignited, arguing that we should discover our own beliefs and find our own way through the world, rather than live within inherited systems. Many came to distrust the nation's major institutions. Concepts that served as cultural glue—freedom, family, democracy, equality—were reintroduced as questions with a variety of answers. Indeed, the '60s persistently asked questions wherever answers had been entrenched. (Generally, spirituality inclines toward questions while religions incline toward answers.) The Transcendentalist theme of self-determined discovery of personal meaning reappeared as a guiding principle. Henry David Thoreau became a bestseller, and Walden Pond a pilgrimage site. There was a serious generational rift for the first time in American history.

This ferment was frightening to many in mainstream America, and the nation managed to cover it over in a few years with the pursuit of other national priorities, particularly economic necessity. The women's and racial equality movements continued to grow, yet they were usually not expressed as part of a spiritual redirection. Still, the subsurface questioning simmered under the media surface, even as hippies, war protests and utopianism receded from public view. As the political pendulum swung toward the conservative, the renewed spirituality that awoke in the '60s grew steadily, continues to grow, and will become one of the distinctive characteristics of the new century. The gash of the '60s was covered by a Band-Aid of caution in the '70s and '80s; all the while, a new skin was growing underneath. The Band-Aid is now being removed, and the new skin reclaims our personal religious potential.

This new skin began to appear in the late '80s. Spiritual individualism spawned billion dollar industries of self-help products, alternative health practices, health foods and new kinds of travel. Do-it-yourself spirituality is a direct outgrowth of the questioning of the '60s. The aggressive secularity of consumer culture could no longer contain our yearnings—although commerce did find ways to tap the emerging spirituality: a spate of bestselling books and then mass media entertainments about angels and mystical spiritual guides. The neo-'60s values invite us to create our own beliefs and live by them, to find our own spiritual way. We are still exploring how to do this.

In the new spirituality, mystical experience becomes significant: as many as three-quarters of Americans say they believe in angels, two-thirds have experienced miracles, and over four-fifths believe God actively performs miracles in the world. These beliefs hold across different religious and racial lines as well as most demographic groups. Over 80 percent of Americans now believe that God is everywhere and in everyone. Psychedelic drug experiences are making a comeback, as highlighted in the bestselling 2018 book *How to Change Your Mind* by Michael Pollan.

Increasingly, Americans are having mystical experiences and inquiring into them on their own, not through their religions. People who have strong mystical insights tend to become less conventionally religious. Those who have near-death experiences, or out-of-body, lucid dreaming, telepathic, energy healing and other powerful mystical experiences, become more spiritually curious yet tend to turn away from traditional religious practice.

In the second half of the '90s, the number of Americans who stated they wanted spiritual growth in their lives increased by one quarter of the population. This is not a fad; it is a resurgence of our American Religious values and identity. It returns to our Jeffersonian roots of personal freedom and the responsibility to develop our own beliefs and find our own paths. Many will follow a private path through organized religions; others will create a collage of practices from the widely available options; still others will quietly innovate their way toward satisfying experiences.

We are experimenting in personal religion today, just as we should be. On an individual and cultural level, we should be testing and trying, experimenting with different combinations of beliefs and practices. The current activity may be demeaned as dabbling, but it may well be the brainstorming work that precedes creative accomplishment.

In a creativity study in the '70s, researchers Jacob Getzels and Mihaly Csikszentmihalyi studied the problem-solving process of visual artists. After presenting the artists with an array of different objects to use in a drawing, the researchers carefully studied the way they prepared, and then drew, the still-life subject. They interviewed the artists afterwards about both processes. In addition, the completed drawings were assessed for quality by an independent panel. The results of the research were surprising: the drawings rated the most original and most artistically valuable were *not* the ones by the artists deemed to be most talented before the experiment began. The best work came from the artists who had handled the greatest number of objects while preparing the subject to be drawn; those who had explored and rearranged the objects most extensively, and who selected the most unusual objects in setting up the still-life, produced the best work.

These findings also apply to success in personal religion. Those who "handle" more kinds of spiritual exploration, who delve with curiosity, and who piece together an unusual collection of practices create the most original and valuable personal religious systems. As a nation, we are now handling many different kinds of spiritual experiences as we prepare for the creative work ahead. The growing experimentation with psychedelic drugs, guided by counselors, is essentially an additional tool in the laboratory of personal religion, applied to achieve a variety of life goals.

# · CHAPTER 18 ·

# CHALLENGING ISMS

WHAT IS THE PROBLEM? If spirituality is increasing, and we have the innate skills of art and religion necessary to create fulfillment, why are so many still spiritually homeless? American culture challenges us with anti-spiritual forces at least as powerful and entrenched as the aspects of our heritage that support personal religion.

What is a culture? It is the fluid entity that holds the spirit of a people. It is the system through which we pass on what we deem important. It is an ongoing re-creation of ways to satisfy pre-cultural needs. (Exactly what it is *not* is the refined sophistication for an elite group, the limited definition we often use.) The etymology of *culture* is much closer to a petri dish than an opera house. The word goes back to a Latin root that split into two meanings: *cultivating*, tending, caring for growth (as in agriculture), and *worship* (as in cult). My sense of the word culture includes both meanings: *the place in which our yearnings are cared for*.

A culture is a medium for growing, as we use the term in laboratories; a human culture is the medium in which the deeper parts of ourselves are nurtured. By this definition, American culture is making us sick. Our culture cares for the growth of the economic and utilitarian parts of ourselves—but our inner growth is stunted. We need not review the sad inventory of symptoms, but remember a few: one of the world's highest incarceration rates, one of the world's highest youth suicide rates, youth violence, a statistical "epidemic" of depression and stress in adults, unprecedented numbers of young people on prescription drugs, decreasing ability to articulate our thoughts and feelings, and countless individuals who yearn for something more.

A culture is the medium in which we grow. The physical environment we grow in is fragile—and increasingly risky to our health, thanks to our abuse of natural resources. (There is no unpolluted place left on Earth; PCBs and microplastics appear in polar bears.) But the inner ecosystem may be even more compromised for growth. Culture shapes the ways we view ourselves and nature, form our expectations and aspirations, consider community and relationships, and work in our imaginations to create the future.

Cultures (like parents) think they pass on their values by what they say; and, certainly, slogans and instructions do have some effect. However, cultures (and parents) teach mostly through their actions, in ancient languages that go beyond words. In those languages, we are surrounded by institutions we do not respect; in love with celebrities who do not merit our reverence; legislated by interests that are not our own; marinated in consumerism as no other people in history; distracted, entertained and stimulated into commercial quick-fix responsiveness; starved of a deeper dialogue. A study in the late-1990s found that the average Polish ten-year-old could identify seventy-five species of plant life; the average American child could identify five flowers and over fifty corporate logos.

We now find ourselves as the economic, military, political and, for better and worse, cultural leader of the world. But there has been an internal cost. Having overlooked inner culture, the economies of the heart and spirit, we are in a recession at the core. We have created unprecedented affluence and worldwide influence—beyond what any society has achieved for its people in human history—but we have not found our way to fulfillment. The answers of profits have overwhelmed the questions of prophets.

Too much of any good thing becomes bad for us. Let's look at four American cultural "isms" that began in healthy impulses and have gone too far: scientism, legalism, utilitarianism and individualism. These are the real problems of our culture, the challenges to our fulfillment.

## Scientism

Science, our trusty tool, has stacked the deck against our spiritual success. Science itself does not trouble the spirit; it is the extension of science outside its appropriate purview, into a belief system some call "scientism," that troubles the spirit. This is science gone bad— not Dr. Frankenstein–bad or biological weapons–bad, but bad in that it reduces love to pheromones. The *Merriam-Webster Dictionary* defines scientism as, "An exaggerated trust in the efficacy of the methods of natural science applied to all areas of investigation (as in philosophy, the social sciences, and the humanities)."

Scientism is neither the wonderful practices nor the accepted procedures of science that have done so much for humanity— both of which are filled with artistry. My brother is a distinguished scientist; when he and I of about our favorite parts of our work, we speak the same language. But scientism is science that has leaked out of its domain of excellence; it is science merged with materialism and morality, suggesting there are scientific-type approaches and answers for everything. Look at the cost of scientism in education, for example. Even though good educators know that standardized testing captures only a sliver of the learning we need students to accomplish, and that high-stakes tests miss the most important learning, we insist so hard on testing in schools that it is now the mechanical tail that wags the live dog. Teachers and systems are forced to teach to the tests, contorting the natural acts of learning to fit the artificial boxes imposed by the demand for convenient quantitative scoring. American students learn much less, and have their love of learning strangled, because of the scientistic belief in testing. And because scientism is an article of faith, we live at peace with the human damage we inflict daily on our children.

Science studies surfaces, observable phenomena, tangible evidence. Scientism discourages meddling in the messy sub-surfaces; it wields the Scientific Method to protect us from the abysses of mystery, ambiguity and subjectivity. Scientism distrusts immediate knowing, the kind of knowing that comprises mystical experience, intuition and aesthetic awareness. Scientism dismisses direct experience, the powerful muscle that builds values, beliefs, inner curiosity, knowledge and vitality. Scientism believes in one kind of knowing, when the full experience of reality and being alive requires several ways of knowing. The arts and religion have a proud history of successful inquiry into unknown spaces; they are the natural complement to science, and the antidote to scientism.

The Scientific Method is superbly effective, but not in the work of art or spirit. America tends to dismiss such inquiries as soft, subjective, unmeasurable; in so doing, we dismiss precisely the investment our hearts and spirits need to make. Scientism skews us to believe that the problems science addresses well are the only problems we should address. Even if individuals don't completely believe in scientistic values, our culture does, and we struggle to justify endeavors that do not adhere to scientistic biases.

The tug of war between science and religion has always been a false dilemma, a multi-century squabble over turf neither really inhabits. As the astronomer/cosmologist Carl Sagan said, "The notion that science and spirituality are somehow mutually exclusive does a disservice to both." The surface struggle has been between scientism and secular religion—power politics fought under scientific and religious banners. Under the surface, science and religion are entirely compatible. Under the surface, the actions of art and religion include scientific processes to pursue inquiries. Conversely, scientists have always used the work of art throughout their inquiries. Creative work in any medium includes many kinds of endeavors—some more scientific, some more intuitive and aesthetic—to create a satisfying new world. Art, religion and science are allies against the common enemies of scientism, materialism, literalism, status quo–ism and mediocrity.

The successes of science and technology have fostered a Western bully-boy sense of certainty that science can solve any problem. They shouldn't be quite so confident; Ken Wilber points out that mystics have claimed that their work is scientific, too—and can be reproduced by others, if the experiments are done correctly. Science has thrived in replicability for two to three hundred years, while mysticism has done so for two to three thousand.

Wilber also argues that the historic dignity of the West stemmed from the fusion of morals, science and art (which might also be described as the good, the true and the beautiful). But starting in the Renaissance, the three spheres began to differentiate, with adherents pursuing their separate truths; by the end of the 18th century, scientists, artists and moral/cultural theorists were doing different things. This led to fragmentation and alienation, and eventually opened up the possibility for science, the most aggressive of the three, to join with the even more aggressive force of industrialism to colonize and dominate the realms of morality and art. With the good and the beautiful removed from science, materialism became the only truth, which has led to our current trouble. If scientism can be pulled back to mere science, we reclaim the spiritual balance of the good, the true and the beautiful.

## Legalism

Legalism is another symptom of America's spiritual imbalance, and it appears in the litigious nature of our society. (An increase in the number of private lawsuits was one of the hallmarks of the fall of the Golden Ages of both ancient Greece and Rome.) I have friends who bought a home from a couple who blithely announced they made their living through lawsuits. They said they had two or three legal cases going at all times, and most were settled for enough money to provide a good living. They had even sued personal friends, and were hurt that the friends no longer liked to spend time with them.

The pressure of legalism extends beyond formal litigation. Legalism is a way of thinking, a sister to scientism, and it squashes the meaning-making impulse and the value of personal morality.

In legalism, we seek to nail down every possible interpretation, eliminate all ambiguity, and try to win.

Some years ago I decided to sell the business I had started and run for seven years. Before finding a buyer, I imposed one condition: whoever purchased it from me had to complete the agreement one-on-one, before the lawyers came in to finish the necessary final steps. I lost more than one prospective buyer over this unconventional condition; they found it, and me, suspect. Eventually I found a buyer (now a friend) who agreed to act in good faith; we figured out what was fair, each of us compromising on areas that counted most to the other. Still, lawyers nearly killed the deal at the last minute, inventing new what-if horror scenarios that had to be protected against. I was disgusted with people during those legal conversations, myself and the buyer in particular; I laid awake at night thinking of all the ways I might get screwed. Finally, over the lawyers' objections, he and I each accepted some human uncertainty and closed the deal. When the crunch came, each chose to trust the decency of the other.

It is not just lawyers. Contractual thinking filters into all aspects of life—our marriages, our childrearing—fostering a give-get sense of relationships. This transactional thinking undermines commitment, making it conditional upon the delivery of agreed-upon services (even if those agreements are tacit). Contractual thinking commodifies fairness, compassion and love, undermining our intimate, intuitive sense of each. In legalism, the only morality becomes the agreements of parties; and those agreements come to define what is good, even if they have no moral content. We decry this slippery morality in some lawyers, yet practice it ourselves in less blatant ways. In this mindset, freedom, community and democracy become tools for getting what you want.

Lawyer-avoidant as I am, I see the damages of legalism in my own life. In the middle years of our marriage, my ex-wife and I battled over many issues. Tired of it, I introduced a new way to deal with our "issues," trying to bring some objective data into our subjective muddle. We would look at all the agreements in our relationship and address ways in which they seemed broken. This made sense to us both, so we proceeded. Every instance where we used this legalistic approach left us both clearer and further from compassion. We found we could *discuss* (etymologically meaning *smash to pieces*), but had less impulse to connect. We had many exchanges but little *dialogue* (etymologically meaning *find shared meaning through words*).

Being more left-brain dominant than my inherently artistic wife, I took to this legalistic approach with zeal. I would make frequent, accurate observations that proved her wrong; I would rack up points; I was finally winning the many-years' arguments. The fact that she was getting unhappier, that we were sharing less intimacy, barely mattered. I was losing our connection and didn't realize it; the legalistic mindset had made my vision one-dimensional, skewing me toward the exclusively logical thinking from which no creative work can spring. I avoided responsibility in my wife's suffering with the historically famous justifications of its being "temporary pain for long-term gain," or "the discomfort of change." My personal legalism squelched compassion. While this is not the full story of this long marriage coming to a close, it was a contributing storyline. Legalism was a weapon I resorted to unconsciously, and it made our lives worse.

## Utilitarianism

*We are a pioneer country. If you can't mend a roof with it,*
*if you can't patch a boot with it, if you can't manure your*
*field with it or physic your child with it, it's no damn good.*
AGNES DE MILLE

*You use all your vital energy on external*
*things and wear out your spirit.*
CHUANG TZU

UTILITARIANISM IS practical-mindedness elevated to a belief system and worldview. Over time, it colonizes the spirit.

Imbalanced America talks religion, but passionately worships at the church of Utilitarian Universalism. Social analysts argue the sources of this national character trait—some tracing it to our Puritan, pioneer and immigrant heritage, some citing the separation of church and state, some propounding the natural decadence cycle of a nation past its peak. Whatever its origin, we live within this gravitational pull toward things and their practical value. While the tangible benefits of such materialism have been unprecedented, the spiritual costs are becoming increasingly intolerable. Utilitarianism wires us to believe that *the more* is *more stuff*, and faith in this belief has the best minds in the country working overtime to promote worship of and through stuff. Utilitarianism disrespects precisely the kinds of human activity, interpersonal bonding and reliance on experience that religion has always served to foster. It makes us narrower as humans, less environmentally aware, less fulfilled, more dangerous. This church where Americans worship causes many of the social symptoms we decry and, ironically, seek utilitarian solutions for.

Utilitarianism requires measurable results, and what gets measured gets managed. Utilitarianism counts religious success by the number of bodies in the pews, and artistic success by the price a canvas can command or how many tickets are sold—thus entrenching the noun definitions in art and religion. It encourages literal thinking and identification: we are religious if ours is one of those bodies in the sanctuary; we have done our art bit if we went to the "Nutcracker" ballet last year or hang some decent stuff on the living room wall.

Follow such guidelines and get an easy A on the utilitarian Ten Commandments test—that is, if you interpret "honoring parents" as sending a check for the nursing home and visiting occasionally, and "taking the Lord's name in vain" as a particular taboo phrase you never use. Jimmy Carter was ridiculed for raising the complex idea that adultery is possible in the mind and heart, not just in the literal act.

American religions market themselves to bring in new participants. As television became the national meeting place, religions offered shorter sermons, drive-in churches, TV and rock music ministries; religious books and bookstores became big business. The Christian rock music industry opened the wallets of concerned parents, as opposed to the much thinner wallets of hard rock- and grunge-loving teens, fostering an extraordinarily lucrative industry. Religion as a product.

The marketing of religion has worked to some degree in the literal sense: some churches get more bodies in the pews, and many billions of dollars have been spent and earned. However, utilitarian marketing fosters transactional religious consumers rather than spiritual explorers. Consumers are the opposite of creators. As religions feed religious stimuli to people, they actually weaken the skills of art required to create religious experience. Like the over-eager parent who responds to a child's declaration of boredom by taking her to an amusement park, some religions distract and entertain participants out of their spiritual ennui— rather than guide them to make something, which is what works for humans (even bored children) spiritually. Religious consumerism fosters a search for quick answers, lively experiences, gratification and a status-positive social congregation; it overlooks the deeper, subtler, sustaining satisfactions of the work of art. When I would dare complain to my mother that I was bored, I would get a scathing look, a dismissive wave of the hand, and the words, "Go make something." Bored churchgoers would do well to follow her advice.

Utilitarianism values what can be seen and touched, and avoids uncertainty, mystery, ambiguity. It relegates abstract ideas to secondary status, is suspicious of intellect, and avoids questions without single right answers. Whatever we may say, we establish our priorities, arrange our time, skew our thoughts to address

Utilitarian concerns. Utilitarian belief systems skim reflection and preclude wonder.

The secular thinking of Utilitarianism is very concerned about time; the word secular originally meant "of a particular time." Sacred thinking steps out of time-consciousness into concerns that extend beyond a particular time. Secular life runs fast; sacred time is slow. After a visit to America in 1842, Charles Dickens said, "It would be well if Americans loved the Real less, and the Ideal somewhat more." Nietzsche wrote, "Don't die of reality." They both use the term "the real" as a shorthand for utilitarian-mindedness after it has colonized the mind and spirit.

"America has lost its values." We hear that often, and we think it when we learn of horrifying abuses of decency. But we haven't lost our values; indeed, we are adhering to them—it is just that our values are those of Utilitarianism. If people literalize their yearnings, they detach from transpersonal values, they lose empathetic connection to the realities under the surfaces of life that unite us. Much as we waggle our fingers about "values," most people pick the values that serve their desires.

In a Utilitarian value system, cash, convenience and comfort—the three Cs—drive most of our choosing. For a practical people, we are governed largely by our feelings; the more pragmatic the value system, the more individual feelings become a basis for choice. The childlike justifications "I feel like doing it" and "I want it" become legitimate bases for action, and increasingly become the only reasons worth considering, with moral, ethical and humanitarian considerations brushed aside. Public opinion is really public sentiment, and those who can influence public sentiment turn the direction of the nation—as every good PR director and politician knows. That which reduces discomfort and uncertainty is good. That which looks good is good. That which is kind, right and helpful is not really important.

A woman chatted to a friend before a workshop I led. As we milled around, I overheard her talking about a minor car accident she had on the way to the workshop. She said it wasn't really either party's fault, but when she called her insurance agent, he had told her what to say on the accident report, and "thank heavens she had been careful about what she said at the accident site." During the workshop, participants wrote monologues in which a character internally debated a moral issue—preparation for engaging with *Hamlet*'s "To be or not to be" soliloquy. This participant wrote about her insurance report. Her character began the monologue driven by financial concerns and cynical manipulation of the insurance game. After some backing and forthing in the speech, the character decided there were bigger issues at stake than the money, and chose to put down the truth in the report. During an afternoon break, I asked her if the insurance dilemma was true for her. She answered me, "Yeah, thanks a lot. You don't know how much this workshop is going to cost me."

Through the work of art, she shifted her value system—from the utilitarian mindset, that saving money is an adequate basis for unethical acts, to another system that holds truth as more important. We need not create works of art to address the big choices in our lives before we act (although there are worse habits to adopt). The actions of art take us to deeper, more universal, more valuable values upon which we can base our decisions. Just wanting something is not adequate justification in a value system deeper than Utilitarianism. The next time you hear someone decry a loss of values in America, tell the person to go make something.

Utilitarian America does have some spiritual advantages we can tap when motivated. Sometimes we manage the humanistic drive and utilitarian tools to addresses problems as few other cultures ever have. This occasional wherewithal has given us some legacy of accomplishing change. In recent decades, the women's movement and the racial justice movement have been historically unprecedented endeavors. Their advances have consistently provoked vigorous counter-reactions that create the impression of failure. Both are currently hitting barriers that seem impermeable, but their history of change over time is remarkable compared to other countries. Social Security dramatically reduced elder poverty, riding over the objections that continue to try to erode its provision for the needy. However, many still angrily decry current racial and gender inequities, still fight to improve the lot of the elderly and the poor, and cringe in shame at the horrid instances of abuse that regularly appear. This healthy rage and its can-do utilitarian toolkit has driven the fastest change in human history.

As a culture, even with the lurches of counter-reaction, we redefined what women are, rewrote the possibilities and expectations, overturned hundreds of years of entrenched thinking in a single lifetime (with help from previous generations). What a statement about the power of our women. De Tocqueville saw American women as the backbone of our spiritual life and future. He was right.

We still struggle with our racism; we are far from redressing our original sin of slavery. But if we look at surveys about racial attitudes over time, on interracial marriage and friendship, we see remarkable advances in the last forty years. I've seen a "whites-only" drinking fountain at a movie theater north of the Mason-Dixon line in my lifetime; that would be unthinkable anywhere in the U.S. today. Even with the increased racial tensions and hideous recent incidents, the long-term trend continues toward tolerance. No population in world history has evolved so far so fast on issues as ancient as subjugation and fear of another race. No other population has gone from widespread visceral disapproval of interracial marriage to widespread acceptance in two generations.

Look at the Americans with Disabilities Act. What a spiritual statement by a culture, again a first in human history. We may have grumbled about inconvenience; we may have resisted and litigated; but as a nation, we put our utilitarian money where our politically correct mouths were, and paid to change the face of a nation ramp by ramp. We walked the talk that says: "We believe in a fair chance for all human beings." Are all venues now accessible? Certainly not, but the utilitarian tool of lawsuits is steadily advancing the spiritual generosity of inclusion.

In writing about human rights two decades ago, I wrote, "Western governments have fostered the focus on human rights, and thus their violations of it appear to be particularly egregious. They certainly have not practiced commitment to human rights with admirable consistency, but for the first time in history there has been a growing sense that merely being alive means we have certain rights that others must respect. This is a profound spiritual accomplishment—even if we are only in the early stages of implementation." That is no longer true of the U.S., as a surge of selfish utilitarianism by those with power has eclipsed our humanism in governmental priorities. Staying aware of long-term trends, though, I am confident America's commitment to human rights will rise again.

## Individualism and Idealism

BEN FRANKLIN EMBODIED and articulated the gospel of individualism, with its most sacred tenet: the chance for an individual to get ahead on his (or *her*, we can now add, Ben) own initiative. This article of American faith has been a dominant thread in our national fabric, in both its idealistic and utilitarian aspects. An American must work hard, do the right things and earn her own good luck to succeed; we have an almost mystical faith that this effort will be rewarded.

Challenged as this beloved story is by troubling statistics of a struggling working class, business failures and bankruptcy, most Americans (and most people) still hold the vision of the land of opportunity and promote bootstrap individualism as an American ideal. I question whether this national persona will persist, as the statistics of upward socioeconomic mobility showed a sharp turnaround beginning around 1980, with the U.S. sinking further and further down the list of industrialized nations, now in the "low mobility" group. The Reagan Revolution, with its "Morning in

America" cheeriness, marked the start of a steep and steady decline in the economic reality of the American dream. How ironic that the banner metaphor commonly used to describe the ideal of American individualism—"lift yourself up by your own bootstraps"—refers to a physically impossible feat.

Bootstrap individual idealism has a long history, as does the seemingly opposite idealism of collective societal visions: the various utopian socialist movements throughout the 1800s, particularly the Transcendental movement of the 1840s, capture the idealistic streak that runs through the American character. Walt Whitman may be the greatest singer of America's civic, social and personal ideal, but this ideal appears throughout our literature, throughout our arts, throughout our stunted political dialogue. Idealism may be the only thing shared by '60s hippies and Ronald Reagan. We believe in the possible improvement of individuals and of society, and in the value of personal hard work to get there no matter what your ideal may be (well, maybe the hippies didn't believe that). Utilitarian America has literalized this to mono-focus on material improvement, without including the moral, psychological, spiritual or intellectual improvement that the Founding Fathers and Transcendentalists aspired toward.

Alexis De Tocqueville came to study America in the 1830s, and to report on the discoveries made in first fifty years of the nation he admired. He saw the strengths, weaknesses and potentials as a caring high school teacher perceives a promising teen. De Tocqueville expressed admiration and concern about American individualism. He saw isolation as a real risk; he worried about people leaving consideration of the society's good to others, as they withdrew within their own walls and needs. Indeed, when he wrote about individualism, he meant becoming too focused on family and friends. Our solitary, lonely sense of individualism has become a more drastic isolation than he imagined. He charged that our individualism could lead us to forget our ancestors and descendants—a haunting warning in the light of what we now do with our elders and to our environment.

De Tocqueville cited three institutions that could moderate the risks of individualism, writing that family, religion and democratic political participation could counterbalance our self-centered tendencies. Look at the current state of those three bastions against socially damaging self-interest. We are all aware of the fragmentation of the traditional family structure. Religion is struggling; attendance has dwindled in mainline churches for twenty-five years—fewer than one-fifth of Protestants and one-quarter of Catholics are in church on any given Sunday. And political participation is poor; voter turnout in the U.S. is lower than for any other major democracy, and we currently fight partisan battles over efforts to make it even harder to vote.

The burgeoning teenage America that De Tocqueville witnessed has grown into the successful, conflicted adult that is our nation today. Indeed, I think our powerful middle-years nation is in a mid-life crisis. Our utilitarianism has seeped so deep that it has invaded the moral vitality De Tocqueville identified as our saving grace.

What about the idealistic humanism that sees the land of opportunity not in terms of personal advancement or material success, but as the opportunity to ask deep questions and to seek new solutions for a nation of good people? This idealistic streak struggles to find more than a token place in American life. It appears in the windy blather of politicians, in the ungrounded demand for "values" and morality; it is sometimes mocked as "touchy-feely," but its impulses express a deeper if undirected reach toward *the more*. When it appears as a quiet urge in our hearts for more contact, more meaning, more depth in daily life—an urge too often drowned out by the noise and demands of our busy lives—it is hardly acknowledged. It may live only as the sad hurt in a heart that knows there is more to living than utilitarian material survival.

The way to revive our individualism with our historically deep idealism lies in the idea of "wholehearted participation." What does it mean to participate? It requires more than just showing up, although that is where it begins. Yet most Americans are not even showing up for religious and political participation, and "families" have changed so much that few resemble what de Tocqueville saw.

We need to shift our definition of participation from the noun (just showing up) to the verb (what you *do* in participation). We must address the actions of the participation in family, politics and religion. Family participation is comprised of a hundred small commonplace actions— investing time, listening, inquiring and giving that communicate love. Religious participation, whether institutional or personal, means starting and pursuing spiritual conversations; a 2018 study found that over three-quarters of Americans (churchgoers and non) rarely if ever have spiritual conversations. It means reading material with helpfully challenging (not only comforting) spiritual ideas; it means curiosity about the presence of and respect for spirituality in daily life and in the lives of others. Political participation means more than responding to political news, writing campaign checks and filling out online petitions. It can mean volunteering for a campaign, showing up for rallies and protesting the unacceptable, and it can also mean living your political beliefs—reducing your carbon footprint, hiring released felons, speaking to homeless people, not silently allowing friends to say sexist things about women.

We do not revive commitment to deep values by insisting, pushing, legislating or ignoring them. Indeed, those impulses catalyze their opposites. When a child is confused or unhappy, we do not shout at her to be positive. The wise parent engages that child in worthwhile play, in hands-on construction in which the child can make something of meaning to himself. Personal religion activates our artistry to create new truths, our own truths, through family, religion, work and community.

And individualism? We can return to the etymological sense of *individual*, which meant *indivisible*. The true individual is neither a cowboy nor an entrepreneur, but a whole person, one capable of *holy* experience.

## · CHAPTER 19 ·

# Now What?
# Implications for...

LET'S ASSUME I have made the case effectively enough that you agree:

- ⮑ *There is a fundamental, ancient connection between the arts and spirituality;*

- ⮑ *this connection still exists in the "actions" and "skills" they both share;*

- ⮑ *both are practiced inside and outside the institutions of art and religion;*

- ⮑ *their joint practice in personal religion fosters the fulfillment many yearn to find in a complex, literal, commercial culture.*

A friend of mine, after powerful weeks of spiritual work in which she accomplished a remarkable transformation in the way she saw the world, said it simply: "Damn. Now what?" Let's look into the "Now what?"—the implications of these agreements: 1. for art and religious institutions, 2. for raising young people, 3. for the workplace, and 4. for sustaining a personal religious practice.

The overarching implication is that we have to grow up. Psychologists tell us healthy development goes through three basic stages: preconventional, conventional and postconventional. These roughly equate with three states of interpersonal dynamics: pre-personal, personal and transpersonal. (Transpersonal dynamics reach beyond the individual to connect with aspects of humankind and of the cosmos.)

We are born in a glorious anarchy of pre-personal need, demand, frustration and bliss at the egotistical center of the universe. (The etymology of *universe* is *everything turned into one*.) Over time, we learn the ways of parents and culture, more or less. Even as we resist some aspects, we accept many more of the norms, and take a couple of decades to learn the rules and preferences of society, including how to form interpersonal relationships. Socialization includes beliefs, values and ways of thinking about life, death, good, bad and reality. As we become "grownups," we become largely conventional; even with our idiosyncrasies and unique histories, we dress like, believe like and act like other "people like us."

Some people stay conventional. They cope with the demands of a complex society, but they stop developing toward their human potential even as they aim for their professional, social or pleasure potential. Others yearn to transform from the conventional into the post-conventional stage, an individual, creative endeavor— artists at work in the medium of daily living.

The most common hallmark of the transition from conventional to postconventional is a hunger, an awareness of *the more*; a realization that William James described as: "Compared to what we ought to be, we are only half-awake. Our fires are dampened, our drafts are checked; we are making use of only a small part of our mental and physical resources." Convention casts a glamour over us (the word for a hypnotic spell in the Middle Ages). Our modern sense of glamour remains hypnotically appropriate in this attractive culture of advertising and celebrity that envelops us in spiritual sleepiness. We must awake from these anesthetics to grow in the aesthetics of a personal religion.

Our post-conventional selves are authentic originals. We perceive with new depth and clarity; we develop along our own paths. We shed the encumbrances of convention that do not reward us experientially, and practice the actions that do. We become world-makers. Interpersonally, we expand from the ability to have relationships with other individuals (the vitality of which is difficult to sustain for long in a conventional person) to the transpersonal state, in which we can also connect to aspects of humanity and greater-than-human truths that were previously invisible.

This developmental sequence is not a mushy, romantic notion; it is an ancient reality that has been articulated in every religion. The metaphors of new sight and rebirth refer to the need to be reborn from the embryonic stage of conventionalism into the new world of post-conventional beginnings.

## 1) Institutions of Art and Religion

THE INSTITUTIONS OF ART AND RELIGION must outgrow the ossification of their conventionality. That is the nature of institutions—they tend to believe they *are* their conventional ways; the etymological meaning of *convention* is *to come together*. In institutions, as in people, convention condenses identity into agreed-upon forms. But each of us is more than that; art and religion are more. Many individuals within the institutions feel the urge for more, for *the more*, and they need the institutions to grow with them.

What would it mean for religions to become post-conventional? What would it mean for the arts establishment, the museums and performance halls, the schools of the arts, to become post-conventional? The answer is the opportunity of this young adult century. Of course institutions, especially institutions as old as art and religion, resist change. But unless the mainstream institutions can develop creatively, art and religion will be pushed further and further to the periphery of American life, becoming historical enclaves for the few. Here are several ways our institutions can grow into post-conventionality.

### Focus on the actions

The art and religion industries, like all industries, emphasize the nouns—turning experiences into commodities and artistry into production and consumption. Of course there are the sonatas and prayers that focus our experiences, but institutions literalize our yearnings; they lead us to think art *is* the painting or performance, religion *is* the body in the pew or on the prayer rug. Artistic and religious institutions are in the experience business. Without successfully nurturing artistic connection and spiritual fulfillment in the present tense, in ways that provoke resonant relevant meaning for a variety of individuals, the church and art gallery are half empty even when they are full.

Religions and art institutions cannot take the inner work for granted, or assume it just takes care of itself. It doesn't. The average American cannot translate an opera ticket into an experience fulfilling enough that they yearn to return (I'd guess fewer than 10 percent can do that); only a minuscule percentage will pay a high price for that ticket in the first place. A visit to a sanctuary and service rarely provides personal renewal for the casual or occasional visitor, and too often does not provide deep nourishment for the regular attendee. The institutions must creatively devise ways to draw people more fully into the experiments of prayer, the experience of reading a painting (and, as every good teaching artist knows, not by telling them about the painting); they must focus on how people create such experiences, and how they can support the development of those skills of engagement.

### New vocabulary

This emphasis argues for a new, shared vocabulary in art and religion. The language already overlaps; leading discussions with musicians from the Philadelphia Orchestra for a documentary film, I heard the words "spiritual," "divine," "mystical" and "whole" spoken as often as "timbre," "trill" and "orchestration." Religions speak of beauty, harmony, grace, choirs of angels and heavenly music. This metaphor-sharing is a beginning.

Give museum newcomers information about pointillism, and they put it in their heads. Guide them to discover what those differ-ent-colored dots do to their eyes and sense of the scene, give them some paper and a good challenge that uses dots (and let a teaching artist work with them), and they create a connection in the heart that changes the way they see the world. Hound the faithful with words like "faith" and "belief," and most slip into autopilot and glaze over. Lead them to inquire into the ways their faith is already manifested in their life choices, and the ways that expression of faith diverges from their stated beliefs, and they begin to explore the realm of the sacred.

### Emphasize competence

The institutions of art and religion could emphasize the innate competence of their participants, rather than their incompetence or the super-competence of others. Preachers sermonize about ways we can be better; docents tell us what is so brilliant about a painting; music teachers show us how we are doing things wrong. This is the modus operandi of most teaching, and it has its place. It just doesn't inspire engagement.

The etymology of *competent* means *capable for striving*. (And ironically, *compete* comes from *striving with*, not *striving against*—as in the original Olympic ideal when races were organized because everyone ran faster within that structure.) People learn better when they are treated as competent. A good teaching artist taps and draws forth learners' competence with engaging challenges that surface what they already know about the subject they are investigating; we all know more than we think about better and worse, about interestingness and originality. The learner can be guided into challenges to make artistic choices and discoveries that illuminate the area of investigation and spark curiosity to learn more. Bingo!—you have an arts participant rather than an uncertain consumer.

Similarly, religions can tap the ways in which participants already succeed spiritually. They can then guide those abilities and relevant experience into interesting, resonant inquiries, and then reflect on the results. We were not taught like this in art or religion—but this is the way people learn best. The role of the institution becomes "the guide" that nurtures competence and provides rewarding occasions for practice and reflection. This is how to nurture healthy motivation, and a sense of belonging in the institution. Successfully "making" personal connections, even small ones, builds curiosity, which builds greater investment in further exploration, which builds habits and commitment.

### Emphasize creating

The Commencement says, "You gotta make stuff you love." What if artistic and religious institutions emphasized making stuff along with their usual emphasis on the great stuff others have made? Both institutions do this with children, but dispense with it for adults. We learn best in a balance of making, perceiving and reflecting; we creatively engage when we have our hands on a subject, not just our eyes. If arts institutions believed that, they would support and celebrate amateurism. Churches would encourage the exploration of different spiritual practices, and what experiences arise in them, and how they relate to an enriched faith; they would guide the discovery and fulfilling expression of personally created statements of belief. They would support the hands-on inquiry process, without limitations on where it leads. Religious practices focus so much on what hands do, because there is such power in the hand-spirit connection, but they rarely apply that awareness to creating things with those same hands.

Institutions with a priority on creating would become resource centers more than repositories or reliquaries. They would provoke inquiry rather than insist on answers. The institutions and their leaders would become more like colleagues than parents or experts—encouraging personal exploration in their medium and giving feedback, not through the lens of denomination or discipline but through the lens of love. As I have often said of great artists, they seek colleagues more than admirers. They want partners in the inquiry processes they care about, even though they usually have to settle for appreciators.

## Multiple truths

If they followed the bullet points just above, the institutions of art and religion would have to ease their attachment to *the* truth, and celebrate the multiplicity of truthful answers. Religions are built on singular truths, even though they know the faithful interpret that truth in various ways. We touched on Niels Bohr's theory of complementarity in the Introduction; it states that opposites are actually two different aspects of a higher unity that exist beyond our capacity to perceive. He pointed out (and he was a physicist) that the distinguishing feature of a small truth is that its opposite is false, while the feature of a great truth is that its opposite is also true. A promise of *the* truth in a complex, turbulent world is comforting. But art and religion must admit that they offer truths, and that there are other truths, and that the truths that matter most are the ones individuals discover personally and know through direct experience. In this imagined setting, the clergy and the connoisseurs would be enthusiastic to learn what participants were discovering, rather than cautious or defensive—the institutions would become research centers for the discovery of significant truths. A close friend of mine decided to convert to Catholicism. She is an unconventional thinker and spiritual explorer; in her precatechumenate classes, the priest discovered her originality and brilliance, and asked her to please not speak up or ask provocative questions or he'd have to deny her initiation.

Arts experts usually forget an etymological truth: a *connoisseur* is not one who knows, but *one adept at coming to know.* A connoisseur is not an expert, not a master knower with impressive words and unassailable opinions, but a master learner. A connoisseur serves us best by demonstrating how to discover new truths, rather than by expounding on the old.

## Be the thing

The challenge of authenticity. The dictum I live by, and that I encourage those I teach and advise to follow, is this: "Be the thing."

Gandhi stated it more elegantly: "You must be that change you wish to see in the world."

What would an arts institution that embodied the highest aspirations of art *experience* look like? How would a church that lived its commitment to sacred *experience* function as a corporate entity? We don't know.

I am often troubled that arts institutions mouth belief in the power of the arts, but have nothing artistic in the way the organizations are managed. It's an "art on the outside, corporation on the inside" model—and it's mostly an old-fashioned corporate culture. There are costs: employees lose their artistic yearning and begin to function like corporate employees; for the "consumers," the power of art is placed in limited, "appropriate" boxes—even as the institutions complain of art's diminished place in society. If indeed art is so important (as I think it is), why is it rejected in the very nature of the corporate entity? Why isn't there more artistry inside the institution? What if the skills of art and the creative passion of art-making infused management structures and practices? The work of art appears in the daily work of individuals within the institutions, and in every line of work. But the arts could do so much better. What if religions were run according to the nature of sacred experience, as monasteries and convents have sought to do?

There is an adage with which I berate my students, the law of eighty percent—80 percent of what we teach is who we are. Our subject matter is important, and comprises 20 percent of our impact; but the real learning derives from the complex human information that the teacher embodies. Our teaching's true power and potential lives in the way we listen, phrase thoughts, respond to questions and ideas, emphasize priorities, pause to reflect, discover something and make a new connection, and in the thousand other cues we send to people. Who were the great teachers in your life? Their live qualities are what made the lasting impression—not the cleverness of their syllabi or the quality of their handouts.

We are all teachers all the time. We teach as we work with colleagues, as we clean up after dinner at home. We have opportunities to teach as we sit on the subway, or wait in a line. We teach with our living example. I challenge artists who teach to steep everything about the way they teach—how they listen, guide and respond—in their artistry. This is not to say that a musician in a classroom answers every question through her violin (although I have students who do that effectively), but that the teaching artist listens to student responses or rudimentary musical ideas with the same depth and delighted interest that she brings to her chamber quartet.

What if all professionals in the arts and in religion took the eighty-percent pledge to personally embody their artistic beliefs in all aspects of their lives? Many in the clergy do take such a pledge, and strive to fulfill it, although few live its artistic aspects. It is a privilege to have a life in these fields, to add our contributions to these most ancient bastions of human potential. If we were to accept this challenge of authenticity, we would change as individuals, and our institutions would transform. We could be that change we wish to see in the world.

Recall the slogan James Carville slapped on the wall of Clinton '92 campaign headquarters? "It's the economy, stupid." Many claim that the disciplined focus on that core message won them the White House. What if all religious and artistic institutions put this slogan on their walls: "It's fulfilling personal experiences of *the more*." Let's Carvillize it (minus the insult) to "It's *the more*." If we were to follow that lead, we would revitalize those institutions with fresh compassion, curiosity and creativity— humankind's greatness—not the three Cs of cash, convenience and comfort.

## 2) Raising Young People

IN JAMES JOYCE'S *Portrait of the Artist as a Young Man*, the character Stephen Dedalus leaves the Catholic Church in which he was raised. A friend asks if he had become a Protestant. He answers, "I said that I had lost the faith, but not that I had lost self-respect."

At age 11, I complained to my mother about the boring Methodist Sunday school she had placed me in, and she responded in a wonderful way. She said I did not have to go there, but I did have to go somewhere. She affirmed that spiritual education was an essential part of growing up, but she gave me choices. She took me to experience all the different kinds of services near where we lived. We visited every Protestant denomination; we went to Catholic and Jewish services. We went to Fundamentalist and gospel services, even to an eerie spiritualist service in which the dead put in an appearance. After our experimentation, I chose to become a Quaker, the silent practice, without clergy, that offers so much in terms of personal freedom and compassionate inquiry. My mother's gift sparked a life of reliance on my personal experience as a basis for religious practice, a belief that all religions have much to offer, and a sense of spiritual development as an essential part of life.

I still strive to hear classical music with the awe I felt when my older brother sat me down to listen to Mussorgsky's "Pictures at an Exhibition" with him. (Part of the indelible mark of that first listening was that my brother was choosing to spend time with me to share something he liked.) I have a friend in her late 70s who still sees pea pods with the same wonder she felt when her grandmother showed her their perfection in a farm garden. All children are born with spiritual affinities and skills. We must tap and educate those skills.

A study questioned people who had been confirmed in a church in the 1960s; twenty years later, fewer than one in three remained in their confirmation denomination, and about half had dispensed with church practice altogether. Yet fewer than 10 percent of those who had left churches altogether, and virtually none of those still involved, said that they had no religious interests. When the young are brought into spiritual and religious thinking and practice, a lifetime of interest gets confirmed.

We are not taking good care of the spiritual development of our young. We love to say we are a child-centered society, but we are not. We give our children a lot, but we do not give to them in ways that respect their creative and spiritual potential. The problem goes beyond fragmented families (only one in five households looks like the "traditional" home of two parents and at least one child) and the hours that children spend in front of screens (now more hours than they spend with teachers).

Children learn by example, by engagement, and through peers. What parents say to a child does have some impact, but is always tempered, and usually overwhelmed, by what they do. Children with parents who were artistically active retain interests in artistic matters throughout life. Those with parents who were spiritually active (not just church attendees without engagement) retain interests in spiritual matters throughout life.

To nurture children, we must live spiritually curious lives. We must practice the actions of art and spirit with our children every day. Remember that those actions happen to be precisely the same ones that develop optimum learning skills: use of attention, capacity to make strong personal connections, open discovery of new things, a capacity for wonder and a taste for inquiry, and so forth. We must model these skills when we function with other adults in the child's sight.

We must draw children into spiritual inquiries—both those that we deal with ourselves and those that arise for them. Are you troubled about starving children in an overseas crisis? Draw your child into the dilemma and into the way you deal with it (waiting until a developmentally appropriate age, of course). Take your child's spiritual questions very seriously, and pursue answers together. The child asks how you know there is a God? Don't dodge the difficulty with a rote response; honor the importance of the question. Deal with it by asking more, by gathering evidence; pursue it over time, together, thus teaching that good spiritual inquiries are explored as an ongoing matter and not like a pop quiz. Build reflective and contemplative habits with your child. Always look under the surfaces. Pray with your children in various ways. Downshift with them to enjoy the fullness of experience in the slow lane.

## Schools

Public schooling discourages the development of passionate inquirers, creators and contributors. Young children are spiritually awake, surrounded by the sense of mystery, filled with wonder, and passionate to inquire into all the marvels of being alive. Schooling channels the questioning, slowly anaesthetizing the sense of mystery and passion to inquire; as sociologist Neil Postman says, "They enter school as question marks and leave as periods." Our standard American schooling (except, in some cases, for the early years) is almost diabolically devised to squelch every natural way young people learn and yearn.

American schooling almost never encourages us to do the things that great learners do by habit: set our own objectives; identify our own relevances; put things together in several ways; follow trails that lead outside established "coverage" parameters of the text or teacher; not-know with relaxation, even pleasure; develop skills of self-assessment; learn to trust our judgment about subtler matters; consider important matters over time; play metaphorically; perceive well using multiple senses. (And persist through eleven-punctuation-mark sentences to their natural finish!) Schooling cares little for intrinsic motivation, the irreducible energy source of real learning. Schooling does not teach young people how to learn.

## Success

For decades, psychologists have surveyed young people to ask what they would like to be when they grow up. The shifting preferences of admired professions have closely reflected social trends in the adult world. In the last couple of decades there has been an unprecedented and dramatic increase in one particular answer. It is not firefighter or astronaut, not rock star or computer whiz—it is "rich." There is no attraction to the doing or creating involved, just the result.

We must teach children alternative definitions of success. They have an endless indoctrination in success as determined by surface measures like grades, appearance, money, possessions, power and celebrity. They learn that success is the power of looking cool to others, having expensive stuff, being sexually attractive, having money or its trappings, being dangerous. Having a gun is having power, on TV and on the playground.

How are we going to give young people the authentic experience of power they need to play with, the experience of success they deserve? We need to teach them to create. You may recall that I introduced the etymology of the word *success* earlier as *having a follow-through*, like succession of royalty—you are a successful painter if your work leaves you more eager to dig into the next painting, not just if your canvasses sell for big money. We must guide young people to develop habits of making things they love, so that they can experience the definition of success that keeps their spirits as well attended to as their checkbooks and closets. Schools purport that their mission is to create lifelong learners, when they are really structured to create lifelong earners. I urge us to commit to developing lifelong yearners.

## 3) Spiritual Action in the Workplace

*Work is holy*
*when the heart of the worker*
*is fixed on the Highest...*
*Action rightly performed brings freedom.*
   *BHAGAVAD GITA*

ATTENTION TO SPIRITUAL and artistic experience at the workplace is slowly building. I know of a dozen centers dedicated to advancing the cause, and another dozen companies that are actively pursuing the development of creativity at the workplace. The poet and business consultant David Whyte wrote a bestseller, *The Heart*

*Aroused*, that dealt with the issue. He writes, "This split between our work life and that part of our soul life forced underground seems to be at the root of much of our current unhappiness."

We invest too many of our waking hours in work to tolerate it as a wasteland of yearning. Too much excellent work results from creatively engaged employees for businesses not to take advantage. The divine does not wait outside the workplace door. Our work must allow us to look under the workplace surfaces to discover new answers to our personal inquiry questions. Ministers and mullahs, pianists and playwrights have the advantage of exploring the questions they are most concerned about through their job descriptions. The rest of us must remember that artistry and spirituality create a quality of experience, not a category of experience or a location for it.

I ask this question of people in business groups: where in your work life do you find yourself naturally slipping into the work of art? After some reminders of the broader definition of "the work of art," every individual recognizes areas of artistry. I ask: What would you love to create at work? Each person can readily generate a creative project that would serve the employer and is personally exciting—as if they were waiting to be asked.

Businesspeople are cautious about acknowledging the spirituality in their work. Some can be coaxed to talk about it, but the divine is not a topic for the workplace. Some progressive companies devise non-religious ways to support spirituality. No, not corporate mantras or whirling dervish breaks. We see the emergence of meditation instruction available in some companies; encouragement of contemplation breaks, yoga classes and meetings that focus not on problem-solving but deep perceiving and intuitive expression.

As individuals, we must take responsibility for our own personal religious practice within our work. We need not make a big public deal about it, but we must stay awake to the fullness of our work experiences. And if our work provides no spiritual sustenance, we must seriously consider taking our passions elsewhere.

## 4) Sustaining a Personal Practice

AN EXPERT IN TIME MANAGEMENT offered a pop quiz to the business executives during his presentation. He placed a five-gallon glass Mason jar on a table, and a number of fist-sized rocks. He placed the rocks in the jar until no more could fit in. "Is this jar full?" The execs all said "yes." "Really?" He reached under the table and pulled out a pail of gravel. He poured gravel into the jar, giving it the occasional shake to help the gravel work into the empty spaces, until it settled and filled right up to the top. "Is it full now?" Some of the executives said yes, and a few said "probably not"—being onto his game. He reached under the table and pulled out a pail of sand. He poured and shook until the sand was up to the top. Again he asked, "Is this jar full?" He heard a chorus of "nos." "Good," he said, and grabbed a pitcher of water and poured till he filled it up to the brim. Then he turned to the group and asked, "What is the point of this demonstration?"

One eager beaver raised his hand and said, "The point is that no matter how full your schedule is, if you really try, you can always fit more things into it!"

"No," the speaker said, "That is exactly not the point. The truth this teaches us is that if you don't put in the big rocks first, you'll never get them in at all."

What are the big rocks in your life? If you want one of them to be a fulfilling spiritual life, place it in first, or you will not fit it in at all. This is the first essential condition of a fulfilling spiritual practice—the time, the space, the priority, expressed internally and externally, to get on with your creative spiritual development.

A question for creators in all disciplines: what conditions do you need to sustain your creative work? That question is not, "What conditions would you like?" Or, "when do you do your best work?" It is a question of essentials. Artists usually jump to a wish list that includes more money, equipment they always wanted, fabulous work space, more time with inspiring colleagues, someone to clean their home. We whittle these wishes down to needs.

The physical needs tend to be few and already available. Artists grudgingly admit they have enough money for the most part to get to the creative work. The more difficult essentials are intangible, and usually have to do with time, with focus and attention, with emotional states and good problems. The barriers are real, but they are imposed more from the inside than the outside. Yes, artists have responsibilities and need to earn enough money, but these needs are manageable if the large rock of commitment is placed daily in the jar.

The conditions artists need are the same we all need to do fulfilling spiritual work. Fulfilled artists are constructively selfish about creating those conditions, so they can successfully engage in the serious play their lives are committed to. Sometimes they are ruthless about maintaining those conditions, sometimes they are stealthy; sometimes they are sloppy and lose their way, or work fitfully. Same with creative spiritual work: some of us are adamant in maintaining our essential requirements, some are subtle, and others—too many—are inattentive or occasional, and get precisely those kinds of results.

TRY THIS.

*List five things you need to do good spiritual work. (Don't say you need to be in a 104-foot foot circle in the middle of nowhere to do good spiritual work, or you are going to flail spiritually at home.) What do you need to tap your competence, to achieve the serious play of being able to identify and pursue spiritual inquiries, to creatively attend to the invisible truths that surround us? What do you need "to bind the pieces of life together tightly?" We must know what we need in order to pursue our best spiritual work, and must be constructively selfish about sustaining those conditions.*

## Courage

I hope courage was one of the five things you came up with in the previous exercise. If not, add it, because it takes courage to sustain a spiritual inquiry in America.

Spiritual courage today does not look like the courage of the martyrs of old. We must internalize those heroic metaphors by remaining open, deep, inquiring and loving in the face of all today's pressures, oppressions, distractions and subtle cruelties to the spirit. The martyred saints, the heroes torn apart by lions, the ascetics and the mystics—we can live their courage in our time without heading into the desert on foot or slaying dragons. Having an active daily practice of spiritual/artistic inquiry is an act of courage in a utilitarian universalist society. Making life choices based on compassion, curiosity and creation rather than cash, comfort and convenience is an act of courage. Courage is not the lack of doubt, fear or despair; it is the capacity to proceed in spite of them.

The quietest courage is that which sustains our creative work over the long haul. "Well begun is half done," the saying goes. Maybe true, and maybe the suggestions in this book can support a good beginning. But the long haul takes courage and grit. Fortitude is the challenge of a lifetime.

David Whyte reminds us, "One of the disciplines of building a rich soul life seems to be the simple act, on a daily basis, of remembering what is most important to us. Poets write poetry as much to remember these primary relationships as they do to tell them with others." People engage in the work of art—creating things—as much to stay in touch with the unexpressed elements of their particular task as they do to bring a new something into the world. The mere doing of our personal religious practices provides the spiritual balance we crave in modern life.

If you were going to give advice to a friend about losing weight and keeping it off permanently, what would you say? You are dealing with issues of sustainability. You would not advise crash techniques and miracle shortcuts for long-term success. You would talk about creating a healthier daily diet, developing exercise habits and changing some behavioral patterns. We know about sustaining healthy practices; we just don't follow the advice. How do we sustain a personal religious practice? We already know the answer: new habits, a healthy experiential diet, regular exercises and changes in some behavioral patterns.

### Authenticity

Sitting in a car in a Kroger supermarket parking lot in Nashville, I watch the railed-off area marked for return of shopping carts. Kroger, like most supermarkets, has compromised: they don't ask shoppers to roll their carts all the way back to the store; they provide a holding pen out in the middle of the parking area to complete the civic duty. I pay attention for exactly seven minutes. I see many decisions made by cart-borrowing shoppers, many different definitions of civic responsibility demonstrated by the action. For some it is good enough to leave the cart in the general vicinity of the corral. Some nose their carts close to other carts, some attend to full nesting. Two improve the status quo by nesting their own cart and improving on the chain of connections, making it easier for the store worker to push them back to the store. This personal choice is not covered by laws; there is no consequence if one does nothing. I watch a morality play of consideration versus convenience. Only three people in seven minutes leave their carts by their cars, making not even a token effort to take the cart toward the indicated area. All three of them are talking on cell phones. (Perhaps they feel the request is not for them, or is unreasonable, or is the store's responsibility, or they just don't care—some belief that allows them to do nothing. Their attentiveness to the phone conversation makes me think they are so absorbed in their own world that the social responsibility doesn't occur to them—a demonstration that William James is right about self-absorption undoing American civic commitment.) Young men are the most conscientious—it surprises me that they hold the highest standard of quality and commitment to achieving it. Maybe because a cart is like a vehicle, and young men love their cars; maybe they had worked at a Kroger as boys, so they know what a help it is. And then, after seven minutes, the Kroger worker arrives—a slow, underpaid young woman who takes her time with the chute and rounds up the strays. It all seems the same to her. She knows what to expect; she believes people hold a wide range of quality, and it is her job to deal with all definitions, clean up people's messes and get the job done. She is steady and with-out attitude. She creates two trains of carts and rolls them, with strength and finesse, one after the other back to the store for people to use, thus ending this act of the ongoing morality play.

OUR LIVES ARE COMPRISED of expressions of our beliefs; that's our authenticity. We must regularly ask why we do the things we do; what are the roots, beliefs and motivations underneath our behavior? The actions we do most frequently and unconsciously are the hardest to see and address—and the most rewarding to uncover. We must work with our daily activities, as actors do with a role. Actors endlessly ask why the character does what he does; they look deeper into the murky undersurface, trying out possibilities. Our lives are our art. Our spirit lives and thrives in the questions we ask, and in the ways we go about answering. The spirit desiccates where there is incongruence between what we believe and what we do, where authenticity is distorted.

Ken Wilber advocates a personal amalgam of spiritual practices. "But this integral approach is still in its infancy, so you have to mix and match. You might take a Hindu practice, a Christian contemplative practice, or a Buddhist meditation practice and combine it with some form of strenuous physical exercise, such as weight lifting or jogging. And those can be combined with some sort of personal psychotherapy practice—keeping a dream journal, going to a psychotherapist—and with a form of community service—working in a hospice, helping the homeless. The idea is to work these various dimensions in yourself, and not to just pick one and exercise it to the neglect of the others."

## Relationships

How do we sustain a spiritual inquiry within relationships? American relationships have become a greater creative challenge as the demand for personal fulfillment has risen in priority and become a big rock in the jar. Couples now try to balance responsibilities, personal fulfillment, hyper-active lifestyles and love. The arrival of children seems to increase the pressure rather than change the deal. This tension is filled with paradoxes, and working with paradox is not an American strength. In more traditional marriages, the balance was clearer—marriage was a big rock both shared in the marital Mason jar. Now, couples struggle with the separate rocks of commitment to a partner and to one's own authenticity, success and fulfillment; with all the commitments we hold, there is not enough space for everything. This argues for simplification and elegance in making life choices, rather than the "having it all" that does not work. Care for the big rocks well, and the pebbles and sand will find their place.

Love is a thrilling personal experience, a spontaneous improvisation within the self and between selves. Love is a willing giving over of self, and a committed relationship is a creative set of agreements, balances and experiments. Love is sacred, filled with intoxicating moments, and it prompts one of the few times we view our lives in terms of lifelong commitments. Some dream of "that one person who will be *the* answer." That search is doomed to fail because it comes from a self that is not self-sustaining. The romantic glamour will wear off. Romantic love is the yearning for connection with the divine, as much as it is a wish for connection to another person. Being in love is contact with the divine. We are spiritually awake; we see anew, find new meaning, upset our habits, look under surfaces, experiment with change, fill with transpersonal empathy and care. As it wears off, we must learn to keep contact with the divine, or the relationship (usually the other person) takes the blame. This is the challenge and opportunity of modern relationships—as the grace of romantic love subsides, the work of art and spirit must rise to create new fulfillment.

A spiritually active relationship does not mean both parties must share the same practices; it means they use the same skills and attend to the other's yearnings. It means they live in commitment to their own inquiries *and* to the grand experiment of an improvisation together.

## Repetition

I have a free-spirited friend who claims her life is without repetitive patterns—she told me this, unprompted, three times in the last six months. Our lives are filled with repetitions. We must get artistic about repetition. Every organized religion uses repetitive phrases and gestures. Every indigenous people use repetition in sacred ceremonies. Every child demands and requires repetition in order to grow. We hear ourselves say the same things and tell the same stories, over and over. Yet many parts of the repetitiveness of our adult lives tend to deaden us.

*Repetition* is an opportunity—etymologically, it means *to seek again*. It deepens us if we attentively seek fresh meaning within the repeating. If we give ourselves to rediscover the core experience within a formal prayer, we find something new. If we fully attend to the experience during a mantra's repetition, we develop the skill to stay awake. I learned about this performing in plays eight times a week on Broadway. It became so repetitive I thought I would go mad—and then I would inexplicably break through to an ecstatic new kind of attention onstage that made the work fresh and thrilling. It became a spiritual practice for me, learning how to experience the opening-night first-timeness, every time, eight times a week, right on cue. It was *better* than opening night because there was so much less backstage micro-drama and adrenaline to distract from the spiritual clarity.

Repetition can become a blessing, because so much of it is familiar and automatic that we are able to devote attention to the inner experiences. We often fall into an unconscious swirl of thinking, feeling and planning during repetitive actions—such a waste. It is the perfect opportunity to practice attending, to detect what is new under the surface right then, to notice themes that appear, to feel how the body feels, how the breath is working. This is a practice as good as a meditation or prayer; indeed, full attention on sweeping the porch, washing the dishes and waxing the car *is* prayer. Full attention on your child or spouse in dialogue *is* prayer. If we can focus full attention on lovemaking, on cooking, on gardening, on the words of a repeated prayer, we are meditating, slowing down, going deep, strengthening the spirit, doing the most important work we can be doing.

The quality of our attending determines the quality of our lives.

# CHAPTER 20

# SEVEN DEADLY SINS

STANDING VIGIL ONE WILDERNESS NIGHT, I was running low on songs and soliloquies to keep me awake in the dwindling hours until dawn. I tried to remember the names of Snow White's seven dwarves, and got confused by half-remembered teenage jokes about Sleazy, Dorky and Floozy. This put me in mind of the Seven Deadly Sins, which I remembered about as well as the dwarves. Nearly asleep on my feet, I began reconstruing the Seven Deadly Sins in the light of personal religion as a way of sustaining good practice.

Medieval Christian scholars were fascinated by the notion of deadly sins. They sought to articulate the biggies—those that condemned not just the body but also the soul to eternal hell, unless the right penitent acts were performed in time. (Incidentally, the number seven was picked for aesthetic reasons, not for any essential theological reason—it had a long mystical tradition and felt like about the right number. Aesthetic reasons always hold validity for me.) That other popular numerical guideline, the Ten Commandments, legislated acceptable behavior, but the SDS pointed to issues of character.

The big seven were an intellectual construct; history makes it clear that this set of seven had much more impact on the thinkers who articulated and preached about them than on the not-gratefully-receiving public for whom they were intended. Churchgoers viewed them as esoteric musings, not unlike the debates about the potential angel count on the head of a pin. The Seven Deadly Sins have probably had more impact on the arts than on individual Christians' daily lives; writers, comedians, satirists and even filmmakers make use of them to this day.

The exercise of reframing those classic deadly sins from the perspective of an authentic personal religion clarifies the ways we send ourselves to experiential hell. For a definition of "sin," let's not use the traditional noun-based sense of a violation of religious principle. Let's use its etymology: *to miss the mark*. This metaphor makes sin a verb, and it offers a sense of alignment, of aim, rather than character dos and don'ts. These are the ways we miss the mark in personal religious inquiries.

## The Seven Deadening Spiritual Misalignments

### 1. To lose faith in creative abundance (Avarice)

To distrust one's capacity to keep creating new meaning and finding ever-deeper fulfillment; to lose the capacity to play

### 2. To adopt the yearnings of others (Envy)

To lose passionate connection to one's creative accomplishments; to stop using the work of others as a springboard to your own work; to doubt that one's own judgment can be trusted

### 3. To lose contact with the experience of satisfaction (Gluttony)

To limit one's yearning to too narrow a range of experience; to crave the experience of fullness without the processes of attention and creation; to become self-absorbed; to lose touch with the pleasures of process

### 4. To literalize one's yearning (Lust)

To blur the distinction between yearning and desire; to distrust love; to despair of making deeper connections; to lose the inclination toward empathy

### 5. To lose interest in the small (Pride)

To lose engagement with the "small-case letter" experiences of art, religion and creativity; to limit the ways one attends; to identify with images of oneself; to believe you know, or perhaps more accurately, to lose interest in the truths that you don't know

### 6. To give up, to lose heart (Sloth)

To lose touch with the "bounce," the impulse toward more that comes with a completion; to let the spirit go to sleep, even though one may be very active; to disregard curiosity; to give the life of one's imagination over to others

### 7. To misplace the creative impulse (Wrath)

To blame one's misalignments on others; to lose touch with the skills of not-knowing; to stop engaging with what's present

ALL SEVEN OF THESE ARE ABOUT IMBALANCE. All result from not making stuff we love, and all can be redressed by making stuff we love. Remember that "stuff" is not literal stuff. It is comprised of experiences—making connections, discoveries, new insights, better questions—and the tangible stuff you make must contain those experiences, or you aren't making the right stuff for your spirit. All seven deadening misalignments represent losing touch with the divine, which thrusts one into a hell of personal experience wherein the natural flow of the divine is absent. Awareness of the misalignments, and the work of art, realigns us.

# PART V
# AN EVOLVING INNER NATURE

# CHAPTER 21

# KNOWING EVOLUTION

SO THERE I SIT OUT THERE in an arbitrarily defined 104-foot circle, having arbitrary experiences at an arbitrarily selected site in an arbitrarily selected wilderness. Is it all so arbitrary? Is it all so arbitrary? It doesn't feel arbitrary. It feels right.

What do I do for a week? Lots of little things, like exercises and stretches. Mostly I just sit or stand and pay attention, naked as the weather allows. I do some formal meditating, but I am not good at it. I look at rocks a lot, thinking about them. (This would never work as a brochure. Maybe I should mention that I lose weight.)

I fast for five or six days, thus the weight loss. For the first twelve years of my annual wilderness retreats, I did one dramatic thing amid the simplicity of the daily activities. (I stopped doing this nine ago because it was time to do so.) I spent one night in a standing vigil, within an eight-foot circle, all night long. This practice too is derived from a Native American vision quest tradition. I guess the term applied to me; I was seeking to deepen my vision, although I was not trying to conjure up totemic animals. I have not had mystical encounters with animal spirits, not even chipmunk entities; during vigils, my only animal encounters have been with mosquitoes. (Although I once shared a long, peaceful stare with a deer, before she slowly ambled off. There was also the snake, which you will read about later.)

The first part of the long, upright night was usually ecstatic. The second part of the night I sang all the songs I knew and performed the speeches I remembered from plays. The last part of the night was just grit, staying upright till dawn, even though my mind and body were barking "give up and sleep."

By dawn the experience had humbled me. I felt honored to participate in a great human tradition, even in such a small way.

I thought of the lineage of heroic spiritual seekers who had done extraordinary things to forge closer ties to the divine. I sent my respects to nameless Native Americans, and those of other native cultures, who withstood far more difficulty than I ever could so they might know the spirit of nature more deeply. I acknowledged men and women who have gone into the wilderness for a month or more to answer their burning questions. I became overwhelmed with respect for meditators who can enter a consciousness devoid of personality, and invest so much time to learn how. I bowed my head as an apprentice to the countless mystics and martyrs, wise women and shamans. I sensed a connection to so many artists who spent lifetimes learning how to paint not only the plum branch but also the forces leading to it. At such times, I felt not only sleepy and grateful for this lineage, but some of what the great spiritual creators in art and spirit (and science) felt, of deeper connections. I felt I had tended the perennial truths, in my own way.

It is more than feeling. It is a knowing. In those moments, I know some things in the way born-again Christians describe knowing Jesus; the way composers and musicians know the way a sequence of notes must go. The way we all "just know" the perfect gift to give or bit of advice for someone sometimes. It is the way scientists say they know something; even though they gather data to confirm the knowledge, there remains an aesthetic aspect of their knowing, expressed in metaphors, applied aesthetically, launching inquiries and living wordlessly in gut knowledge. Indeed, I notice how scientific my thinking is out in the wild, not merely in analyzing the midnight sound of approaching critters, but in piecing together thoughts throughout the day. *Science* etymologically means *to know*, and out there I know in all the ways I can.

This book reports what I know. I use my skills of art to get a firmer grasp on the divine in my life, and to share what I know in hopes it can do the same for you. Quite frankly, I dislike writing books; the process is about as much fun as standing up all night for no logical reason. But liking or disliking is not very important. Under the surface, I am drawn to both exercises. My yearning for divine experience pulls me along, like a half unwilling child who lets out occasional whimpers of "do I have to?" I do and don't have to, and I continue the arduous practices because that parent part of me, the St. Francis part that is looking, knows the value of what is to be found.

THERE IS A MINDSET I EXPERIENCE that keeps me returning to nowhere. It is difficult to describe. At the beginning of my week in the wild, there is so little to do that my need to be active gets fairly pitiful—let me move that tent again, six inches should do it. After a day, the doing-imperative settles down. I do what needs to be done, but focus less on the task itself and more on the its role in the larger unfolding experience. The underwear needs to be washed; I participate in this marvelous improvisation that feels far from arbitrary, and underwear care becomes a sequence in the unfolding story, no more or less significant than high-profile activities in my busy professional life. I slip into a different way of looking at things, just the way successful art can slip us into a different way of looking at things. I am a player in the story as well as one watching it unfold. It is as if the scientific part of me (attending to the washing and how to do it really well) and the spiritual part of me (attending to the experiencing in its fullest context) are both fully engaged at the same time—and both use the skills of art to accomplish their tasks well. The challenge of this dual role is greater than anything else I do.

Ants know what to do. Weeds are great at their work. As I experience the dual role of participating fully in the unfolding story and witnessing the story unfold at the same time, I know I am doing what I am supposed to do.

I had this feeling one year when I arrived, exhausted, at the wilderness circle I had come to adopt as a beloved annual site. It was miles of bushwhacking from the nearest trail—it had a good view from this one flat spot, right on a lake that isn't on a hiker's map. I dropped my pack, stepped to my favorite sitting spot, and saw the snake. A thick eight-foot snake with the diamond-shaped head that says "poison" coiled up in the sun. (I later learned it was a timber rattlesnake.) I backed up. What to do?

There was no other usable site around this small lake, and I didn't want to go searching merely out of fear. So I stood back, waiting to see what would unfold. I watched it. It was sunbathing. Snakes don't attack people unless threatened, I vaguely recalled. That made sense looking at it from ten feet away, not in theory but here in reality. So I sat with my back on the rock where the snake sunned on the other side, for a couple of hours. Four feet apart but with three-foot-high rock between us. Death right there and feeling even more alive. When the sun cast a shadow on the snake, it slipped into the water and swam away. I made my decision to stay, and if it returned, to cohabit peacefully with the animal that could kill me.

The snake returned every sunny afternoon, and we sat, back to back (if coiled snakes have backs) against the same warm rock. That retreat week was particularly deep. For a week I noted how the physical symbol of death, not just a felt-sense of it, sharpened the tang of the present. I was given a pain-free visit to the perspective of the dying. The situation and the snake didn't feel dangerous; they felt generous, lucky, kind. Immanent death wasn't a problem; it was and is an invitation to stay awake as things unfold.

## Unfolding

THE LITERAL ETYMOLOGY of the word *evolution* is *opening that which was rolled up*, or more simply *unfolding*. As I fully engage my skills of art and spirit in the ordinary doings of the wild, being awake in a place, I experience a sense of unfolding. I know I am part of an evolution of some kind. I inhabit the metaphor of my life as one part of a grander unfolding story. As I decode the music of a brook, or welcome a poisonous snake as companion, or later write thoughts on a page about the experiences, the activity becomes a contribution to human development.

We carry two definitions of evolution, one explicit and one implicit. We recognize the scientific one, Darwin's savage species competition with its survival of the fittest. This interpretation of the facts is taught in schools and makes sense on many levels; it fits the biological and anthropological record and applies to other human games as well, like economic competition and dating. Recent scientific writings present updated angles on this evolutionary story, and tell it slightly differently than Darwin did, but they don't change the predominant competitive and creative survival plotline.

There is another evolutionary story that we sense but don't cite. This story is supported by evidence too, but not the kind a scientistic culture enjoys. We experience, we *know*, this unfolding; every spiritual tradition that reveres wise people and recognizes greatness of spirit knows about this evolutionary plotline. When a person performs an act of extraordinary generosity or selflessness, when a person suggests a new way of looking at things that makes pieces of experience fit together, we recognize and revere that person's development. We even refer to the person as "evolved." We know an evolved spirit when we meet one.

Humankind is evolving in two directions at the same time, one physical and one spiritual. Do the two kinds of development relate in some way? We think of the impersonal competitive plot with its memorable cruelty as the "real" evolutionary story—perhaps because it flatters us with our triumph over other species, perhaps because it is such a juicy tale, perhaps because its tangible results are evident in the biological record. Perhaps because we may yet lose this game if our environmental ravages start killing off our own species in larger numbers. The spiritual unfolding is experienced in subtler ways, although the evidence of its triumphs and failures is glaringly evident in history and in daily life.

We are members of the subgroup *Homo sapiens sapiens,* which differentiates us from the larger group that includes now-extinct players like Neanderthals; this is the lineage from which we come— the Latin etymology repeats the word "wise." The story of this supposedly double-wise subgroup is not merely the ongoing tale of inhuman cruelty, power mongering and relentless greed of the "killer apes," as the Darwinian narrative suggests (or the "selfish gene" Richard Dawkins suggests more recently). The human story is also filled with great sacrifice, illogical love, heroic altruism and a dedication to learning more about *the more*. The story science tells has tilted toward Darwinian selfishness and ruthlessness, even though the development of cooperative behaviors that promote unity is every bit as important in species development as the aggressive and competitive behaviors. There is strong evidence among chimpanzees and bonobos of conflict resolution activity, aid to the disadvantaged, resource sharing and equitable exchange of services. Indeed, bonobos, which are genetically closer to humans than are chimps, are a female-centered species, egalitarian, and almost without violence. Bonobos seem to have substituted sex for aggression, with sex becoming an integral part of all social relationships. No wonder they don't refer to bonobos in schoolbooks.[38]

The mathematician Kurt Gödel demonstrated that we must look beyond the attributes in any seemingly disconnected set of elements in order to find a unifying principle. The two evolutionary stories are not separate and disconnected; look under the surface, and they are linked. They unfold together.

We participate in physical evolution, even though our individual role is small. (But not so small that things like recycling, taking public transit and voting do not matter.) When we actively inquire into any of the big questions that surround evolution— why do we evolve? where is evolution heading?—we join in the spiritual story of humankind. The relationship between these two kinds of participation appears in the circular image of yin and yang. Our participation in physical evolution, struggling within complementary opposing forces, is held in delicate balances of light and dark, yin and yang. Our participation in spiritual evolution is expressed by whole circle itself, containing both yin and yang—

indeed, the whole circle is called yin-yang. Human evolution includes both contending elements *and* the awareness that can see the whole story in its dappled beauty.

To see the yin-yang circle that contains all the contending aspects we live among, we must take that "little step back" in consciousness that widens our awareness. Physical evolution happens inside the circle; spiritual evolution perceives the circle. I wash my underwear inside the circle, and am simultaneously aware of the scene within the circle as if from above.

These two evolutionary stories intermingle as our sense of science becomes more mysterious and our sense of the divine becomes more known. Quantum mechanics, superstring and chaos theories provoke profound reinterpretations of reality; hundreds of books and essays have ridden the waves of science into the mystical and ontological terrain of spiritual inquiry. Some call it speculative ether, but it springs from the *terra firma* of science. Conversely, "scientific" thinking about spiritual issues is growing too, as research into paranormal phenomena (like the medical efficacy of prayer and meditation, or the measurement of psychic abilities) brings the divine out of the ether and more toward the tangible.

Let's take a mundane example to demonstrate this convergence of science and spirit. I pick up a rock in the woods near my home. My small town was founded in 1669, and someone may have picked up this same rock to contemplate it back then. What has changed in that 350 years? The rock itself has evolved a little—perhaps not noticeably, but it probably has some dramatic stories detailing its sad loss of chips and molecules.

The rock has the same reliable rocky qualities: it is hard and stable. But it is not so simple. The rock is evolving toward some other form, even if it is transforming more slowly than our preferred pace. However, in my 21st century–awareness of the rock, I realize the atoms that make up that rock are comprised almost entirely of "non-matter, " of "air," rather than a dense mass of hard stuff. (Remember that if the nucleus of any carbon atom in this rock were the size of a grapefruit, its nearest electron would be a half a mile away. That is true for every atom in this solid rock). Scientific advances have transformed the rock's most obvious feature, its hardness, into something of a mystery: it's comprised almost completely of air. Just forty to fifty years ago when we Boomers were in high school science class, we were taught that there were three kinds of elementary particles in the atoms of this rock (you can still probably name them). Now scientists know of sixty-one types of elementary particles—and counting.

Our awareness of the complexity of things keeps growing. That rock becomes more complex and wondrous. I experience it in a different way than my pre-revolutionary counterpart; I must hold simple certainties, like knowing what a rock is, more lightly and with curiosity; I must acknowledge that I both know and don't know what the rock is, at the same time. As the physicist Freeman Dyson puts it, "Instead of a few succinct equations to summarize the universe of physics, we have a luxuriant growth of mathematical structures, as diverse as the phenomena they attempt to describe." [39] I am more aware than the 1669 rock-holder that simplicity is not so simple, that there are worlds of unfolding mystery within ostensibly straightforward worlds, and hardness is both a foot-bruising and a mind-stretching reality. I have hard evidence for awe right in my hand; in 1669, she held the rock as a certainty. She may have found the rock beautiful; I find it sublime. The experience of beauty is orderly and peaceful. The sublime is more; it has a dash of pain, a streak of divine awe shot through it.

Evolution is a property of all living systems, including our awareness. The evolution of consciousness invites me to consider that the rock and God have things in common. Both matter. Both are partly evident, partly unknown, and ultimately unknowable. Both invite us to attend and reward us if we do. Both are understood differently by humans over time. Both can be seen as beautiful, useful, pointless, profound, ultimately truthful and dead or alive by different human interpretations that they don't care about. Both function in timeframes beyond our own. Both make a good focus for spiritual and artistic inquiry. As Freeman Dyson muses, "We stand midway between the unpredictability of atoms and the unpredictability of God. Atoms are small pieces of our mental apparatus, and we are small pieces of God's mental apparatus. Our minds may receive inputs equally from atoms and from God. This view of our place in the cosmos many not be true, but it is compatible with the active nature of atoms as revealed in the experiments of modern physics."

Spiritually evolved people tell us that God and the rock are made of the same stuff. Enlightened awareness from many traditions reports there is only one stuff, and it doesn't matter what we call it. Indeed it is not even "stuff"— stuff is a noun, and nouns live in separateness. It is the verbs of the divine and the rock that are somehow the same. Though that idea makes no logical sense, I have glimmers of those universal verbs in the wild. The rocks in the brook that make it sing, the awareness I bring to discover that song, the way all the elements are bound together in that moment—all contain the same verbs of improvised unfolding.

I have often written this before: nouns tend to separate us, and verbs tend to bring us together. That truth even applies to our relationship in this book, even as it sparks agreement as I hope it does; the nouns of ideas and opinions herein may resonate, but they set us up as two separate people connecting. The experiences I have had—the verbs that led to the those words and ideas—if you resonate with them, they make us one in a greater unfolding.

# CHAPTER 22

# THRIVING CREATIVELY

WHAT IS YOUR SENSE OF EVOLUTION? Do you picture a long Veteran's Day parade of species improvements? Do you envision the science-class poster with a row of increasingly upright humanoids? Actually, the evolution of species works more like a school cafeteria, where chaos, barely restrained in delicate balances, sometimes explodes into mayhem. Scientists tell us biological evolution is inherently spontaneous, indeterminate, improbable and unpredictable—the species that a savvy handicapper would bet on are not the ones that win.

In the improvised drama (or comedy, depending on your lens) of evolution, there is a period of stability, a catastrophe, and then a burst of diversity in life as the environment and leftover species recover. The story of evolution is the story of sameness punctuated by explosions of creative vitality, followed by a sorting out of the creative contributions that narrow them down elegantly, inexorably, to the most successful. In other words, a reasonable description of any complex creative process. The elements: status quo, crisis, creative profusion and then integration of the best new ideas into a new status quo. The stakes are high: in an environmental crisis, many die off, most famously those dinosaurs that couldn't make the crocodile cut in their particular creative adaptation contest.

The same universals embedded in the Darwinian story apply to our spiritual evolution. The laws of nature are the laws of human nature. The principles of species survival are the same as those for the spirit:

⤳ In clearing the environmental stage, extinctions take the brakes off the evolutionary creativity and allow inventive survivors to exploit new opportunities. Evolution teaches us not to be too perfect, too narrow, too cautious, too confident—the flexible, adaptive and inventive survive. We (and every species) owe our identity and opportunity more to our ancestors' creativity in times of crisis than to their toughness. The species that survive are those with diverse abilities developed in response to previous challenges—those that experimented during the quieter times.

Spiritually, it is not the toughest who thrive. Those who hold rigorously to their beliefs, those who are most like the previous generations, are less prepared for success in the reality of a turbulent, diverse, challenging environment. They get left behind. Those whose spirits have explored and experimented, have made mistakes and acknowledged them, develop what it takes to grow with the challenges, changes and catastrophes.

The work of art is a natural way humans develop and sustain this necessary spiritual vitality. I happened to be working in Minneapolis when a Minnesota arts high school student was murdered in a random drive-by shooting. The media buzzed around the school, interviewing students. Watching the news from my hotel room, I saw one TV reporter, typically, stick a microphone in a student's face and say, "It must be hard for you to deal with all the extreme emotions." She answered simply, "We are artists. We know how to deal with extreme experiences. And we take care of each other." End of interview.

🖎 Evolution is overabundant and opportunistic. Species produce a madhouse array of variations, adaptations and mutations, few of them beneficial. There are mounds of crumpled, rejected pages around evolution's writing desk; the process is preposterously inefficient and ultimately effective. Evolutionary survival pounces on the variations, those few chance occurrences that successfully provide an edge. For millions of years evolutionary opportunism succeeded in the primordial soup, and it still applies in the consumer and idea marketplaces.

Spiritual evolution is also inherently overabundant and opportunistic, two key qualities psychologists identify in creative individuals. "Ideational fluency," the generation of many possible solutions, is the most common way we recognize and measure creative capacity. This capacity is partly innate and partly developed (nature *and* nurture); the key to developing it is using it often, and the key to using it is to take pleasure in exploring multiplicity over the cut-to-the-chase satisficing habits of daily life. After a lifetime of study, Nelson Goodman, the founder of Harvard's renowned arts learning research center Project Zero, was asked how to make students more creative. "Simple," he replied. "Give them harder problems."

In our spiritually creative overabundance, we endlessly make metaphors, analogies and new ideas; we find new ways of thinking, doing and looking at things. This is the spiritual equivalent of mutation, or cellular variation. In the work of art, we choose among these options, opportunistically grabbing the one that works best; we make natural selections again and again. When we are creatively evolving, we play seriously with improvement in choices large and small. We can't help ourselves—we are the species that makes things and then makes them better. Our creative instinct also takes joyful advantage of chance, of things that just pop up from the person next to us on the bus or from an enigmatic adage in the *I Ching*.

⮕ The biologist Rupert Sheldrake proposes that the productive tension between creativity and habit allows for all evolution. Either force alone will kill off a species, if taken to its natural extreme; unsettled creativity leads to chaos, and too much habit leads to narrowness and a deadly lack of resilience.

Spiritual growth requires a dynamic balance between creativity and habit. Those who are inadequately grounded in the world—or, conversely, those who are too entrenched—do not progress. We need habits to support our growth, and to provide enough stability and safety so that we can invest our attention productively and creatively. All species, from marsupial to managerial, prefer the status quo and strive mightily to keep it, whether it is pleasurable or not. At the same time, we must inquire into new ideas and practices and adopt changes that work, even if they are initially uncomfortable. We must hold our habits lightly, using them creatively as we innovate, explore and adopt the best of the new—be it genetic, scientific or aesthetic.

Evolution navigates a path between the opposing conservative and progressive forces that pull on it, in an ongoing, high-stakes game of cosmic politics. The dynamic tension gives evolution its predominant chaos and eventual elegance. We are drawn toward greater complexity *and* toward simplification at the same time, as artists are—creating a cycle of elegance in inquiry. Researchers find this distinctive pattern in creative people: 1) they are attracted to the unresolved complexity, the difficulty, in an interesting problem; 2) they generate many ideas in their work on the problem, and seek to distill the simplest-possible discoveries; and then 3) they are attracted again to more complex extensions of the discoveries. Einstein, the great inquirer, speaks for nature when he posits: everything should be made as simple as possible but not simpler. He also said, "Creativity is intelligence at play."

Evolution takes risks. Every successful species' evolutionary path is littered with failed experiments, piled high with mistakes and good ideas that came before their time. Mistakes are healthy; the creative vitality that produces them is essential. Few things are worse for long-term species success (or individual spiritual or artistic development) than short-term, easy success.

The British science writer John Barrow writes, "To live in complex ways you must live dangerously because coping with danger necessitates the evolution of complexity."[40] Spiritual evolution requires risks. We must explore things we do not understand, begin things without knowing how they will turn out. Fear of failure stunts development; it is a certified creativity-killer. Our willingness to have an experiment flop is essential to finding inquiries that succeed. In the work of art, we call this constructive waste; the sketches that get discarded, the scenes that are cut during previews—all are essential parts of the creative process, which is laughably inefficient and profoundly successful.

IN THE DARWINIAN STORY, the super-objective of all species is clear: survive. Armadillos did not develop shells to look cool. If peacocks or persons do things to look good, there is a survival motive underneath. But the drive exceeds mere survival; species also seek to thrive. The impulse to thrive helps explain that seemingly contradictory human tendency to act selflessly, to give a life to save another's. In spiritual evolution, individuals contribute to the ongoing development of consciousness, beyond what we need to merely survive. This drive to thrive appears in our yearning, in our admiration for "enlightened people," in our self-help and selfless impulses and efforts, in our lifelong learning.

These two kinds of evolution, physical and spiritual, are not two different stories. They are one story, ours. Our spiritual development has been quieter, a seeming subplot within the high drama of red-toothed nature. We have done so well in the species survival game that our main adversary is now ourselves. So, reasonably, now would be the time that the overlooked spiritual plotline emerges into prominence. We now depend on our spiritual development to survive and thrive. The skills of art and spirit are becoming the tools to survive and thrive that opposable thumbs, controlled fire, weapons, agriculture, the steam engine and computers have been. Here are several ways those skills have helped us prosper.

Humanity has thrived because we can do so many things with our attention. Among our great accomplishments is pattern recognition. We succeeded on the African plain and then in harsher environments because we were skilled at recognizing patterns—in seasons, adversaries, prey, communication, plant life, information, interpersonal relating and more. We must now use our artistic-spiritual skills to recognize patterns in previously invisible areas (within physics, genetics, culture, spirituality), to find structure amid the complexity and to discover integrative patterns that hold the seemingly irreconcilable opposites. Pattern recognition is a fundamental act of meaning-making. And we are the species that makes meaning, as inexorably and more frequently than we make war.

This truth is so elusive, it requires repeating—only spiritually evolved people can abide this existential paradox, a koan at the heart of our species: we make meaning. The meaning we make doesn't really mean anything. And it is worth making anyway.

We have developed the evolutionary advantages of imagination and self-reflection. John Dewey described imagination as the capacity to see the world as if it were otherwise. We generate many possible alternatives, and that leads to better solutions. Humans also developed the capacity to assess how things are going inside, not just outside. This ability to "handle" personal experience as a medium for exploration has proven advantageous, boosting creativity and offering additional and subtler ways to challenge the status quo. Our awareness of experiencing (our consciousness) has promoted species self-improvement by making reflection a natural tendency. Self-reflection tends to support cooperation among individuals, creation of alternatives to purely instinctual response, greater awareness, greater empathy. Don't confuse self-awareness and reflective capacity with self-absorption or narcissism, both of which choke cooperative capacity.

In her book *Not for Profit: Why Democracy Needs the Humanities* (page 95), philosopher Martha Nussbaum notes the essentialness of a civil society's empathetic capacity: "Citizens cannot relate well to the complex world around them by factual knowledge and logic alone. The third ability of the citizen, closely related to the first two, is what we can call the narrative imagination. This means the ability to think what it might be like to be in the shoes of a person different from oneself, to be an intelligent reader of that person's story, and to understand the emotions and wishes and desires that someone so placed might have."

In the psychic kitbag that helps our species thrive we also find our capacity to realize that we do not know. We know we must continue to learn, each one of us, to develop our species. When we are curious, we are our human selves. We are hardwired to inquire. Those who can not-know well become our most valuable pioneers.

The kitbag also holds that "bounce." A tiny spark of new interest springs from a completion, provoking the next connection, the next insight, the next discovery. That innate "and" of the spirit is one of our greatest gifts. The simplest expression of this species advantage is the moment of curiosity that arises a hundred times a day—at least within the fittest of our species, the ones who enable us to succeed.

Aesthetic awareness and appreciation are not the elite, effete niceties that the terms connote; they are hard-earned species advantages. Narrative, pattern recognition, sentence structure, myths, turns of phrase, the appreciation of beauty—all create greater order. It was an evolutionary benefit to organize random impressions, to find subsurface connections, to gravitate toward the beautiful solution, to unite a community through images and common actions, to strive for efficiency and elegance. We use our hardwired aesthetic impulses to accomplish these essential goals. Research shows that we are drawn toward both the more attractive physiognomy and the more attractive solution, our evolutionary wiring at work. We are inherently artistic beings because the work of art works for the species. The physicist Niels Bohr wrote, "The fact that religions through the ages have spoken in images, parables, and paradoxes means simply that there are no other ways of grasping the reality to which they refer. But that does not mean that it is not a genuine reality. And splitting this reality into an objective and a subjective side won't get us very far."

Pleasure is an important evolutionary indicator. Whether something is pleasurable or aversive is generally a clue to its evolutionary benefit or detriment. Often, what feels good is connected to a species need; to "like" or "dislike" something is the tip of the tip of the deep pleasure iceberg. The two-second opinion, even its binary expression, even in its Facebook gesture, is based in something worth inquiring into. That inquiry can go deep. A simple question—what do I see that makes me like or dislike it?—begins to open things up. If something feels good, inquire into whatever it is to discover what it holds that we need. Feeling good in a deep way indicates personal evolution at work. The capacity to develop a wider palette of pleasures, to distinguish between them, and to develop an increasing taste for deep pleasure are evolutionary advantages.

Humans, like many animals, have thrived through our capacity to play. Playing develops essential skills, as it does for bear and lion cubs. The human adumbration on this skill is serious play, and the fittest humans play with everything—ideas and problems, within relationships and work. Serious play is the work of art in any medium, and engages us fully to thrive through that medium. John Huizinga, the great theorist of play, wrote, "The concept of play merges quite naturally with that of holiness...archaic ritual is thus sacred play, indispensable for the well-being of the community, fecund of cosmic insight and social development but always play in the sense Plato gave it—an action accomplishing itself outside and above the necessities and seriousness of everyday life. In this sphere of sacred play the child and the poet are at home with the savage. His aesthetic sensibility has brought the modern man closer to this sphere than the 'enlightened' man of the 18th century ever was."[41]

## Creating Consciousness

WE PRACTICE FOR OUR SPECIES' SURVIVAL challenges by making stuff. The work of art, practiced in many parts of life, is the serious play that supports the spiritual evolution of our species. E. O. Wilson describes humans as "the poetic species" with a "mythopoeic drive to understand, explain, innovate, discover, and explore the unknown reaches of the mind [and human experience] by means of myths and images."[42] Yearning is evolutionary creativity playing through us. I know from weeks in the wild and not so wild that if we get quiet enough, if we get out of our own way, two things happen: we start to create (new ideas, new metaphors, new understandings), and we start to understand things in greater complexity.

Irrational ways of knowing are not an evolutionary dead end, but a magnificent legacy. The ultimate species advantage is not just to have a wide array of ways of knowing things, or even to use as many as possible in different situations, but also to add awareness to these abilities and use them intentionally. To know and to inquire is our ultimate challenge, and consciousness is our most advanced evolutionary capacity. In over-stimulated, hyper-commercial America, conscious attention is the greatest scarcity. The scarcest U.S. commodity used to be money; then it became time; now the most precious commodity is the conscious use of our attention.

Consciousness is hard to describe. It is the new advantage on the evolutionary block. Those who are adept with this capacity gain a radical experiential difference on top of ordinary perceiving. This experience of full consciousness is the "most different" thing humans can encounter in life—the equivalent of meeting an alien from another galaxy while eating breakfast in a diner. Seekers get glimpses and flashes of full consciousness, but mostly live in a gray area that is lit by that bright awareness but dulled by life's murkier aspects. In terms of making life choices, we know we are on the right track as we become more conscious. We know it because we feel the deepest pleasure. Joseph Campbell said, "follow your bliss, and you will be helped by a thousand unseen helping hands that were not there before." Consciousness is an evolutionary advantage, not an esoteric distraction. We know this because the more conscious people become, the more compassionate, generous, wise, attuned to nature and joyful they become. Not always, and not always clearly, but that's true in general.

What does it mean to become more conscious? It does not mean we must learn to crank our knees into lotus positions and recite mantras. It means we can learn how to do certain things with our minds, our attention, our psyches, our "other ways" of knowing. There are many excellent approaches and good schools to developing these inner abilities, which apply not just in silent, candle-lit rooms but also in the improvisations of real life and real work. Whether we practice within an organized religion or not, whether we are dedicated meditators or not, our live, creative, personal religious practice develops our consciousness as far as we can go in a lifetime.

The Darwinian story of evolution doesn't predict much about the direction of humanity, except that our greed may well lead to our demise. The story of our spiritual evolution, however, offers some hints about our future. Look to those spiritually "evolved" individuals. The characteristics they share imply the direction our species is heading. They are compassionate. They are generous. They teach all the time. They are as curious as children. They create artistically and live post-conventionally. They are filled with, and guided by, the divine. Humanity is heading toward compassionate divinity; slowly, lurchingly. Because of our evolutionary impulse, we move toward *the more* even as the quality of our political, institutional and commercial nation remains mired in the less.

There have always been spiritually evolved teachers and individuals, amid the gigantic human mass of cruel and mindless destroyers, survivors, builders, helpers and those who just try to get by. But there are more seekers and spiritually interested learners than ever before. There is an enormous global faculty of teachers and leaders of the spiritual growth and human potential movements, many of whom have gigantic followings. There is no way to measure the size of the "market" for personal religion, or calculate how many of their admirers are serious versus casual students, but look at this top-of-my-mind listing of teachers who are prominent in the West—Adyashanti, A.H. Almaas, Fritjof Capra, Pema Chodron, Deepak Chopra, Paulo Coelho, Dalai Lama, Ram Dass, Matthew Fox, Gangaji, Joan Halifax, Thich Nhat Hanh, Sam Harris, Jean Houston, Jon Kabat-Zinn, Landmark Education, Byron Katie,

Sam Keen, J.Z. Knight, Caroline Myss, Mark Nepo, Eckhart Tolle, Desmond Tutu, Ken Wilber, Marianne Williamson, even mega-stars Oprah Winfrey and Tony Robbins. They write bestselling books, reach huge audiences around the world, post widely viewed teachings on the web, teach in-person in many ways. There are dozens more of comparable fame in the West, and hundreds more of significance all around the world. These are just those who are currently alive; there are many hundreds more who have died but left legacies through books that still get studied and followers who teach. Each of these teachers lead learners on a slightly different path toward the same summit. There is no way to count the size of their engaged audience, nor to gauge the depth of their impact, but it is safe to assert that the planet has never before seen so many teaching so many. These teachers all affirm that interest has grown in the last generation and continues to grow.

Yes, this global yearning also results in dubious contributions—for example, yoga, an ancient spiritual pathway, sometimes becomes a workout regime with light spiritual overtones for many practitioners; tantra instruction gets marketed alongside sex toys; meditation is prescribed to reduce blood pressure. So be it. The commercialization doesn't negate the size of the influence; indeed, it probably affirms and contributes to it.

The personal religion congregation has never been larger, and the collective growth in consciousness has never been so strong. Let's remember this overlooked truth as we struggle and rage at the daily difficulties, despairs and idiocies we face. It's another paradox that might ring the way Niels Bohr proposed, as quoted earlier: "How wonderful that we have met with a paradox. Now we have some hope of making progress." This is is the best of spiritual times, while it is also—not the worst of times, but certainly a time of global cruelty, conflict and confusion.

# CHAPTER 23

# METHOD ACTING

THE QUIET LEISURE IN THE WILD enables me to attend to the natural ways I inquire into things. I recall John Dewey's idea that the inquiry process suggests a willingness to participate in the future by exploring present actions. The historian Will Durant notes that "Inquiry is fatal to certainty."

With the underwear washed, and no possible excuse for moving the tent again, it occurs to me that inquiring into my present experience might be interesting. What does that mean? How do I do that? I don't really know, since no one ever taught me—but I do know on some level, so I just do it. I start paying attention to whatever comes up. As thoughts or feelings arise, I do not let them go, as one does in meditation; I attend to them curiously, as if they were little creations. I do not simply inquire logically, although logic is a frequent part of the process. I use multiple ways of digging in, drawing on different methods improvisationally as needed, as the sculptor or surgeon reaches for different tools according to the nuance of intent. Also like the sculptor and surgeon, I improvise a process, a method, that includes science and art. As Ludwig van Beethoven wrote to a young admirer, "Do not only practice art, but get at the very heart of it; this it deserves, for only art and science raise men to the God-head."

The appearance of the Scientific Method in the Renaissance was a radical advance in thinking, a great marker in our evolutionary story. The term was coined by Francis Bacon, and its roots go back to the philosophical practice of deduction by ancient Greek natural philosophers, who were the precursors of "scientists." Descartes' "Discourse On Method" addressed how we can know things, organizing the idiosyncratic thinking approaches of the past into a more effective system. He believed we must not accept anything as being true unless we can clearly and distinctly perceive it. Logical, rigorous, honest. It proposed a mathematical model for reflection and inquiry.

In 1725, Isaac Watt was the first to use of the idea of "science" as a separate category of inquiry in his essay "Logic." Until then, science was not separated from art by a narrow definition. Previously, we had the medical arts, the art of brickmaking, and the arts of architecture and music, all filled with logical pursuits and methodical thinking as well as aesthetic inspiration. The Greek meaning of the word science, *to know*, derived from an earlier root meaning *to separate or divide*. Until the mid-19th century, that implication of subdividing things into pieces and sorting and studying the pieces applied to any study; there was a science of how to grind wheat and a science of playing the flute. Science was the way we discovered the parts, and art was the way we brought things together.

For hundreds of years, Western civilization has applied and shared the Scientific Method to pursue knowledge. Our fealty to logical thought has guided our incredible accomplishments in the hard sciences and our work in the social sciences, business and government. In 1644, Descartes proposed "cogito ergo sum"—I think, therefore I am. His notion that thinking is our human way into the deepest questions, that thinking is our fundamental identity, launched the heyday of logic that leaves us so accomplished and so imbalanced today. We have outgrown it as a credo and as a best practice. At this stage of our psychic development, thinking is one of many ways toward truth, and it cannot get us there by itself. As the laws of creativity tell us, creativity requires logic and analogic (the creative capacity to identify a truth by connecting it to something else) in a dynamic tension.

In the twentieth century, the Scientific Method met challenges. Its fundamental tenets—that mathematics provides unassailable truth, that the measurable is the knowable, and that objectivity is essential—were undermined. It relied on one definition of reality, while humanity came to acknowledge that reality is more complex. Freud launched our acknowledgment of inner worlds; Einstein offered a deeper link between the two fundamentally separate worlds of matter and energy. Quantum mechanics forced us to compromise our clear understandings of the separateness of observer and observation, our trust in the reliability of cause and effect. We had to admit the uncertainties within certainty, the limitations of measurement, the possibilities of truths beyond our imagining. Things that seem separate may not be; things that logic certifies may not be true. Rocks are almost entirely non-matter; light bends and is sometimes a particle and sometimes a wave.

The mechanical metaphors of Newton and Descartes described the workings of the brain as a retrieval system, and more recently as a marvelous computer. The currently emerging metaphors for the brain are more aesthetic than mechanical. The Scientific Method was the underlying how-to manual for figuring out the world; the Aesthetic Method is the inquiry approach for arriving at multifaceted, integrated understandings of the way it is.

The Scientific Method is still enormously useful in scientific procedure, in teaching, in figuring things out. However, as we inquire into the nature of rocks, or whatever we might do sitting out in the wild, we naturally apply the Aesthetic Method to find the other truths. This is the natural way we work when we invest ourselves fully. It includes the reliably effective Scientific Method *and* all the logical ways we try to get at a truth. Plus it taps other ways we recognize truth: the gut feel, the emotional sense that something is or isn't quite right, the intuitive hunch, the sense of the beauty of an idea, the intimate experience of rightness.

Scientists use the Aesthetic Method when they find their way toward a theory, or in choosing how to pursue a line of inquiry. They have hunches and a sense of the beauty in their work, just as artists and entrepreneurs do.

Following the Aesthetic Method, we playfully, adeptly juggle several ways of knowing how to go toward deeper truths. Love, art, play, sex, food, comedy, insight, ecstasy, sacredness—all the best things in life defy our logical grasp. They require and reward the widest array of inquiry skills we can bring.

The Scientific Method is no longer enough to advance our species. It can help, but it has proven to lead us into serious species-survival trouble because of its narrowness, because it detaches from other ways of knowing what is good for us. When, as Ken Wilber argues, the good, the true and the beautiful separated, science and its preferred Method grabbed the opportunity and guided Western development. We have more recently cultivated the Aesthetic Method, which reunites the good, the true and the beautiful to guide us toward fuller truths.

# · CHAPTER 24 ·

# Auxin and Improvisation

ANOTHER THING I RE-LEARN in the wild every year is that I have to let things go. It takes me a couple of days to let go of my concerns, to stop planning. I have to let go of my work projects for a time. I slowly give up everything attached to activity outside my 104-foot universe. As I do so, the deep pleasures start to burble up. Giving up the known releases discovery of the new that has been there all along. It is human auxin.

Auxin is a plant hormone that spurs growth. It is critical in phototropism (stems growing toward light) and gravitropism (roots growing down). Without auxin, plants don't know which way to grow; worse, they cannot grow at all. Where do plants get this crucial phytohormone? Only from one source.

Auxin is produced by dying cells. As cells die, they release auxin, which is essential for growth. Death of the old produces growth of the new. Death of the old *first*; then release to create the new. That is also my experience in the wild: let go of the old, then begin to create something new out of the old material.

If we cannot let go of the status quo, we cannot grow— which means we start to die. Auxin reminds us that yearning is not enough. We do not evolve just because we want to. Shedding what we know, letting things go, triggers new growth. The willing release from the world as we know it produces the spiritual auxin that drives our healthy growth.

Remember the distinction between art and entertainment drawn many pages ago? Entertainment happens within what we know, and art happens outside what we know. Artistic experience is our human auxin. We willingly release the status quo and enter a world of possibility. Once released from the known, the actions of art, which are also the actions of spirit (differing only in style and medium, as we have seen), play seriously in a nameless place to create a connection, an idea, an individual, a world anew.

In that nameless place of art, we are less attached to ego and personality and see patterns that connect under surfaces. When we release ourselves from the status quo, that auxin-burst is a creative bounce. That tiny impulse to create is a microcosmic way in which we are colleagues with God, a way we are in tune with the divine.

That is one of the things I know out there in the wild. I know that people who are having spiritual experiences are having artistic experiences, and vice versa. And I know that my own creative impulse is made of the same stuff as someone else's, even though it leads to different creations. The impulse is universal, transpersonal. I know that the way my heart and mind are working when I am making stuff, or when I am around others who are making stuff they love, is the divine way it was meant to be. It is the same impulse that drives the tomato to fruit. As Alice Walker writes, "The nature of this flower is to bloom."

In the wilderness circle I realize anew that all this visible stuff is permeated by the same omnipresent creative impulse. It is harder for me to see that inside my home rectangles with their computers and obligations. Out there in a circle in nature, I see the improvisation we are part of—one incredible, ongoing improvisation of interdependence and interplay. We are creating it together.

SINCE WE ARE CREATING THE UNDERSTANDINGS in these pages together as partners, let me share a few things artists know about improvisation. First, some improvs "work" better than others. That means that some bring together various elements and individuals in attuned patterns that "click." They are more exciting, more cohesive, more beautiful and fun—for actors and audience. These "flow" encounters generate more energy than they require. As we discovered in Part II, the quintessential key that allows such experiences to occur is that all the participants must say "yes" to what happens.

An actor begins an improvised domestic scene with, "Honey, I hate it when you get all tense like this." If the actress says, "I am not tense, and I have never seen you before," the scene continues, but it has no flow, no creative collaboration. If she says, "What do you expect when you eat the pear in the still life I am painting?" they have somewhere fun to go together. The key is the mindset of yes. Yes to everything, even the illogical, the uncomfortable, the I-don't-know-where-this-will-take-us risky offerings. That yes surrenders control; it releases the creative auxin that allows for growth. It allows the improvisers to make something delicious and satisfying. "Yes" allows the collaborating artists in any medium to create something extraordinary.

It is a mindset to bring to each day. In this mindset, the improv does not have better and worse parts; it is all perfect, unfolding exactly as it should, rich with surprises and opportunities, given the infinite complexity of the forces that have led to that moment. "No" believes in imperfection, and thus gets exactly those results. "Yes" unfolds the way the divine unfolds everywhere, and makes the experience more exciting, more cohesive, richer, more beautiful and fun—for us and for those we have contact with. As I wrote above, some improvs work out better than others. As the great spiritual teacher Ramana Maharshi said, "The world is perfect just as it is, and could do with a lot of improvement."

Improvisation needs an audience to be fully realized, to get its shot at quality; there must be a witness to the creative work. Musicians may improvise together in rehearsal, as actors and dancers do, but it is different when others witness the interaction. It gains focus; the play gets more serious; the stakes rise because the risk and potential significance increase. Sacred potential begins. Remember that the etymological sense of *sacred* is *set apart for special noticing*.

Who is my audience when I am improvising a week in solitude? Some might say the witness is God. I think it is the divine aspect within me that witnesses the improvisation, that "little step back" we take in our minds to see, without attachment, what is happening. I can accept the term "God" to refer to that awakened aspect of the self. It is a shift in perspective, a way of seeing the play of inner and outer reality. "We are looking for who is looking," as St. Francis said. When we find that divine aspect of ourselves, we see everything differently. We leave the world of the way it is, with its yin and yang of contentions, to see the yin-yang way it truly is. We release the auxin of creative growth and recognize that it's all divine. Our capacity to step back and see the divine, creates the divine.

TWICE IN MY LIFE, I experienced enlightenment. That is a big bomb to drop on page 300. I have avoided it because even those who live in the state can't describe it well, and my own fumbling attempts to define it would probably make you roll your eyes and skip those pages, as well as diminish the other parts of this book that I hope you find helpful. To me, enlightenment is white—the non-color that contains all colors. It is the clear place in which we see that everything simply is as it is, and is okay like that. More than okay. It all is connected. It's beautiful, not in an aesthetic way but in its truthful way. Somehow, in that state, I recognized that the way I was experiencing things was the way many others who had been given access to this state experienced it. You recognize it as the place so many have talked and written about because it is so "other" than everything you've experienced before. Although time feels different there, it is a place you want to stay. I didn't get to stay, much as I wanted to.

After getting to visit this place, and then watching it slip away, many fervently attempt to get back. Trying doesn't help. All you can do is be grateful and do whatever you can to increase your readiness to take entry again, should it be provided. I haven't dedicated myself to that goal, choosing other priorities in my days, so I think my visiting time is probably done. But I learned from those gift experiences, and have tried to share that gift in these pages.

My experiences of enlightenment were just for a day each time. The two days happened six months apart, about ten years ago, strangely in the same location, a small house beside a pond on Cape Cod, when I was alone. I was surrounded by trees and quiet, but it wasn't the wilderness. I wasn't fasting, or withholding books and paper, or staying in a circumscribed area. It was gently ordinary; there was a comfortable bed, and there were nature walks, and tea. My goodness but the tea tasted good.

The state of full consciousness was not the incremental peace that reliably emerges in my wilderness circle; it was unmistakable Truth, the place that the founders of religions and wisest sages have known. It was a gift. In both instances, I felt something approaching the night before, a bubbling up of irrational giddy gratitude. I awoke into awakened-ness. I received the gift at those particular times, I believe, because of the prior year when I had disrupted established life patterns and was "religiously" attentive to the issues you find in this book. Not at the time, but afterwards, it felt like a reward for the year of dedication. At the time, it felt: "Ahhh, so this is the ultimate truth of how it is."

I didn't do much on those days, mostly just sat in awe and gratitude. I wrote some notes to myself that clarified questions I had been struggling with in my life. I didn't know if I would remember experiences of this state, hence the notes. I had already written the first draft of this book a few years before, and had set it aside to gestate. One note I wrote to myself on the first of those enlightened days was simply this: *Go back to the book on personal religion when the time is right. Give back what you have to give.*

# CHAPTER 25

# COMING HOME

I LOVE COMING BACK from the wild after a week. It seems as adventurous to encounter the "normal" world as it did to head out into bearland or mountain lionville. Slipping into the car seat feels like limo luxury; driving at five miles an hour on a dirt access road feels like the Grand Prix. I see so clearly, notice so many things, realize how peculiar and frail our version of normalcy is. I know I look dangerous in my wild-eyed, unshaven scruffiness. People return to their parked cars and lock them after they glimpse me. I once cleared out an entire convenience store when I was paying for gas. I am raw, available, courageous, maybe a little smelly, but able to make good connections with anyone if they dare. I *am* dangerous—I see through the status quo. Everything is amazingly fun.

There was this greasy diner where I had a huge breakfast right before setting out one year. The waitress paid me perfunctory attention, and I tried to chat with her—it was going to be my last exchange for a week so I wanted to make it good. I failed. One long week later I returned for my first hot food, first contact with people. Heads turned as I entered, a few stayed turned as I made eye contact and smiled, genuinely fascinated to see faces. Unafraid, joyful. They were interested and wary. I got the same waitress; Maeve, her name tag read. I asked, and she didn't remember me from a week before. Made sense, I was a different person then. I told her I had just spent a week in the woods. I said I hadn't eaten much all week, and she said I must be hungry. I asked what might be good for easing back into a regular diet, and she said oatmeal, and even though it was afternoon, she would get the cook to make some if I didn't mind the wait. For once, I had all the time in the world.

She came back with some orange juice I hadn't ordered and told me I should have this too. So I did. She asked me about my week, and I told her the basics of doing nothing for seven days. She didn't ask the usual questions or express the usual aversion to such a thing. She asked me if I prayed. At other times, an alarm would have rung in my head—sticky situation up ahead—but not this day. I told her I prayed a lot, but that maybe my praying didn't look like other people's idea of prayer. She sat down in the booth across from me. And we didn't say anything for almost a minute.

She got up to serve other customers. She came back with a glass of water for me. And she said, "I know I live near beautiful natural places, but I don't go out there much because I hate bugs. The hour before the diner opens is like a prayer for me. I don't tell them that at church. It is quiet, and with just a few lights on it is like a church in here. Except for the smell. I walk around slowly and smoothly doing what has to be done. No music or anything. Just the sounds of a person in a place. I don't think I could live without that."

The sound of a person in a place. I knew exactly what she meant. The connection between us was species-deep. She smiled as she brought me the oatmeal, but we didn't have much more to say. She brought me the check, and we met standing as she went to the cash register to take my money. Such joy filled me—the deep connection between us, the imagined beauty of this diner in the divine half-light with Maeve moving reverently through it. We made our formal exchange; just a nod and a look closed the adventure. I sat in the car and wept with gratitude at the power of the human spirit to connect so deeply so quickly. It happened because I was as open as an artist to the creative opportunity of the moment. It happened because Maeve was far more remarkable than I ever would have guessed, and she dared to grab the opportunity.

With my hands on the steering wheel that would guide me home, I vowed to do whatever was necessary in this disorganized world to sustain the awareness of being a person in a place. I vowed to share the holiness of that moment with others in every way I can.

# EPILOGUE

ONE AFTERNOON IN THE WILDERNESS, there was this flying grasshopper. It landed a few feet from me as I leaned back against a tree, doing nothing. It looked at me for some moments, and then went on with its work, which seemed to have something to do with food. At first it seemed like any grasshopper, not that I brought an entomologist's eye to the greeting. After it stayed around for a while, I began to notice its particular habit of bobbing its front end in a rhythmic way and moving in completely unpredictable directions. What drives these seemingly arbitrary choices, I wondered?

I had my legs crossed and didn't dare move for fear of frightening my guest. It hopped onto one of my bare feet. I could feel it there, slightly tickling as it touched and moved around the outside of one foot. I recalled a pattern in my life. On every major vacation I had taken in the last many years, I had injured a foot along the way or just before. I had often mused about the meaning of this pattern, and had become more careful of my holiday feet, but still managed to acquire a bruise or cut. The grasshopper continued to make a circuit of the foot, walking the perimeter. It took minutes to complete the foot circuit, and I waited for it to leap away. It didn't. It made the awkward move to the other foot; it moved to the edge and began a circuit of that. For another few minutes, it walked the perimeter of this other foot, and just as it finished, it unceremoniously flew off. I didn't know quite what to make of this experience, but it felt like a blessing.

I still can't name what those minutes were all about, but I do know three things: 1) I have not injured my feet since that day; 2) I find similar blessings being given to me almost every day; 3) I did not tell anyone about the grasshopper right away, and before I did, a friend showed me this poem:

## The Summer Day

by Mary Oliver

*Who made the world?*
*Who made the swan, and the black bear?*
*Who made the grasshopper?*
*This grasshopper, I mean—*
*the one who has flung herself out of the grass,*
*the one who is eating sugar out of my hand,*
*who is moving her jaws back and forth instead of up and down—*
*who is gazing around with her enormous and complicated eyes.*
*Now she lifts her pale forearms and thoroughly washes her face.*
*Now she snaps her wings open, and floats away.*
*I don't know exactly what a prayer is.*
*I do know how to pay attention, how to fall down*
*into the grass, how to kneel down in the grass,*
*how to be idle and blessed, how to stroll through the fields,*
*which is what I have been doing all day.*
*Tell me, what else should I have done?*
*Doesn't everything die at last and too soon?*
*Tell me, what is it you plan to do*
*with your one wild and precious life?*[43]

# Endnotes

[The author has made every effort to accurately credit sources; any errors will be corrected in future editions.]

1 William James, *The Varieties of Religious Experience* (Touchstone, Simon & Schuster, 1997), page 59.

2 *This Longing: Poetry, Teaching Stories and Selected Letters of Rumi,* translated by Coleman Barks and John Moyne (Shambhala, 2000), page 28. Permission granted by Coleman Barks.

3 This concept of "spiritual homelessness" comes from the writing of Robert Wuthnow, especially in his book *Spirituality and Spiritual Practice* (Wiley, 2007).

4 Lynda Sexson, *Ordinarily Sacred* (University of Virginia Press, 1992), page 105.

5 The formative group of initial teaching artists at Lincoln Center Education (later Lincoln Center Institute, which later became Lincoln Center Education again) included Tom Bullard, Conrad Cummings, Jonathan Levy, Joanne Robinson, David Shookhoff, and Stan Walden, working with Philosopher-in-Residence Maxine Greene.

6 The core idea of this activity was originated by teaching artist David Shookhoff, who was my teacher when I was first learning to be a teaching artist at Lincoln Center Institute (now Lincoln Center Education) in 1979.

7 William James, in *The Varieties of Religious Experience*, as quoted by Harold Bloom in *The American Religion* (Simon & Schuster, 1992), page 25.

8 Sam Keen, in an interview in *Yes!* Magazine, Winter 1997/98 issue, page 35.

9 William James, *The Varieties of Religious Experience*, Centenary Edition (Routledge, 2003), page 359.

10 Gathered from Robert Wuthnow, *Inventing American Religion* (Oxford University Press, 2015).

11 Idea found in Ellen Dissanayake's *Homo Aestheticus* (The Free Press, Macmillan Inc., 1992), page 69.

12 Jaroslav Pelikan, *The Vindication of Tradition: The 1983 Jefferson Lecture in the Humanities* (Yale University Press, reprint edition 1986).

13 Martin Buber, as quoted in Karen Armstrong's *A History of God* (Ballantine Books, 1993), page 387.

14 Laurens van der Post, *Jung and the Story of Our Time* (Vintage Books, 1997), page 216.

15 Karen Armstrong, *A History of God* (Ballantine Books, 1993), page 394.

16 Hippolytus, *Heresies*, 7.21.4

17 Martin Buber, *The Way of Man* (Citadel Press Book, Carol Publishing Group, 1998), page 38.

18 Ibid. 15, 4.

19 Ibid. 17, 41.

20 For a fuller investigation of the ways attention works, I refer the reader to several chapters in my book *The Everyday Work of Art* (iUniverse, current edition).

21 Jaquest Derrida, *Of Grammatology*, translated by Gayatri Chakravorty Spivak (Johns Hopkins University Press, originally published in 1967), page 50.

22 John Keats in a letter to his brothers, 1817.

23 From "Adonais" by Percy Bysshe Shelley.

24 Carl Jung, "On the Relation of Analytical Psychology to Poetic Art," Baynes, H.G., (trans.), *British Journal of Medical Psychology* 1923, Vol. 3, page 219.

25    Aldous Huxley, *The Perennial Philosophy* (Perennial Library,
      Harper & Row Publishers), page 271.

26    George Lakoff and Mark Johnson, *Metaphors We Live By*
      (University of Chicago Press, 1980), page 157.

27    Ibid. 4, 190.

28    Ibid, 4, 121.

29    Joseph Campbell, as quoted in Jean Houston, *A Passion for
      the Possible: A Guide to Realizing Your True Potential* (Harper San
      Francisco 2004), page 127.

30    I credit Pierre Hadot, and his remarkable book *Philosophy As
      a Way of Life* (Wiley-Blackwell, 1995), for inspiring this list of
      ideas. Though his thoughts differ from these, his work sparked
      this section.

31    Nathaniel Branden, *The Art of Living Consciously* (Touchstone,
      1999), page 62.

32    John Dewey, from *How We Think*, in *The Later Works: 1925–
      1953, Volume 8, 1933*, Edited by Jo Ann Boydston (Southern
      Illinois University Press, 1986), page 177.

33    In his fine book *Art in Action: Toward a Christian Aesthetic*
      (Eerdmans, 1987), Nicholas Wolterstorff argues that America
      has limited the definition of art to this particular kind of aes-
      thetic reflection.

34    Ellen Langer, *The Power of Mindful Learning* (Da Capo Books,
      1997).

35    Plato, *Laws*, Book 7, paragraph 803.

36    "The Man with the Blue Guitar," copyright © 1937 by
      Wallace Stevens; from *The Collected Poems of Wallace Stevens*
      by Wallace Stevens. Used by permission of Alfred A. Knopf,
      an imprint of Knopf Doubleday Publishing Group, a division
      of Penguin Random House LLC. All Rights Reserved.

37    Ibid. 1, 267.

38    These ideas come from Frans de Waal in *Good Natured, The Origins of Right and Wrong in Humans and Other Animals* (Harvard University Press, 2009), and *Bonobo, The Forgotten Ape* (University of California Press, 1998).

39    Freeman Dyson, "Will Man Survive in the Cosmos?" article in *The Washington Post*, April 3, 1988.

40    John D. Barrow, *The Artful Universe* (Oxford University Press, 1995), page 32.

41    Johan Huizinga, *Homo Ludens* (Beacon Press, paperback, 1955), page 25.

42    Edward O. Wilson, *On Human Nature* (Harvard University Press, 2004).

43    "The Summer Day" from *House of Light* by Mary Oliver published by Beacon Press, Boston; copyright © 1990 by Mary Oliver, used herewith by permission of the Charlotte Sheedy Literary Agency, Inc.

# Index

## A

Abraham 82, 118, 217
Adyashanti 35, 59, 291
Aesthetic education 7, 26
Aesthetic method 295–296
Almaas, A.H. 291
Americans with Disabilities Act 241
Armstrong, Karen 85, 100, 178, 307
Aurelius, Marcus 195
Authenticity 263
Auxin 8, 297, 299, 301, 311

## B

Bacon, Francis 293
Barrow, John 285, 310
Beard, George M. 226
Bhagavad Gita 258, 310
Bible 42, 78, 79, 144, 215, 222, 319
Blake, William 156, 157
Bloom, Harold 225, 307, 310
Bohm, David 38, 192
Bohr, Niels 38, 158, 252, 288, 292
Borgman, Jim 96
Boy Scout Handbook 79

Branden, Nathaniel 150, 309
Buber, Martin 84, 85, 97, 101, 307
Buddha 41, 72, 82, 163, 205, 207, 215, 217
Buddhism 100, 178, 182, 196

## C

Camino de Santiago, El 163
Campbell, Joseph 131, 134, 145, 290, 308
Capra, Fritjof 291
Carter, Jimmy 237
Carville, James 254
Cézanne, Paul 96
Chabris, Christopher 39
Chaos Theory 103
Chesterton, G.K. 222
Chodron, Pema 291
Chopra, Deepak 291
Christianity 131, 218–220
    Catholic 74, 178, 204, 215, 226, 254, 255
    Christian rock 238
    Medieval Christian scholars 268
    Protestants 220, 244
    Southern Baptists 224
Christians 85, 219, 268, 274
    Orthodox 219, 309
Chuang Tzu 236
Clinton, William 221, 254

Coelho, Paulo 291

Coleridge, Samuel Taylor 141

Commencement 162, 251 *See also* Ten commencements

Confucius 215

Constantine 219

Cooper, David 91

Coward, Noel 55

Creative prayer practice 162, 178

Csikszentmihalyi, Mihaly 229, 309

Curiosity 105

## D

Dalai Lama 118, 291

Danto, Arthur 48

Darwin, Charles 131, 277

Dawkins, Richard 278

Declaration of Independence 221

De Mille, Agnes 236

Deep pleasure principle 162–167

Descartes, René 293, 294, 295

De Tocqueville, Alexis 226, 241, 243, 244

Dewey, John 26, 55, 150, 151, 287, 293, 309

Dickinson, Emily 182

Dionysus 130, 215

Discomfort 202

Dorotheus of Gaza 195

Drucker, Peter 173

Dyson, Freeman 280, 281, 310

## E

Eisenhower, Dwight 222

El Greco 45

Evolution 211, 212, 276, 277, 278, 279, 280, 282–285, 286, 289, 291, 308

## F

Faust 132

Fox, Matthew 291

Franklin, Benjamin 242

Freud, Sigmund 295

Fuller, Buckminster 132

fundamentalism 131, 225

## G

Gandhi, Mahatma 253

Gangaji 291

Gardner, Howard 114, 190, 309

Gautama 82

Getzels, Jacob 229

Gilgamesh 130

Glass, Philip 95

Gnostics 219

Gödel, Kurt 278

Goldberg, Natalie 75

Golden Rule 63

Goodman, Nelson 284

Gordimer, Nadine 165

Grace 30, 67, 76, 77, 108, 120, 167, 171, 185, 226, 244, 249, 266

Greene, Maxine 27

## H

Halifax, Joan 291

Hamlet 23, 24, 37, 56, 240

Hanuman 132

Harris, Sam 291

Harry Potter 132

Hawking, Stephen 131

Hebrew 144, 215

Hegel, Georg 142

Hinduism 19, 41, 49, 100, 131, 215, 264

Hippolytus 86, 307

Holocaust 88

Horowitz, Alexandra 95

Houston, Jean 118, 291

*How to Change Your Mind* 228

Huizinga, Johan 154, 289, 309, 310

Huxley, Aldous 124, 308

## I

Ignatius of Loyola 195

Inner facts 32–36, 40, 42, 87, 106

Iyer, Pico 21

## J

James, WIlliam 12, 31, 44, 64, 140, 216, 247, 263, 307, 309

Jerusalem 217

Jesus 82, 128, 130, 136, 146, 205, 217, 218, 219, 220, 221, 222, 274

Joyce, James 254

Jung, Carl 75, 84, 116, 118, 133, 307, 308

## K

Kabat-Zinn, Jon 291

Kant, Immanuel 91

Katie, Byron 35, 291

Kazantzakis, Nikos 195

Keats, John 113, 307

Keen, Sam 47, 164, 292, 307

Kitchen Table Wisdom 149

Knight, J.Z. 292

## L

Lamar, Kendrick 45

Landmark Education 291

Langer, Ellen 154, 309

Lao Tzu 215

Legalism 234, 236

Literalism 125, 126, 233

*Little Prince, The* 79

Luther, Martin 215, 220

# M

Macbeth  27–29

Maharshi, Ramana  100, 299

Man With a Blue Guitar, The
   185

Marley, Christopher  221

Maslow, Abraham  118

Materialism  34, 58, 65, 77,
   232, 233, 234, 237

McCowen, Alec  78

Merton, Thomas  170, 179

Metaphor  7, 46, 56, 72, 75, 84,
   109, 123–127, 129, 130,
   131, 133, 137, 139, 152,
   157, 186, 188, 192, 203,
   248, 262, 274, 284, 290,
   295, 308

Michelangelo  66

Milan, Edict of  219

Miller, Alexa  114

Mochon, Daniel  174

Mohammed  82, 130, 215, 217

Moses  60, 130, 132, 161, 214

Mullins, E.Y.  224

Myanmar  217

Myss, Caroline  292

Mythology  130–134

# N

Nepo, Mark  292

Newton, Isaac  295

Nussbaum, Martha  287

# O

Old Testament  85, 131

Oliver, Mary  305

Olympic ideal  250

Optimism  105

Orpheus  215

Ovid  155

# P

Pascal, Blaise  142

Pattern recognition  212, 287

Persephone  75, 132

Perennial philosophy  49

Personal Practice  260

Pharisees  218

Philadelphia Orchestra  249

Picasso, Pablo  37, 122

Pilgrimage  97, 163, 227

Plato  154, 155, 163, 165, 289

Plymouth Rock  221

Pollan, Michael  228

Portrait of the Artist as a Young Man
   254

Prayer  63, 64, 65, 178, 179,
   181, 308

Protestant  178, 221, 226, 254,
   255

Puritans  101, 144, 221, 222

Pythagoras  215

# Q
Quantum mechanics  279, 295

# R
Ramana Maharshi  100, 299
Ram Dass  291
Ramen, Rachel  149
Reagan, Ronald  242, 243
Reformists  220
Relationships  198, 265
Relaxation  11, 49, 113, 143, 168,
    169–171, 182, 190, 191
Religion  12, 13, 17–26, 28–34,
    36, 38, 40, 42, 44, 46, 48,
    49, 51, 55, 56, 57, 59, 60,
    62–64, 68–70, 73, 74, 76,
    77, 80–82, 86, 87, 90,
    91, 100, 113, 114, 118,
    120–123, 128, 130–132,
    136, 138, 142, 147–149,
    151, 157, 158, 162, 166,
    168, 169, 171, 177, 178,
    195–197, 200, 211, 214,
    215, 216–219, 221–224,
    226, 228–230, 233, 237,
    238, 244–250, 252, 254,
    266, 268, 269, 291, 292,
    301
Rembrandt  36
Renaissance  234, 293
Repetition  195, 266, 267
Rilke, Rainer Maria  45, 191

Ritual  17, 23, 50, 68–70, 129,
    154, 218, 289
Robbins, Tony  292
Rukeyser, Muriel  130
Rumi  19, 44, 148, 182, 307

# S
Saint Peter  90
Saint Simeon Stylites  34
Sanskrit  85, 215
Scientific Method  232, 233,
    293, 294, 295, 296
Scientism  232, 233
Secularism  222
Sexson, Lynda  23, 128, 130,
    307, 308
Shakespeare, William  24, 27,
    28, 55, 76, 119
Shepard, Sam  55
Shulman, Jason  122
Simons, Daniel  39
Social Security  241
Sondheim, Stephen  57
Stevens, Wallace  185
St. Francis of Assisi  41, 97,
    134, 275, 300
St. John of the Cross  100, 146
St. Mark's Gospel  78, 317
Sufism  189
Symbols  7, 74, 75, 123, 124,
    125, 127, 129, 131, 133,
    137, 139

T

Taoism 218

*Tao Te Ching* 79

Ten commencements 161, 162, 164

Thich Nhat Hanh 170, 205, 291

Thoreau, Henry David 227

*Thousand Gratitudes, A* 50–51

Tippett, Krista 21

Tolle, Eckhart 35, 292

Torah 168

Tradition 71

Transcendentalists 243

Turgenev, Ivan 171

Tutu, Desmond 292


U

Utilitarianism 236, 237, 238, 239, 240


V

Venus of Willendorf 148

Virgin Mary 123

*Virgin Soil* 171

von Bingen, Hildegard 100


W

Walden Pond 227

Watt, Isaac 294

Weber-Fechner 88

Whitman, Walt 49, 243

Whyte, David 258, 262, 310

Wilber, Ken 233, 234, 264, 292, 296, 310

Williamson, Marianne 292

Wilson, Edmund 31

Winfrey, Oprah 292

Wittenberg 220

Wordsworth, William 47

Wotan 132


Y

Yahweh 85

yin-yang 279, 300


Z

Zarathustra 215

Zen 59, 97, 106, 113, 143, 158, 170, 191

Zoroastrianism 215

## Personal Note From the Author

AT AGE 20, I MADE A CONSEQUENTIAL DECISION that echoes through this book. I was a sophomore at Middlebury College in Vermont and decided to transfer to a fast-track divinity school program at Yale University. It was 1970; I was a conscientious objector to the Vietnam War; and my fierce pacifism required action. I was accepted to Yale and preparing for probable career in the clergy, when, on a lark, I auditioned for and was cast in a play at Middlebury, *Under Milkwood* by Dylan Thomas. The experience had such a profound impact on me that I made a sharp turn in my life plan, and transferred instead to Emerson College to study acting. This led to further MFA study of theater at Stanford University, and then a successful career as an actor. There was a surprising pattern in my acting career—I was frequently cast in plays that dealt overtly with spiritual themes. I wasn't happy in the life of a New York actor—hated doing eight performances a week, didn't like the pressure to get commercials and voice-overs, didn't enjoy doing soap operas—so I edged away into teaching artistry, a field that was in its infancy and within which I found much more creative satisfaction. My last major role as an actor was performing the yearlong American tour of *St. Mark's Gospel*—a one-man, bare-stage telling, made famous by British actor Alec McCowen, of the King James Version of the Gospel. I memorized the text, rehearsed the performance, and spent a year performing it hundreds of times on major and minor U.S. stages, going deeper and deeper into this fusion of art and spirit. That fusion has remained the compass in my subsequent four decades as a freelance consultant, speaker and workshop leader, program designer, writer and even wilderness adventurer. There is always a spiritual component to the work I commit myself to, and there is always an artistic aspect to the spiritual work in my personal life. That's where this book comes from. That's why there are many personal stories in the book—I have never written so autobiographically before.

## Acknowledgements

I THANK THE MANY SPIRITUAL TEACHERS who fed my yearning over the sixty years of this learning journey. Too many to name; none I ever knew in person.

Thanks to the friends and colleagues who sparked and incubated the ideas in these pages: Nancy Baker, Dahlia Cabe, Denise Dillenbeck, Le Clanché Du Rand, Carl Frankel, Isabelle Grandin, Evry Mann, Jane Perry, Peter Rojcewicz, and my late friend Michael Schwartz. Thanks to Tilman Reitzle and Patrick Scafidi for guiding with the completion process.

Deepest thanks go to Tricia Tunstall and Amy Miller who supported me and this project in so many ways for so many days, including many improvements in the actual text, but mostly in their abundant eagerness to talk about the ideas in these pages and their unconditional love. Thanks to other readers who helped me over the finish line: Henry "Chip" Arnold, Noah Gittell and John Zweig.

## About the Author

ERIC BOOTH is the author of six previous books, including *The Everyday Work of Art*, *Playing for Their Lives* (co-authored with Tricia Tunstall) and *The Music Teaching Artist's Bible*. He is widely called "the father of the teaching artist profession," has received the nation's highest award in arts education, and has spent many years on the faculties of Juilliard, Lincoln Center Education, The Kennedy Center, and Tanglewood. He is a frequent keynote speaker, project leader and workshop teacher, around the world. His personal website, with many of his essays and other writing available, is *ericbooth.net*.

To communicate with the author and/or to sign up for occasional emails about the book and new thoughts connected to it, go to the website: *tendingtheperennials.com*

Made in the USA
Middletown, DE
19 May 2019